# The Duckfoot Site

Volume 2

Archaeology of the House and Household

OCCASIONAL PAPERS OF THE CROW CANYON ARCHAEOLOGICAL CENTER

Richard H. Wilshusen, General Editor

# The Duckfoot Site

## Volume 2

## Archaeology of the House and Household

*Ricky R. Lightfoot*

With a Foreword by William D. Lipe and Richard H. Wilshusen

OCCASIONAL PAPER NO. 4
CROW CANYON ARCHAEOLOGICAL CENTER
Cortez, Colorado
1994

Library of Congress Catalog Card Number: 94-68616
ISBN 0-9624640-5-8


Production coordinated by Lynn L. Udick
Copyedited by Mary C. Etzkorn
Layout and production of camera-ready copy by Louise M. Schmidlap
Artifact photography by Rick Bell
Cover illustration by Jane Baigent
Printed by Thomson-Shore, Inc., Dexter, Michigan

Distributed by The University of Arizona Press, 1230 N. Park Ave., Suite 102, Tucson, Arizona 85719

An earlier version of Chapter 2 was published in *Kiva,* Vol. 57, under the title "Architecture and Tree-Ring Dating at the Duckfoot Site in Southwestern Colorado," by Ricky R. Lightfoot. © 1992 by the Arizona Archaeological and Historical Society. Adapted with permission.

Portions of Chapters 3 and 4 (including Table 4.1 and Figures 3.1, 3.4, 3.5, 4.1, and 4.2) first appeared in "Abandonment Processes in Prehistoric Pueblos," by Ricky R. Lightfoot, in *Abandonment of Settlements and Regions: Ethnoarchaeological and Archaeological Approaches,* edited by Catherine M. Cameron and Steve A. Tomka. © 1993 by Cambridge University Press. Adapted with permission.

Permission was obtained to quote or paraphrase from the following works:

"Land Tenure Systems and Prehistoric Land Use: Perspectives from the American Southwest," by Michael Adler. Paper presented at the 57th Annual Meeting of the Society for American Archaeology. © 1992 by Michael Adler.

"The Changing Face of the Community in the Mesa Verde Region, A.D. 1000–1300," by Michael Adler and Mark Varien. Preliminary draft of paper presented at the 2nd Anasazi Symposium. © 1991 by Michael Adler and Mark Varien.

"Replication of an Early Anasazi Pithouse," by Gilbert D. Glennie and William D. Lipe. Paper presented at the 49th Annual Meeting of the Society for American Archaeology. © 1984 by Gilbert D. Glennie and William D. Lipe.

"Engineering the Pithouse to Pueblo Transition," by Richard H. Wilshusen. Paper presented at the 49th Annual Meeting of the Society for American Archaeology. © 1984 by Richard H. Wilshusen.

To Melissa, Nivale, Piedra, and Savanna, with love.

# Contents

# Illustrations

# Tables

# Foreword

The publication of this monograph completes a two-volume report on research focused on the Duckfoot site, a Pueblo hamlet occupied in the late ninth century A.D. The great majority of the field and laboratory research was directed by Ricky Lightfoot, the author of this volume and senior editor of Volume 1 (Lightfoot and Etzkorn 1993). The first volume reports in meticulous detail on the excavations, architecture, artifacts, ecofacts, and human remains encountered at the site and provides a brief, site-specific synthesis of the results. Volume 2 focuses on the problem of understanding household size, composition, and activities at the Duckfoot site. In order to make inferences about households, Lightfoot first had to understand the site's archaeological record; hence, a substantial portion of the book is devoted to analyzing archaeological formation processes. The Duckfoot archaeological record was especially appropriate for the intensive and ambitious analyses that Lightfoot undertook. A settlement of four pit structures and 19 above-ground rooms, the site was occupied for about a generation—from the mid– to late A.D. 850s to about A.D. 880. Lightfoot had hundreds of tree-ring dates with which to place various construction events at the site and a nearly complete sample of the artifact record, since virtually the entire site was excavated.

As with any archaeological research, the Duckfoot Project is rooted in the history of research in its region and in American archaeology in general. In addition, this project played an important role in the development of the Crow Canyon Archaeological Center as a full-fledged research organization. The Duckfoot excavation was the first major project undertaken by the Center after it opened in 1983. The Center's predecessor—the Crow Canyon School—had conducted archaeological education programs that in some cases included students in professionally led excavations (Berger 1993), but the School did not have its own research staff and continuing research program. The newly organized Crow Canyon Center took on the challenges of developing a research program; this included obtaining adequate funding, facilities, and staff, as well as creating systems for provenience control, laboratory analysis, and publication. The Duckfoot site was in many ways the "guinea pig" for facing and solving these problems. The publication of this monograph thus marks a coming of age for the Crow Canyon Archaeological Center, demonstrating its ability not only to carry field projects through the descriptive reporting stage, but to produce significant problem-oriented publications based on those projects.

In its research orientations, the Duckfoot Project is in many ways the offspring of the Dolores Project, an immense multiyear study that focused on the archaeological sites impacted by the construction of McPhee Reservoir in the Dolores River valley of southwestern Colorado (Breternitz et al. 1986). Because the heaviest occupation of the reservoir area was during the Pueblo I period—A.D. 750–900—

numerous sites of this period were sampled, and models of Pueblo I environ-
ments, settlement patterns, demography, cultural adaptations, sociocultural organization, and sociocultural change were developed. The work at Duckfoot was
initiated in part to test a Dolores model of social organization with data from a
Pueblo I site located outside the Dolores area and in a somewhat different
environment. Lightfoot's work supports many of the substantive conclusions of
the Dolores Project researchers but amplifies or provides alternatives to them in
others.

This volume is also a product of current emphases in American archaeology.
When archaeology was seen primarily as a kind of history of material culture,
the changing technology, styles, and cultural relationships of a people could be
studied largely by analyzing the artifacts found in trash layers. As archaeology has
broadened to include studies of social and economic organization, work such as
Lightfoot's has become central to the field. By analyzing houses and the activities
of the people who occupied them, Lightfoot focuses on the household—a fundamental building block of society. Understanding how prehistoric societies were
organized and how they functioned has also required archaeologists to ask more
penetrating questions about the formation of the archaeological record—that is,
about what kinds of past behavior are reflected in the structures, features, and
artifacts that excavations uncover. In this monograph, Lightfoot provides text-
book examples of how the archaeological record can be "read" to support
inferences about prehistoric household organization and activities.

The first half of the volume has a strong methodological slant and addresses
questions important for any site. How do we use multiple dates to interpret the
building and remodeling of a number of connected or closely related structures?
How do we explain how a site was abandoned? How do we estimate how many
pottery vessels were used over the life of the site? How do artifact deposition
rates relate to the size of the site's population, the length of time it was occupied,
and the activities carried out there?

In many archaeological contexts, it is difficult to date sites more precisely than to
a span of several hundred years. The remarkable success of tree-ring dating has
enabled Southwestern archaeologists—at some sites—to date construction events
to within a few years. Duckfoot is one of those exceptional sites, and Lightfoot
does a masterful job of integrating evidence from tree-ring samples, architecture,
and stratigraphy to build one of the finest-grained intrasite chronologies to be
found anywhere in the archaeological literature. This enables him to focus on the
archaeological record of individual households and to bring his analysis of spatial
and temporal patterning at the site to at least the household level. For archaeologists working in the Eastern United States, Alaska, or Central America, this is
next to impossible at most sites. In places such as Hawaii and the Northern
Plains, it may be possible to identify the archaeological record of households, but
it is often difficult to date them to within a 20-year period, or a human genera-

tion. The detailed chronology that Lightfoot was able to construct for Duckfoot made possible much of his success in analyzing formation processes and, ultimately, household organization.

The second half of the book is concerned with this latter topic—how people organize themselves into household groups, and whether there is a single kind of household organization in Puebloan prehistory. Lightfoot analyzes evidence from the content and spatial arrangement of activity areas and structures to address basic issues of the size, functions, and interrelationships of households at Duckfoot. This is the most intriguing part of Lightfoot's analysis and the part that other archaeologists may find most controversial. Whereas Lightfoot concludes that a single, nuclear-family-based household ordinarily occupied each "Prudden unit" (a single pit structure and associated roomblock), many other Southwesternists would infer that several households occupied the same facilities. Although Lightfoot makes a strong case that there were never more than three households at Duckfoot, there are alternative interpretations of the data that would support an inference of five or six households. Fortunately, the descriptive data for site architecture, stratigraphy, features, assemblages, and chronology are presented in sufficient detail in these volumes to permit alternative interpretations to be investigated. In fact, the marvelous potential of these two volumes is that they provide us with the materials for a methodological and substantive debate over how to recognize and characterize households in the archaeological record and over the issue of whether Pueblo household organization changed through time in the northern Southwest.

There is another compelling aspect to this study. The excavation of the Duckfoot site and some key analyses of its artifacts were accomplished as a partnership between professional archaeologists and lay participants in educational programs. It is rare for archaeologists to work this extensively with the public in a major excavation and even more rare for two major monographs to result from such a collaboration. If American archaeology is to flourish in the coming years, we must have more collaboration with the public. We must also do more to engage one segment of that public—American Indians—in the study of the past record of human life on this continent. Finally, we must have more studies of basic human organization and behavior, such as Lightfoot offers us in this superb analysis of early Pueblo households, if we are to understand how and why societies changed through time. If we can do all these things, it is possible that humanity as well as archaeology will be the better for it.

WILLIAM D. LIPE
Professor of Anthropology
Washington State University

RICHARD H. WILSHUSEN
Director of Research
Crow Canyon Archaeological Center

# Acknowledgments

I thank the many people who read different versions of this volume: William Lipe, Timothy Kohler, John Bodley, J. Jefferson Reid, and Richard Wilshusen. I am especially grateful to William Lipe for his inspiration, guidance, and assistance throughout this project, from fieldwork through publication. In the final stages of manuscript preparation, Mary Etzkorn's datachecking and editorial comments greatly improved the coherence of the text. Lynn Udick's and Louise Schmidlap's experience in desktop publishing and Rick Bell's expertise in photography greatly enhanced the appearance of this volume. Tom May did an excellent job of drafting the site maps (Figures 1.1, 1.2, 2.1, 3.1, 3.3, 5.1, 6.2, and 6.3), providing baseline illustrations that could be adapted to fit various needs throughout the book. These figures subsequently were converted into computer files and individually modified by the Publications staff, resulting in Crow Canyon's first major computer graphics project for publication. Jane Baigent rendered the superb pen-and-ink drawing that appears on the cover.

I extend my sincerest thanks to the staff, Chairman's Council, and Board of Trustees of the Crow Canyon Archaeological Center, who have supported me immeasurably throughout this project. Crow Canyon researchers, educators, consultants, and interns have worked together as a team since 1983, and I am proud to be a member of the team. Special thanks are also due the approximately 4,000 participants—many of them schoolchildren—who served as field and laboratory crew over the course of the study. As with any undertaking of this magnitude, there were many individuals who contributed to the success of the project; although the assistance of each was individually acknowledged in Volume 1, I would like to take this opportunity to collectively thank again everyone who contributed time, labor, and financial support.

I gratefully acknowledge the people who owned the Duckfoot site at the time we were excavating: Carol Claycomb, Eugene Crawford, James Crawford, and Wesley Dunlap. They allowed us to excavate on their land, and they generously donated the entire collection to the Anasazi Heritage Center (Bureau of Land Management, Dolores, Colorado), where it is available for future study and public enjoyment. The staff of the Anasazi Heritage Center, especially LouAnn Jacobson and Susan Thomas, arranged for us to photograph artifacts for this volume, and their assistance is greatly appreciated. The Wenner–Gren Foundation for Anthropological Research funded the refitting studies, which were instrumental in understanding formation processes and household organization at Duckfoot.

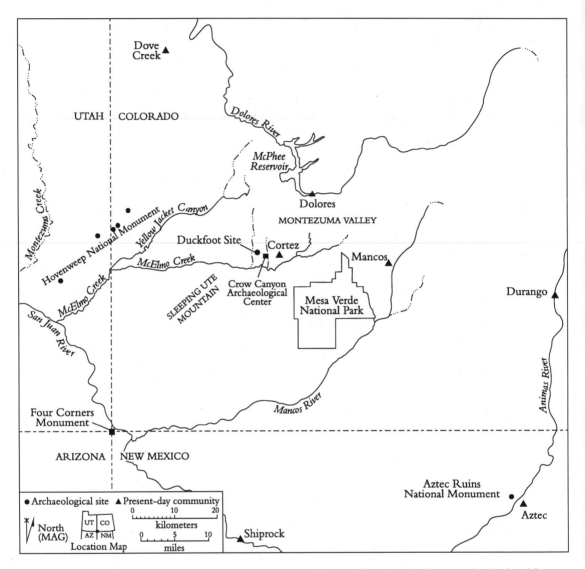

**Figure 1.1.** *Map of southwestern Colorado showing the location of the Duckfoot site and other natural and cultural features discussed in text.*

# 1

# Introduction

Archaeologists have long been interested in the social organization of prehistoric societies. In recent years, studies of social organization have focused on households as the primary organizational building blocks of society. By learning how households were organized, what activities they performed, and how they interacted with each other, we can gain a better understanding of past cultures. One objective of this study is to test a model of early Pueblo household organization in the northern Southwest. I accomplish this by using excavation and laboratory data from the Duckfoot site, a late-ninth-century ancestral Pueblo hamlet in southwestern Colorado (Figure 1.1).

Our understanding of prehistoric household organization is limited to what we can infer from the material remains of the archaeological record. Architecture provides one source of information about how activities and interactions were structured, but architecture does not tell the entire story. In this volume, a model of household organization derived from architectural patterns at prehistoric Pueblo sites is evaluated using other sources of archaeological data. These other sources of data include features and artifacts, which require some assessment to determine their applicability to questions of household organization. For example, archaeological assemblages of artifacts from structures may tell us more about how a site was abandoned than about how it was used. Therefore, a substantial portion of this volume is devoted to studying how the artifact assemblages formed, as a prelude to using those assemblages to make other interpretations.

To make interpretations about household organization on the basis of archaeological data, it is essential to consider the natural, cultural, and archaeological processes that have influenced the content and patterning of material assemblages. The nature of the archaeological record and the archaeological process makes studies of social and political organization difficult because we cannot observe the behaviors that are of interest. We make inferences about activities and cultural behavior in the ancient past on the basis of physical evidence that we observe in the present. First, we must consider what kinds of physical remains and spatial patterns the activities of interest will produce. Then we must learn to distinguish those remains and patterns from others produced by activities and processes that are not of interest. In addition, we must consider what kinds of natural and cultural processes have affected the archaeological remains since they were deposited. Of paramount importance in interpreting an excavated archaeological assemblage is an understanding of site chronology and abandonment processes.

In this volume, I present a detailed case study of the archaeology of households at Duckfoot in an attempt to understand how archaeological assemblages, features, and architecture reflect household organization. This study contributes to current debates about how early Pueblo structures were used and how early Pueblo households and residence groups were organized. Understanding early Pueblo household organization is important because of the implications for estimating population size and for understanding human interactions and suprahousehold organization in prehistoric Pueblo sites.

## The Duckfoot Site

Detailed descriptive information about the Duckfoot site is provided in Volume 1 of this report (Lightfoot and Etzkorn 1993). The site, which was occupied from the mid– to late A.D. 850s to about 880, consists of 19 contiguous surface (above-ground) rooms, four pit structures, and a midden, or trash, deposit that is 20 to 30 cm thick and covers an area of approximately 350 m² (Figure 1.2). An isolated surface structure (Room 20) is located west of the roomblock; because its affiliation with the rest of the site is not clear, this room is excluded from consideration in most of the studies presented in this volume.

The Duckfoot site gets its name from a pottery artifact that was found just beneath the modern ground surface on the first day of excavation in 1983 (Figure 1.3). The artifact, which is about 8 cm tall, has a nearly triangular base with three small eminences that appear to be the toes of a webbed foot. This base is attached to a cylindrical leg that clearly was once affixed to a pottery vessel— probably a stylized duck- or bird-effigy vessel—that would have been supported on two legs. Near the end of the fifth and final

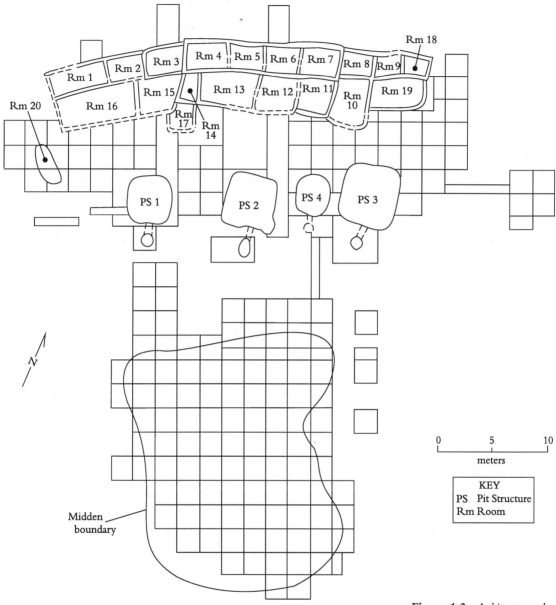

**Figure 1.2.** *Architecture and extramural excavation units at the Duckfoot site.*

season of excavation, the second duck foot was found in the fill of a large, basin-shaped pit in the eastern end of the courtyard area; however, the vessel itself was never recognized in the large sherd assemblage from the site. One miniature vessel from Duckfoot is a stylized bird effigy, but it has a smooth, deliberately flattened base that clearly was never attached to legs or feet. Several sherds in the

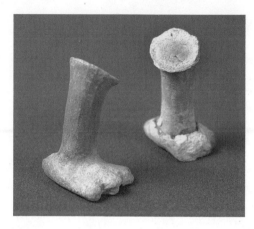

**Figure 1.3.** *Pottery artifacts resembling duck feet. The feet and legs are believed to have supported a pottery container, probably a duck-effigy vessel. The item on the left, found on the first day of excavation, is the artifact after which the site was named. Height (left) = 8.1 cm.*

Duckfoot collection have stylized duck wings, but they are not from the portions of the vessels necessary to establish that they belong to the specimen that once stood on the legs and feet in question. Duck-effigy vessels are rare but not unknown in Pueblo I sites in the region (Roberts 1925).

The Duckfoot site was almost completely excavated over a five-year period from 1983 to 1987. Excavations were conducted by the Crow Canyon Archaeological Center, a not-for-profit organization whose staff of professional archaeologists and educators supervise participants of all ages (junior high students through senior citizens) in experiential education programs, some of which involve participation in field and laboratory research (Figure 1.4). After a brief training period, participants enrolled in the Center's programs assist in excavation, laboratory processing, and basic analysis of artifacts.

## The Duckfoot Site as a Case Study

The Duckfoot site was originally selected for excavation because it was a well-preserved example of a typical hamlet dating to the late Pueblo I period.[1] Archaeologists commonly sample only a portion of any one site in order to preserve the remainder for future research. The nearly complete excavation of the Duckfoot site was justified by the potential to conduct intrasite comparative studies that would have been hampered by a more limited sampling approach. The knowledge that the site represented only a small sample of a larger community of similar and apparently contemporaneous settlements in the immediate area also justified the extensive excavation.

---

1. The Pueblo I period lasted from approximately A.D. 750 to 900 (Kane 1986; Rohn 1977); in this volume, A.D. 840–900 is considered the late Pueblo I period.

**Figure 1.4.** *High school students excavating in the roomblock at Duckfoot.*

The Duckfoot site was selected as a case study in site formation and household organization because its architecture was well preserved, the floor assemblages were rich and varied, the excavated sample was large, and the site, for the most part, represented a single, well-dated occupation. There were only minimal indications of vandalism, and the site had not been disturbed by erosion, modern agriculture, the clearing of vegetation, or other activities associated with modern development. In addition, because site-formation processes could be identified and controlled for at Duckfoot, I recognized the potential that the investigation had for contributing to the development of methods to be used in the study of formation processes and household organization. Many of the structures at Duckfoot had burned, which resulted in the rapid collapse of the roofs and the sealing of floor artifact assemblages in place. The discovery of artifacts and features in meaningful associations on these floors provided an excellent opportunity to learn about the activities that were conducted at the site and possibly the organization of the social groups who occupied it.

## Environmental Setting

The Duckfoot site is located approximately 5 km west of Cortez, Colorado. It is near the eastern edge of the Colorado Plateau, an area of geologic uplift characterized by deeply dissected tablelands and mesas. More specifically, Duckfoot, at an elevation of 1945 m (6380 ft), is at the western edge of the Montezuma Valley, which is drained by McElmo Creek. The Montezuma Valley is surrounded by prominent landforms, including the San Juan Mountains to the east, with peaks over 4270 m (14,000 ft); Sleeping Ute Mountain to the southwest, with laccolithic peaks rising to 3040 m (9980 ft); and Mesa Verde to the south, with its steep northern escarpment at 2590 m (8500 ft). The site is on moderately deep, eolian, silt loam sediments overlying the Cretaceous-period Dakota Sandstone. It is located on the crest of a ridge between two drainages that flow southward into McElmo Creek; these drainages are located in Alkali Canyon, approximately 1 km west of the site, and Crow Canyon, approximately 2 km east. The vegetation in the area immediately surrounding the site represents two biotic communities: the Great Basin Desertscrub (Turner 1982) and the Great Basin Conifer Woodland (Brown 1982). The dominant vegetation in undisturbed areas today consists of widely spaced pinyon pine (*Pinus edulis*) and Utah juniper (*Juniperus osteosperma*) interspersed with big sagebrush (*Artemisia tridentata*) and a variety of other shrubs, including mountain mahogany (*Cercocarpus montanus*), Utah service berry (*Amelanchier utahensis*), squaw apple (*Peraphyllum ramosissimum*), bitterbrush (*Purshia tridentata*), Gambel oak (*Quercus gambelii*), and Mormon tea (*Ephedra viridis*). Herbaceous plants forming the understory include a variety of grasses (Gramineae), legumes (Leguminosae), composites (Compositae), mustards (Cruciferae), mallows (Malvaceae), borages (Boraginaceae), and cacti (Cactaceae) (Lightfoot, Etzkorn, Adams, and Walker 1993:6). Riparian vegetation grows in the canyon bottoms. The climate records for the 30-year period ending in 1980 in nearby Cortez indicate that the area around Duckfoot receives an average of approximately 32 cm (12.7 in) of precipitation annually, which is distributed fairly evenly throughout the year. The mean annual temperature is 9.3°C (48.8°F), with a mean January temperature of −2.8°C (26.9°F) and a mean July temperature of 22.2°C (71.9°F) (National Climate Center 1983).

## Archaeological Background

The Duckfoot site is in the southwestern corner of Colorado in an area variously referred to as the Mesa Verde region, the Four Corners region, and the northern San Juan region. The northern San Juan region is the most inclusive, consisting of the area drained by the San Juan River and its northern tributaries. The Mesa Verde region consists of the area including and surrounding the prominent landform and national park by the same name; the mesa is the location of many ancient Pueblo cliff dwellings. The Four Corners region is defined loosely as the area surrounding the arbitrary, but unique, point in the region where the four states of Colorado, Utah, Arizona, and New Mexico meet.

Some of the more important early studies of Pueblo I settlements in the region include those of Morris (1919, 1939), Roberts (1930), Martin (1938, 1939), and Brew (1946). During the 1970s, work at Mesa Verde National Park was conducted by Hayes and Lancaster (1975), and in the late 1970s and early 1980s, the construction of the McPhee dam and reservoir on the Dolores River necessitated the large-scale investigations of the Dolores Archaeological Program (DAP) (Breternitz et al. 1986; Kane 1986; Petersen and Orcutt 1987; Kane and Robinson 1988; Lipe, Kohler, Varien, Morris, and Lightfoot 1988; Petersen 1988; Wilshusen 1991). The DAP sampling strategy allowed researchers to characterize the diversity of sites in the project area; over 100 sites, including many dating to the late Pueblo I period, were partly excavated or tested (Robinson et al. 1986:Table 1.13). As a result of this long history of research and, in particular, the extensive work conducted by the DAP, much was known about Pueblo I population, economy, architecture, and social organization, as well as the environment of the northern San Juan region. This strong background of regional knowledge about the Pueblo I period made the case for conducting a problem-oriented research project even stronger.

The ancestral Pueblo population in the Mesa Verde region was both dense and aggregated by the late Pueblo I period. Architectural clusters comparable to "unit-type" pueblos (Prudden 1903) first appeared during the early Pueblo I period, and these were often aggregated into multiple-household roomblocks and roomblock clusters. Many sites dating to this period include several roomblocks of over 50 rooms, which are clustered into large villages or communities.

The layout of the Duckfoot site is similar to that of other late Pueblo I settlements in the northern Southwest. Roomblocks dating to this period typically consist of double rows of rooms, with storage rooms to the north and domestic (habitation) rooms to the south. A row of pit structures (often called pithouses or sometimes "proto-kivas") lies 4 to 6 m south of each roomblock. The pithouses are separated from the roomblocks by open courtyards, and their ground-level roofs would have been part of those courtyards. Midden deposits are usually located several meters south of the pithouses. The variation in size of Pueblo I pit structures suggests that they varied greatly in their range of uses and in the size of the social groups who used and maintained them (Blinman 1989; Varien and Lightfoot 1989; Wilshusen 1989b). The floor areas of late Pueblo I pithouses vary from less than 10 m² to 64 m² (Kane 1986; Wilshusen 1988a); pithouses are believed to be domestic structures in which certain ritual activities also took place. Great kivas (pit structures with floor areas greater than 75 m²) were not abundant in early Pueblo times, but at least 12 dating to the Basketmaker III and Pueblo I periods have been reported throughout the northern Southwest (Lightfoot 1988; Vivian and Reiter 1965). Great kivas are often interpreted as community-wide, integrative structures (Adler and Varien 1991; Adler and Wilshusen 1990; Plog 1974; Wilshusen 1991).

Subsistence during the Pueblo I period in the northern Southwest was based primarily on agriculture, with corn and beans being the major crops (Adams 1993; Decker and Tieszen 1989; Griffitts 1987). Several important cultural developments took place during the Pueblo I period, including a shift from widely dispersed, shallow pit structures with small, isolated storage rooms to fully subterranean pit structures and multiroom pueblos. The population pattern in the northern Southwest shifted from one characterized by loose clusters of dispersed, one- to four-family settlements to one characterized by large villages (Wilshusen 1991). At the same time, the population, which formerly had been more-or-less evenly distributed across the region, began to congregate in the higher elevations (Eddy et al. 1984). The change in the distribution of settlements corresponded to a climatic shift from relatively cool, moist conditions to warmer temperatures, lower winter precipitation, and higher summer precipitation, especially at higher elevations (Petersen 1988). Thus, the coalescence of population into higher-elevation areas has been interpreted as a response to a climatic regime that favored higher elevations for dry-land farming (Eddy et al. 1984:38; Petersen 1988). Eddy et al. (1984) conclude that the dry-farming belt during the Pueblo I period was largely confined to the area between 2010 m (6600 ft) and 2260 m (7400 ft). A study of Pueblo I villages in southwestern Colorado by Wilshusen (1991) basically confirmed the strength of this pattern. However, the Duckfoot site and a group of nearby contemporaneous settlements in the Crow Canyon area are located well below the lower limit of this postulated dry-farming belt.

Wilshusen (1991) studied Pueblo I village formation in southwestern Colorado from the Utah border east to Durango and from the New Mexico border north to Dove Creek. He recorded 30 Pueblo I villages and 10 more Pueblo I sites that may have been large enough to be considered villages. Wilshusen had sufficient data to use 22 of the villages in his analysis, and all but one lie above 2010 m. The one Pueblo I village on Wilshusen's list that lies below 2010 m is the Cirque site, which is approximately 3 km east of Duckfoot, on the east rim of Crow Canyon. The elevation of the Cirque site is 1890 m (6200 ft); Duckfoot is at 1945 m (6380 ft). Wilshusen (1991) estimated the population of the Cirque site to be 25 households, or about 125 to 175 people. Approximately 486 ha (1200 a) surrounding the Duckfoot site have been surveyed (Honeycutt and Fetterman 1991) and 11 other Pueblo I habitation sites have been recorded. Even with a more conservative estimate than Wilshusen's, the Cirque site and the other Pueblo I habitations in the area around Duckfoot represent a population of more than 250 people. Thus, although most Pueblo I sites were located above 2010 m in elevation, it appears that topographic and edaphic factors on the east-facing slopes of the western Montezuma Valley resulted in the inclusion of some lower-elevation sites within the Pueblo I dry-farming belt (Petersen 1988:Figure 57).

# Site-Formation Processes and Household Organization

Well-preserved and extensively excavated sites like Duckfoot offer the opportunity to develop methods that may be useful to other archaeologists working with less well preserved assemblages and more-limited samples. In this study, I attempt to explain some of the processes that helped to create the archaeological record at the Duckfoot site so that, in turn, we may better understand the relationship between the systemic, or behavioral, context and the archaeological context.

The archaeological record exists because artifacts, features, and structures that were created and used by people in the past still exist and can be studied in the present. We can use these physical traces of past behavior to make inferences about the culture that produced them, but we must keep in mind that they do not provide a clear and undistorted reflection of past behavior. The physical traces in the present must be linked to behaviors in the past by way of theory-dependent arguments. The empirical generalizations and theoretical principles upon which these linking arguments are based constitute "middle-range theory" in archaeology.

The assemblage-formation studies described in this volume are part of the development and testing of middle-range theory. Although the study of assemblage-formation processes is a legitimate and worthwhile endeavor in its own right, the goal of this volume is to use the results of such studies to address questions of household organization in prehistoric pueblos. The evaluation of assemblage-formation processes is prerequisite to using floor assemblages for addressing problems of general anthropological interest.

## Site-Formation Processes

Using archaeological data to study aspects of past social organization involves analysis of the spatial patterning of artifacts, features, and structures. However, the patterning of these material remains is affected by many factors other than the interactions relating to social organization. Some early attempts at anthropological archaeology failed because the researchers attempted to conduct ethnographic analysis using archaeological data, while failing to adequately account for the contextual vagaries of the archaeological record. This volume addresses a variety of issues relating to the processes by which sites are formed and the processes that produce the distributions we find archaeologically.

Archaeologists must rely on material remains and their spatial contexts to make inferences about the people, activities, and cultures of the past. The reason we can define sites, structures, and activity areas in the archaeological record is that there is a relationship between the location of activities and the material residues they produce:

> The basic assumption allowing us to deal rationally with archeological assemblages is: *The form and composition of assemblages recovered from geologically undisturbed context are directly related to the form and composition of human activities at a given location* [Binford and Binford 1966:291; emphasis in original].

We might extend this reasoning to add that if individual actions and social practices were random, sporadic, nonrepetitive, and spatially unconstrained, there would be little hope of making sense of the archaeological record. Especially in habitation sites, individual actions and social practices are largely prescribed by culture, marked by repetition, and confined by architecture and features. I do not mean to imply that the relationship between an activity and its material residues is simple and uncomplicated. Certain activities, such as housekeeping and refuse discard, may actually alter a spatial and temporal relationship that existed briefly between the manufacture of a tool and the distribution of the manufacturing by-products. The point is that tool manufacture, tool use, housekeeping, and refuse discard are all part of the repertoire of cultural processes that influence the relationship between the activity itself and the final deposition of the artifacts associated with the activity. Ascher (1961, 1968) warned against regarding the archaeological record as a clear reflection of past activities:

> Every living community is in the process of continuous change with respect to the materials which it utilizes. At any point in its existence some proportion of materials are falling into disuse and decomposing, while new materials are being added as replacement. In a certain sense a part of every community is becoming, but is not yet, archaeological data [Ascher 1961:324].

In presenting his "time's arrow" perspective, Ascher (1968:52) referred to the tendency of the universe to move in the direction of disorder and chaos. Ascher argued that this trend toward disorder begins not after abandonment but throughout the occupation of a settlement. Ascher (1961:324) noted that "what the archaeologist disturbs is not the remains of a once living community, stopped as it were, at a point in time; what he does interrupt is the process of decomposition." The material record is not only being ordered by cultural processes, it is also being disordered, recycled, discarded, and mixed by cultural and natural processes.

Schiffer continued to develop theory and methods for evaluating and explaining the complex processes that contribute to the formation of the archaeological record. Schiffer emphasized the range of cultural variables that determine the structure, rather than the form and content, of the archaeological record (Schiffer 1972:156). He argued that it is essential to conceptually and analytically distinguish the *archaeological context,* in which we observe artifacts and ecofacts in the present, from the *systemic context,* in which these same materials were used by humans in a cultural system. He opposed the perspective implicit in Binford's (1964:425) statement that "the loss, breakage, and abandonment of implements and facilities at different locations, where groups of variable structure performed different tasks, leaves a 'fossil' record of the actual operation of an extinct society."

Schiffer called for archaeologists to more rigorously develop the methods and the theoretical framework for explaining the relationship between past behavioral systems and the structure of the archaeological record. Schiffer's efforts have increased archaeologists' awareness of the complex relationship between activities and the refuse that those activities produce. The focus on assemblage-formation processes in this volume is an outgrowth of these trends in modern archaeology. The objective is to make better use of the archaeological record and to make better inferences about past activities and behavior associated with artifacts and features in the systemic context.

## Household Organization

Studying aspects of social organization and interaction is fundamental to anthropology, and since the 1960s, archaeologists have attempted to address anthropological problems in their studies of past cultures. Archaeologically, we may never achieve the richness of detail and understanding of social organization that are attained by ethnographers, but we have the potential to understand changes in organization through time on a scale that cannot be achieved ethnographically. We also have the potential to define a range of historical behaviors that is richer than the range that can be observed in the present. As archaeologists, we do not have living informants and we cannot observe social interactions, but it is possible for us to infer basic social structures and patterns of interaction using the distribution of material remains in the archaeological record.

First, we must separate the notion of *family,* defined on the basis of real or fictive kinship and affinity, from that of *household,* which is defined on the basis of behavior. If we define the household on the basis of activities and social interactions, then it becomes an appropriate unit for analysis in comparative cross-cultural studies, and it becomes an important unit of analysis archaeologically. Behaviorally defined social groups are of particular interest archaeologically because we have the potential to interpret the relevant cultural behavior from the material record.

Certainly by the 1950s, anthropologists recognized the importance of distinguishing between families as kinship units and households as coresident groups (Bohannon 1963; Keesing 1958). Bender (1967) argued that, despite the fact that researchers were distinguishing between families and residence groups, they were implicitly applying the term *household* to mean coresidence and shared domestic functions (for example, economic cooperation and the socialization of children). Although coresidence and shared domestic functions are often linked, they are not necessarily so. Wilk, Netting, and others (Wilk and Netting 1984; Netting et al. 1984) have proposed that social scientists define households not morphologically but behaviorally, as the smallest social group with the greatest frequency of interactions. This definition is vague, but it encompasses the variability that anthropologists have found in the ways that different cultures meet their basic social, economic, and residential needs. Defining the household in terms of our own value-laden folk perceptions of household and family is bound to be inadequate because such a definition will fail to account for important structural distinctions in household organization in other cultures.

Individual households are the minimal social units that form the building blocks for higher-order social groups, and they exist in some form in every society. Households have social, material, and behavioral elements (Wilk and Rathje 1982). Socially, the household is composed of specific individual members who usually have specific kin and affinal relationships to each other. Materially, the household generally has dwellings, activity areas, and possessions. Behaviorally, the household has certain activities it performs for its members, such as producing and distributing food or income, reproducing its membership, and controlling the transmission of its possessions from one generation to the next. Understanding the structure and behavior of household groups is essential to understanding the suprahousehold organizations that are usually the focus of settlement-pattern analyses.

## The Nested-Hierarchy Model

Archaeologists have long recognized that architecture in some way reflects the organization of activities and social groups (see review in Wilcox [1975]). To this day, architecture remains one of the most important tools for inferring social groups in prehistoric settlements. Architectural patterns and site layout have often been used as the basis for modeling Pueblo I social organization (e.g., Kane 1986). Such models assume that there is a relationship between the arrangement of architectural spaces and the size and relationships of the social groups who occupied and used those spaces. Early Pueblo structures are arranged in functionally distinct rows north to south (storage rooms, domestic rooms, pit structures), whereas they are organized into more or less redundant suites east to west. In this volume, a *dwelling unit* is defined as a domestic room and its associated (usually one to three) storage rooms (Figure 1.5 and Table 1.1). One to three contiguous dwelling units may be associated with a pit structure and a courtyard area, and together these constitute an *architectural suite*. Two or more architectural suites may be joined together, and along with a midden, they form a *roomblock cluster*. A small settlement consisting of one to a few small roomblock clusters with a total of fewer than 50 rooms is a *hamlet;* a larger settlement consisting of 50 or more rooms is a *village*. A *community cluster* is a constellation of hamlets and villages whose residents could have had regular, face-to-face interaction. According to the nested-hierarchy model, the Duckfoot site would be classified as both a roomblock cluster and a hamlet in a community cluster that probably included the Cirque site and additional smaller sites in the vicinity.

In a model of social organization derived from architecture, social groups are inferred from architectural patterns. In this volume, a *dwelling group* is the group of individuals who occupies a dwelling

**Figure 1.5.** *Spatial units that form the basis of the nested-hierarchy model of social organization. The example shown here is similar to the Duckfoot site, where the roomblock cluster is also a hamlet. Refer to Figure 6.1 for an illustration of the units above the level of the roomblock cluster.*

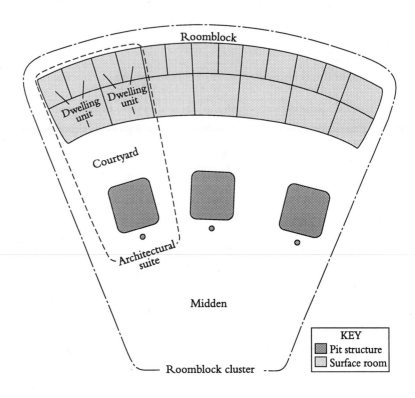

unit, a *household* occupies an architectural suite, a *roomblock group* occupies a roomblock cluster, and a *hamlet group* occupies a hamlet. If a hamlet consists of only one roomblock cluster, as it does at Duckfoot, then the roomblock group may be synonymous with the hamlet group. The group that occupies a village is a *village group.* A *community* is a group of people who occupy a number of separate hamlets and villages that are close enough to each other for the people to have regular, perhaps even daily, face-to-face interaction. With the exception of "household," the social-group terminology parallels the architectural terminology because the former is inferred from the latter. The social model presented here might best be defined as a "nested-hierarchy" model. At each level of organization, lower-order social groups are "nested" within higher-order groups. The hierarchical aspect of the model might best be explained by what Johnson (1982) defined as a sequential hierarchy of consensual decision making rather than a simultaneous hierarchy of political authority.

The question that is addressed throughout this volume is whether data from the Duckfoot site support the interpretation of household organization that is derived from the nested-hierarchy model. The

Table 1.1. Social Groups and Their Corresponding Architectural Units in the Nested-Hierarchy Model of Social Organization

| Social Group | Architectural Unit | Architectural Description |
|---|---|---|
| Dwelling group | dwelling unit | one domestic room and one to three storage rooms |
| Household | architectural suite | one pit structure, one to three dwelling units, and an associated courtyard |
| Roomblock group | roomblock cluster | two or more contiguous architectural suites and a midden area |
| Hamlet group | hamlet | one to a few closely spaced roomblock clusters totaling fewer than 50 rooms |
| Village group | village | one or more closely spaced roomblock clusters totaling 50 rooms or more |
| Community | community cluster | an associated group of villages and/or hamlets |

model as I have presented it here differs from most previous nested-hierarchy models of early Pueblo social organization in that it associates the household with an architectural suite rather than with each domestic room. This interpretation has implications for prehistoric population estimates: If each household was associated with an architectural suite rather than with a domestic room, population density during the late Pueblo I period might have been lower than previously estimated.

## Overview

In this chapter, I have presented a model of early Pueblo household organization that was developed on the basis of architectural patterns at residential sites in the region. This model provides a framework for interpreting household organization at Duckfoot. In the second chapter, I discuss the architecture at Duckfoot, with particular emphasis on the sequence and chronology of construction, occupation, and abandonment. In anticipation of using artifact and feature assemblages to evaluate the architecture-based interpretation of household organization at Duckfoot, I present a discussion of issues relating to site- and assemblage-formation processes (Chapter 3). In Chapter 4, I estimate the total quantity of pottery discarded at the site, and on the basis of that estimate, I simulate a "typical" pottery-vessel inventory (a list of the vessels that typically would have been in use at one time). I then compare the actual archaeological assemblage of vessels from structure floors with the simulated, or expected, vessel inventory. In Chapter 5, I use the floor assemblages of artifacts and features to analyze the distribution of activities across the site. In the network analyses described in Chapter 6, I look at interior access between rooms and document the distribution of parts of broken vessels in an attempt to infer social interactions between the occupants of different structures. Finally, in Chapter 7, I use the results of the various analyses to conclude that households were organized at the level of the architectural suite, an interpretation that differs from the conclusions of previous researchers and that has implications for estimating prehistoric population size. In addition to underscoring the need to reevaluate population estimates, I hope that the study methods and results reported in this volume will contribute to future studies of household organization.

# 2

# Architecture and Tree-Ring Dating

Traditionally, architecture has been used to infer the organization of prehistoric social groups in the Southwest (see review by Lipe and Hegmon [1989]). I continue in that tradition because architecture defines the stage for social interactions, enhancing interactions within groups, while restricting or controlling interactions with outsiders. Building design reflects both a traditional way of doing things and a perceived need for certain amounts of space for specific activities (Hegmon 1989; Rapoport 1990). The nested-hierarchy model of social organization presented in Chapter 1 provides a framework for inferring social-group arrangements on the basis of architectural layout alone. In this volume, I use additional types of architectural data, as well as the distributions of artifacts and features, to evaluate the validity of this model. In this chapter, I use architectural details and building styles to interpret the sequence of construction at the Duckfoot site. Next, I evaluate this interpretation by analyzing the distribution of tree-ring dates from individual structures and groups of structures. This analysis relies on techniques developed by Ahlstrom (1985) for analyzing tree-ring dates from structures and sites.

Through analysis of construction details in the roomblock at Duckfoot, I define three "room suites," each of which consists of one to several dwelling units and each of which is associated with a separate pit structure. I refer to the room suite, the pit structure, and the intervening courtyard area as an "architectural suite." The use and changes in use of these three architectural suites are evaluated in subsequent chapters.

# Duckfoot Site Architecture

The Duckfoot site (Figure 2.1) consists of a single-story pueblo with 19 contiguous surface rooms and four pit structures. Archaeological survey in the area around Duckfoot indicates that there are at least 11 sites within a 3-km radius that may have been contemporaneous with Duckfoot. One of these is a small village, the Cirque site, which includes several roomblocks and pit structures, including an oversize pit structure. It is possible that the residents of these sites were members of the same community and had regular face-to-face interaction (Wilshusen 1991).

Rooms at the Duckfoot site are predominantly earth-walled structures built of locally available silt loam sediments and unshaped or minimally shaped stones, especially in the lower walls. Several building styles are evident in the way that stones were used in these predominantly mud walls. Some of the walls, such as the one surrounding Rooms 4 through 7, were made of unshaped sandstone blocks that had been laid in horizontal courses, of which three to four still remain. Existing walls in other rooms (for example, in Rooms 2, 8, and 15) were constructed predominantly of large, thin, minimally shaped sandstone slabs set on edge at the bases of the

**Figure 2.1.** *Architectural map of the Duckfoot site. Room 20 is not shown.*

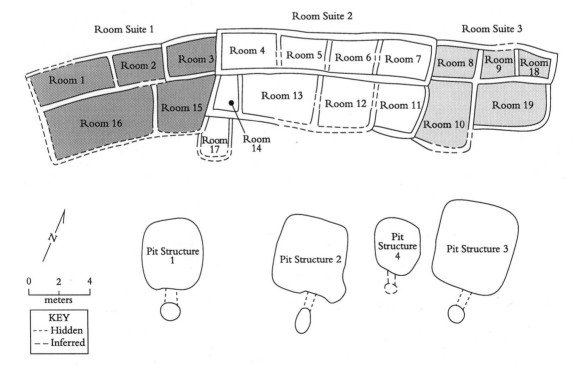

walls. In some cases, the horizontal-block and vertical-slab styles were used in different walls of the same room (for example, in Rooms 11, 12, and 13). In still other cases, the different styles were combined in the same wall (for example, in Rooms 2 and 3). The south and east walls of Room 19 were of jacal, or post-and-mud, construction, which is common in the Southwest and in many other arid parts of the world. The jacal construction is indicated by an alignment of post holes and a small remnant of a mud wall seen in the stratigraphic profile of the room. In general, the northern and interior walls of the roomblock are better preserved than the southern exterior walls. This may be the result of a combination of factors relating to both construction and weathering. The northern (storage) rooms consistently appear to have been built more soundly than the southern (habitation) rooms. The need for sturdy, rodent-resistant, stable-temperature storage facilities might have resulted in an emphasis on storage rooms built to last (Gross 1987). In addition, the southern walls would have weathered more rapidly and severely than the interior and northern walls because they were subject to more extreme cycles of warming and cooling, wetting and drying, and freezing and thawing.

# Using Architecture to Interpret Construction and Remodeling

Interpreting construction sequences in masonry structures is a relatively routine operation. Careful observation allows one to determine whether two walls were bonded together, and thus were built at the same time, or abutted, and thus were built at different times. The interpretation of construction sequences in mud-walled structures is much less precise. Often there are slight differences in appearance or materials that reveal continuity or interruption of a wall; these changes may be equivalent to wall bonding and abutment, respectively. Using the same basic logic that one would use to interpret construction sequences in masonry walls, I propose three principles to be used in the interpretation of mud-walled structures. First, continuity of a single construction style in an uninterrupted wall reflects a single building event (as in the north and south walls of Rooms 4 through 7). Second, where walls of two different construction styles intersect, the wall of the style that continues uninterrupted past the juncture (either straight across or around a corner) is earlier than the wall of the style that terminates at the juncture (for example, the east wall of Room 7 was built before the south wall of Room 8, and the northwest corner of Room 4 was built before the north wall of Room 3). This principle is the mud-wall equivalent of the abutment principle. Third, if two wall segments of one style are interrupted by a perpendicular segment of wall of a different style, construction of all three segments was contemporaneous (for example, construction of the wall dividing Rooms 4 and 5 was contemporaneous with construction of the continuous north wall of Rooms 4 and 5). This is the mud-wall equivalent of the bonded-juncture principle.

Another relative-dating principle implicit in some of the inferences in this study is that pit structures and room suites were not built independently. The construction of a fully subterranean pit structure produces a surplus of sediment, and the construction of an earthen roomblock requires a large volume of sediment (Glennie 1983; Varien 1984; Wilshusen 1984, 1988c, 1989a). At Duckfoot, the roomblock walls were built with silt loam that occurs in the local soil B horizon and which therefore requires excavation. The surplus sediment from the prehistoric excavation of the pit structures would have been a logical source for this construction material. Varien (1984) built an experimental Pueblo I–style room suite without excavating a pit structure. He discovered that the demand for construction-quality sediment was no small obstacle; even though he used substantial amounts of stone, the three-room suite required almost 10 m$^3$ (about 15 tons) of sediment. I estimate that if the walls in the Duckfoot roomblock were 20 cm thick, 2 m high, and 70 percent earthen construction (that is, 30 percent stone and wood), and if there were 10 cm of dirt on the roof, then a layer of sediment 1.2 m thick excavated prehistorically from Pit Structures 1, 2, and 3 would have provided enough sediment for the construction of the roomblock.

On the basis of archaeological data, we can make several generalizations about ancestral Pueblo sites in the late A.D. 800s in the northern San Juan area: (1) Pit structures and surface roomblocks typically occur together and not in isolation; (2) the two types of structures are contemporaneous; and (3) there is a significant quantitative relationship between the volume of sediment excavated from a pit structure and the size of the associated roomblock (Wilshusen 1984, 1988c, 1989a). Therefore, it seems safe to assume that room suites and adjacent pit structures were built together at Duckfoot.

## Roomblock Construction

The first construction in the Duckfoot roomblock was in Room Suite 2 and was probably concurrent with the construction of Pit Structure 2. The first wall to be constructed was that enclosing Rooms 4, 5, 6, and 7 (Figure 2.1). The dividing wall between Rooms

4 and 5 was built at the same time, as evidenced by a "tied" juncture at the north end of this cross wall. Next, the dividing walls between Rooms 5, 6, and 7 were added. Sometime after the construction of these northern rooms, Rooms 12, 13, and 14 were built. Room 11 was then added to the suite, with its walls abutting the walls of Room 7 to the north and Room 12 to the west. On the basis of the wall junctures between Rooms 3 and 4 and between Rooms 7 and 8, it is clear that Room Suites 1 and 3 were built after Room Suite 2. It is not clear which of the two was built first, and there is nothing in the architectural data that rules out the possibility that they were built at the same time.

In the western addition (Room Suite 1), it appears that Room 3 was attached to the west end of Room 4, and sometime later, Rooms 1 and 2 were added (Figure 2.1). Next, Rooms 15 and 16 were added to the front of Rooms 1, 2, and 3. Pit Structure 1 lies directly south of Room Suite 1, and together these structures are interpreted as Architectural Suite 1. The north-south wall that separates Rooms 15 and 16 does not align with the north-south wall that divides the adjoining back rooms (Rooms 2 and 3). The dwelling unit does not conform to the typical room pattern described in Chapter 1. There are three back rooms (Rooms 1, 2, and 3) and two front rooms (Rooms 15 and 16), but Room 2 could have been associated with either front room (15 or 16), or it could have been shared by both. After the initial construction of this room suite was complete, Room 17 was added in front of Room 14, as part of Architectural Suite 2.

At the eastern end of the roomblock, Rooms 8, 9, 10, and 18 appear to have been built at or near the same time; Room 19 apparently was added later. Pit Structure 3 lies immediately south of this room suite, and together the pit structure and the rooms are interpreted as Architectural Suite 3 (Figure 2.1).

## Pit Structure Construction

Pit Structures 1, 2, and 3 are evenly spaced and well aligned with the three room suites. The size, shape, and location of Pit Structure 4 appear to have been influenced by the prior existence of Pit Structures 2 and 3, and therefore Pit Structure 4 is interpreted as a later addition to the site. Small pit structures such as Pit Structure 4 are known to have been late additions to other sites in the region dating to approximately this same period. For example, at Grass Mesa Village in the Dolores River valley, small, late pit structures were common, representing over 40 percent of the 109 pit structures found during testing (Lipe, Morris, and Kohler 1988). The spatial context was similar at Grass Mesa as well, with the smaller pit structures having been built between existing structures or in the fill of earlier, abandoned structures. Some of the existing roomblocks and pit structures were thought to have still been in use when the small, late pit structures were added. In only one case at Grass Mesa were room suites built in association with one of these pit structures (Morris 1988). Blinman (1991) has recently argued that the small, late pit structures at Grass Mesa may have been built in the early A.D. 900s, postdating a postulated hiatus in the A.D. 880s. The tree-ring dates from Pit Structure 4 at Duckfoot show that there was no interruption in the occupation of this site, and although Pit Structure 4 was built later than the other structures at the site, its use was clearly contemporaneous with the use of the other structures.

## Roomblock Remodeling

Remodeling in rooms at Duckfoot is evidenced primarily by changes in the feature assemblages of the rooms. The changes included the capping of old features and the addition of new ones (*capping* refers to the deliberate filling and sealing of a pit feature, usually with clean sediment). Four rooms at Duckfoot show evidence of significant remodeling, and in three of those cases, the remodeling appears to signal changes in the way the rooms were used.

Room 10 is a front room that originally had a hearth, but at some point the hearth had been capped, which effectively removed it from use. In addition, a large cist had been excavated into the floor, truncating the hearth, and another cist and three bins were probably added at the same time. The bins and the cists consumed much of the available floor space in the room, which suggests that the room was used primarily for storage after it was remodeled. Room 15 is a front room that has a deep, centrally located cist, similar to the one in Room 10, and a shallower cist along the west wall. It is possible that Room 15 originally had a hearth, but if so, all signs of it were obliterated by the construction of the cist in the center of the room. It is not clear if Room 15 was originally used as a domestic structure, but the presence of two cists and the absence of a hearth suggest that it was not a domestic structure at abandonment.

Room 5 also underwent changes in the final period of the Duckfoot occupation. The direction of change in this room is opposite that inferred for Rooms 10 and 15. Room 5 probably was a long-term storage room until late in the occupation, when it was altered to accommodate domestic activities. A small fire pit was excavated into the floor, and a bin was built in the northeast corner. A shallow pit in the northwest corner had a number of thin sandstone slabs associated with it, which suggests that a bin may have been built in that corner as well. The diversity of artifacts recovered is more consistent with what one would expect on the floor of a domestic room than on the floor of a long-term storage room.

Room 4, a long-term storage room, apparently was used for some domestic activities during the period of abandonment, but the kinds of permanent facilities that were added to Room 5 are not present in Room 4. A large burned spot covered with several centimeters of ash was found on the floor of Room 4, and broken and burned bones of small mammals (mostly *Lepus* [jackrabbit] and *Sylvilagus* [cottontail]) were recovered from the ash and the floor surrounding the burned spot. This evidence is not believed to indicate a change in the basic function of this long-term storage room; rather, there seems to have been a period of brief and expedient use of the room for cooking. It is even possible that this use of the room took place soon after the site was abandoned, as this cooking pattern is not typical of other structures at Duckfoot or at other Pueblo I habitation sites.

## Pit Structure Remodeling

Earth-walled structures are subject to decay and require almost continuous maintenance because of the effects of weathering on the sediments used in construction. In addition, wooden construction members are subject to decay because of the action of bacteria, fungi, and insects, as well as weathering. Ethnographic data from around the world indicate that structures built of earth and timbers have relatively short use lives, ranging from four to 10 years (see the review of the ethnographic literature by Cameron [1991]).

The strongest evidence of major pit structure remodeling is in Pit Structure 3, where the main roof-support posts had been replaced. Four post holes, three of which still contained remnants of posts, were interpreted as being part of the final roof-support system (Lightfoot, Etzkorn, and Varien 1993:112–113). In addition, three other capped post holes were identified adjacent to the southeast, southwest, and northeast roof-support post holes, and in the northwest corner, there were two capped pits that could have held earlier roof-support posts. Replacement of the main support posts suggests that the roof was probably removed and completely rebuilt rather than just repaired.

Some researchers (e.g., Gilman 1987) have suggested that the number of pit features in the floor of a structure can be used as a measure of the relative length of use of the structure. The assumption is that pit structures were used in similar ways and that, through time, pits were added to the structure floors at some relatively constant rate. The assumption that all pit structures were used in similar ways may not be valid. Certain activities undoubtedly required more pit features than did others. For example, an everyday activity such as cooking may have required only a single pit feature that was used for decades. On the other hand, a ceremonial event that occurred only occasionally might have required the construction of a temporary altar with four posts. If one pit structure had been used more often than others for such ceremonies, then pit features would have accumulated much faster in that structure, even though it was the same age as the others. The range of activities may not have been the same for all pit structures, the use life of pit features may not have been equivalent, and there is no compelling reason to believe that pit features should have accumulated at a constant rate over time.

Nevertheless, Table 2.1 lists the number of pit features found in the floors of pit structures at Duckfoot. Some of the pits are described as "capped," which indicates that they were filled and then deliberately covered with sediment before abandonment. Thus, capped features are "old" pit features that were no longer in use, as opposed to uncapped features, which were open and available for use at abandonment. Ranked by the total number of pit features, Pit Structure 3 is first, with 61 pits; Pit Structure 2 is second, with 35 pits; Pit Structure 4 is third, with 34 pits; and Pit Structure 1 is last, with only 16 pits. These numbers suggest that Pit Structures 2 and 4 were used for about the same length of time, whereas Pit Structure 3 was used nearly twice as long, and Pit Structure 1 was used about half as long. If Pit Structure 3 was extensively remodeled, as was suggested above, then all the pit features in its floor could have been replaced at that time. If all four pit structures were abandoned at about the same time, then the number of pit features suggests, first, that the structures were built at very different times and, second, that Pit Structure 4 was occupied as long as Pit Structure 2 and much longer than Pit Structure 1. These interpretations are not consistent with those made on the basis of architectural evidence, and—as discussed in the following section—they are not supported by tree-ring dates.

Table 2.1. Pit Features in Pit Structures

| Pit Structure | Pit Features | | | |
| | In Use | Capped | Unknown | Total |
| --- | --- | --- | --- | --- |
| 1 | 8 | 7 | 1 | 16 |
| 2 | 16 | 17 | 2 | 35 |
| 3 | 24 | 34 | 3 | 61 |
| 4 | 17 | 15 | 2 | 34 |

# Using Tree-Rings to Date Construction and Remodeling

Tree-ring dates are "independent dates" (Dean 1978a:226), which means that they are derived by methods that are totally independent of archaeological context and systematics. In the case of tree-ring dating, the "dated event" is the production of a layer of xylem cells in an individual tree in a particular year. If the outermost growth ring of the tree is intact, the date represents the year that the tree died; this is typically the "reference event" that is of interest to archaeologists (Dean 1978a:226). The fact that the wood ended up in an interpretable archaeological context allows us to construct an argument that relates the "reference event" (the death of a tree) to an archaeological "target event" (for example, the building of a structure). The argument generally involves a "bridging event" (for example, the cutting of the tree by humans) to relate the dated event to the target event.

Building on Dean's discussion of the logic of archaeological dating, Ahlstrom (1985) developed some general principles and techniques for interpreting assemblages of tree-ring dates from structures and sites. Ahlstrom (1985:42) specified the bridging and target events that are commonly used in archaeological dating and proposed several principles that underlie the interpretation of tree-ring dates from structures (Ahlstrom 1985:57–59). These may be summarized as follows:

- Clusters of cutting dates provide evidence that timbers were newly cut for the construction they date.
- Construction generally occurred soon after the timbers were cut.
- Large clusters of noncutting dates can provide evidence of wood cutting and construction.
- Dates that are anomalous with respect to a presumed construction event come from timbers that were eroded, reused, stockpiled, or used to repair a structure (dates from repair timbers follow the construction date; dates from the other categories of timber precede it).
- In the absence of a cluster of dates, the latest date from a structure may provide the best estimate of when construction occurred.

Ahlstrom (1985:59–60) also discussed some criteria for evaluating date clusters. These criteria include the following: the number of dates in the cluster, the span of time represented (for example, a tight cluster is five years or less, whereas a loose cluster spans more than five years), the proportion of cutting to noncutting dates, the relative strength of multiple clusters in the same distribution, and the extent to which a distribution approaches an "ideal" distribution.

Ahlstrom (1985:64) described an "ideal" scenario, which would result in an unambiguous distribution and a correct interpretation. The scenario is basically this: The occupants of a site cut live trees in a single year to procure all the wood needed for a structure, and they finish construction in that same year. Later, an archaeologist excavates the structure and collects a sample from each timber. Finally, a dendrochronologist analyzes the samples and determines that the cutting date for each specimen is the same. This situation never occurs in the real world, and instead we are faced with the task of interpreting assemblages of dates that include all types of "noise" created by the collection of dead wood, the reuse and stockpiling of beams, the erosion or deterioration of samples, and so on. The archaeological examples that come closest to approximating the ideal scenario are those that, when plotted on a graph, produce an extended left tail, a strong right peak, and a truncated right tail. The left tail is accounted for by all the processes that produce dates earlier than the construction date. The strong right peak, or "terminal cluster," generally approximates the construction date, and the truncated right tail represents wood added after construction for remodeling, repair, or use as fuel. Ahlstrom (1985) found that stem-and-leaf plots (Hartwig and Dearing 1979:16–19) were useful for analyzing groups of dates from structures. Stem-and-leaf plots are essentially horizontal histograms that display the general distribution of dates, while allowing one to see the individual dates that produce the distribution. The "stem" is usually displayed as a vertical column of numbers representing centuries and decades A.D., and the "leaves" are the final digits of each date, which form the horizontal bars of the histogram.

The sequence of construction inferred for the Duckfoot roomblock on the basis of architectural evidence suggests that Room Suite 2 was built before Room Suites 1 and 3. A completely different sequence of construction is suggested for pit structures if the number of pit features is used as a measure of the relative length of the use of each structure, a method that I question. Tree-ring dates provide a means of assigning more specific dates to the construction, occupation, and abandonment of Duckfoot. The dates are largely confined to structures that burned at abandonment. The Duckfoot site is extremely well dated, with 375 tree-ring dates from 13 rooms (including Room 20), four pit structures, several courtyard features, and midden deposits. Fifty-two percent (194) of these dates are cutting dates (that is, those with a notation of r, rB, or B), and an additional 5 percent (20) are "v" dates, which are near-cutting dates that are treated in this study as cutting dates (Ahlstrom 1985:38,

1989:364).[1] Many of the 161 noncutting dates (that is, those with a notation of ++ or vv) also fall within clusters of cutting dates or a few years before. Clusters of noncutting dates—especially in combination with cutting dates—can be treated as if they were cutting dates. As Dean (1978b:148) argued, "the probability that weathering, burning, or shaping of a number of beams could remove exactly the right number of rings to cause the beams to date within a few years of one another is low."

Figure 2.2 presents a stem-and-leaf plot of all 375 dates from the Duckfoot site. This summary graph shows a fairly robust terminal cluster of dates representing the total period of occupation. The distribution has a gradually sloping left tail from an early outlying date of A.D. 689 to about A.D. 850. There is an almost continuous string of dates in this left tail between A.D. 824 and 850, with a minor peak, or cluster, of dates in the late A.D. 820s and 830s. There is a strong terminal cluster consisting of 262 dates (70 percent) between A.D. 850 and 876. In the discussions of individual architectural suites that follow, I present additional graphs that support the following general interpretations: (1) Construction at Duckfoot began during the mid– to late A.D. 850s; (2) remodeling and construction occurred almost continuously until A.D. 873; and (3) the site was occupied until at least A.D. 876. The site may have been occupied until the early A.D. 880s, but one would expect at least a few dates after 876 if the occupation continued for more than a few years after that date (Hantman 1983). Pit Structures 1, 3, and 4 at Duckfoot burned, which accounts for the abundance of tree-ring samples col-

---

1. Dates provided by the Laboratory of Tree-Ring Research at the University of Arizona are reported with a suffix that aids in interpretation. The following suffixes are associated with the Duckfoot samples: B = bark present; r = less than a full section is present, but the outermost ring is continuous around the available circumference; v = a subjective judgment that the date is very close to a cutting date; vv = there is no way of knowing how far the last ring is from the true outside of the tree, and many rings may be missing; ++ = a ring count is needed beyond a certain point because cross-dating ceases; + = one or a few rings may be missing near the outside of the specimen, but the presence or absence of the rings cannot be determined because the series does not extend far enough to provide adequate cross-dating. The interpretation of tree-ring date notations in the present volume differs slightly from the approach used in Volume 1 (Lightfoot and Etzkorn 1993). In Volume 1, the only dates treated as noncutting dates were those with a vv suffix. Dates with a suffix of r, rB, B, or v were always treated as cutting dates, regardless of the presence or absence of an additional qualifier (+ or ++). In the present volume, in addition to vv dates being interpreted as noncutting dates, *any* date accompanied by a ++ qualifier is also treated as a noncutting date. Thus, a date of 851++B would have been interpreted as a cutting date in Volume 1 but is interpreted as a noncutting date in Volume 2.

```
A.D.
680s 68  9
         **
     76  6
770s 77  46
     78  27899
790s 79  0699
     80  00012334567
810s 81  112344678
     82  02222445566677888888888999
830s 83  00001112222223445555566778889
     84  1112233344556677888888999
850s 85  0000111122222222222233333333444444444455555555566666666677777888888888899999999999999999999
     86  00111111122222222223333333333444455555555555555555555555555555555666666666666666666666666666777888 9999
870s 87  00011111111111111222222222222222222222222222222222233333333333344445 66
```

Key: ** = break in scale of *y*-axis
underlined = cutting date
unmarked = noncutting date

**Figure 2.2.** *Stem-and-leaf plot of all tree-ring dates for the Duckfoot site. Each numeric digit in the bars of the histogram represents the third digit of one tree-ring date. For example, in the fourth bar from the top, there are five dates in the A.D. 780s: 782, 787, 788, and two 789s. Three of the five are cutting dates.*

lected from these structures. Seventy-four percent (276) of the dates from the site are from Pit Structures 1, 3, and 4. Twenty-three percent (85) of the dates are from samples collected from rooms, and these samples are fairly evenly dispersed across the roomblock.

## Architectural Suite 2

This unit includes the central suite of rooms (Rooms 4–7, 11–14, and 17) and Pit Structure 2. On the basis of building styles and wall junctures, this suite is believed to be the first architectural unit constructed at the site. Pit Structure 2 was not burned, and the single tree-ring date of 822vv is from a sample collected from the lower fill. This noncutting date is not very useful for estimating the date of construction, but an inference may be drawn from the associated suite of rooms in the roomblock. The rooms most likely built in association with Pit Structure 2 are front rooms 11, 12, 13, and 14 and back rooms 4, 5, 6, and 7. Of these, Rooms 4, 6, 11, 12, and 13 yielded tree-ring dates; these are shown in Figure 2.3. The distribution has a very flat left tail, a terminal cluster at A.D. 855–857, and a short right tail extending to A.D. 873. This distribution is interpreted as indicating construction in about A.D. 857 and occupation extending into the mid-870s. The cutting dates in the A.D. 855–857 range are all from Room 13, and the latest dates in the distribution (right tail) are from Rooms 6 and 11. The spatial relationship between these central rooms and Pit Structure 2 makes it reasonable to argue that this unburned pit structure was also built in the late A.D. 850s.

## Architectural Suite 1

Building details suggest that Architectural Suite 1 was built after Architectural Suite 2. Pit Structure 1 has a date distribution that, in

```
A.D.
770s  77  46
      78  29                 Key: underlined = cutting date
790s  79  069                     unmarked = noncutting date
      80  0017
810s  81  14
      82  0577888
830s  83  29
      84  467889
850s  85  001222234445555566666677
      86  56
870s  87  123
```

**Figure 2.3.** *Stem-and-leaf plot of the tree-ring dates for Room Suite 2 (Rooms 4, 6, 11, 12, and 13). Each numeric digit in the bars of the histogram represents the third digit of one tree-ring date.*

**Figure 2.4.** *Stem-and-leaf plot of the tree-ring dates for Pit Structure 1. Each numeric digit in the bars of the histogram represents the third digit of one tree-ring date.*

```
A.D.
780s  78  89
          **                    Key:  ** = break in scale of y-axis
830s  83  1122                        underlined = cutting date
      84  134568                       unmarked = noncutting date
850s  85  13333444699
      86  233333455555555555555555555555555555555566666666666666666
870s  87  23
```

general, conforms to the ideal scenario described by Ahlstrom: an extended left tail, a small, tight cluster of A.D. 853 and 854 dates, a strong terminal cluster of 865 and 866 dates, and two early 870s dates (Figure 2.4). Three of the four main roof-support posts in Pit Structure 1 yielded cutting or near-cutting dates in the A.D. 860s (863+r, 865vv, and 866+r). The distribution of dates for Pit Structure 1 suggests two possible interpretations. The most obvious is that the pit structure was constructed in A.D. 866, with the earlier dates representing the use of dead wood or salvaged timbers in construction. A less obvious, but equally plausible, interpretation is that the smaller cluster of A.D. 853 and 854 dates represents initial construction in the 850s, with the 865 and 866 cluster dating major remodeling or rebuilding in A.D. 866.

Room Suite 1 has tree-ring dates from Rooms 2, 3, 15, and 16, which are displayed together as a stem-and-leaf plot in Figure 2.5.

**Figure 2.5.** *Stem-and-leaf plot of the tree-ring dates for Room Suite 1 (Rooms 2, 3, 15, and 16). Each numeric digit in the bars of the histogram represents the third digit of one tree-ring date.*

```
A.D.
820s  82  2688
      83  0                    Key:  underlined = cutting date
840s  84  237                         unmarked = noncutting date
      85  246788                       bold = Room 3 date
```

The 14 dates from Room Suite 1 have a terminal cluster in the late A.D. 850s and no dates later than 858. The number of dates is small, but the presence of a tight terminal cluster suggests that the west end of the roomblock was built in the mid- to late 850s, perhaps A.D. 858. The cluster of dates in Room Suite 1 coincides with the small cluster of dates in the mid- to late A.D. 850s in Pit Structure 1. The distribution of dates throughout Architectural Suite 1 suggests that the rooms and Pit Structure 1 were built in the mid- to late A.D. 850s—possibly as late as A.D. 858—and that Pit Structure 1 was substantially remodeled around A.D. 866.

## Architectural Suite 3

Construction details in the roomblock suggest that Architectural Suite 3 was built after Architectural Suite 2, although its relationship to the construction of Architectural Suite 1 cannot be determined. Pit Structure 3 has the largest number of floor pits, which some would argue indicates a longer use life than for the other pit structures. Pit Structure 3 also has the largest number of dates (113, not counting those from the postabandonment pit, Feature 2) from a single structure, with 84 of them being cutting dates (Figure 2.6). About two-thirds of the dates from Pit Structure 3 are after A.D. 850, but there is a pronounced secondary peak from A.D. 830 to 838, with 13 of the 18 dates from the decade of the 830s being cutting dates. There are also 13 dates between A.D. 830 and 835, inclusive. Most of the dates from Pit Structure 3 are in the A.D. 850s and 860s; 16 samples produced cutting dates of A.D. 859. Although it is possible that Pit Structure 3 was originally built in the A.D. 830s and maintained until the late A.D. 870s, cross-cultural data on the use lives of earth-walled structures (Cameron 1991) suggest that this is unlikely. The early cutting dates more likely are from timbers salvaged from a structure at an earlier site. Juniper is much more resistant to decay than is pinyon, and the predominance of juniper (eight samples) over pinyon (three samples) and ponderosa pine (two samples) in specimens with cutting dates in the A.D. 830s is consistent with the argument that these early timbers were salvaged. Another piece of evidence that argues against the earlier cluster indicating the construction date for Pit Structure 3 is the relative paucity of dates between A.D. 835 and 855 compared with the abundance of dates, especially cutting dates, between A.D. 855 and 876. The charred re-

```
A.D.
760s  76  6
      77
780s  78  7
      79  9
800s  80  5
      81  3467
820s  82  24489
      83  000122445555567788
840s  84  238889
      85  112222334555556788899999999999999999
860s  86  0112222233333355566666666667779
      87  02223334466
```

Key: underlined = cutting date
     unmarked = noncutting date

**Figure 2.6.** *Stem-and-leaf plot of the tree-ring dates for Pit Structure 3, excluding those for Feature 2, an intrusive pit excavated into postabandonment deposits. Each numeric digit in the bars of the histogram represents the third digit of one tree-ring date.*

**Figure 2.7.** *Stem-and-leaf plot of the tree-ring dates for Room Suite 3 (Rooms 10, 18, and 19). Each numeric digit in the bars of the histogram represents the third digit of one tree-ring date.*

```
A.D.
800s  80   06
      81
820s  82   5 8 8         Key:  underlined = cutting date
      83                        unmarked = noncutting date
840s  84   1 9
      85   0 3 8 9
860s  86   1 4 8
      87   3
```

mains of the southwest corner post yielded a noncutting date of A.D. 870, indicating relatively major remodeling or rebuilding after that date, even though the total number of dates after A.D. 870 is small. The two A.D. 876 dates are the latest dates from the entire site. I interpret the assemblage of dates from Pit Structure 3 as indicating initial construction in the late A.D. 850s, probably A.D. 859, with continuous occupation and frequent repairs until A.D. 876.

A postabandonment reuse of the Pit Structure 3 depression is indicated by the presence of a pit, Feature 2, that had been prehistorically excavated into the collapsed roof debris that covered the structure floor. Tree-ring samples from this burned, slab-lined feature yielded eight "vv" dates, none of which are included in Figure 2.6 or were discussed above. All the dates from Feature 2 are A.D. 861 or earlier, and they probably represent reuse, as fuel, of some of the charred beams from the collapsed roof of Pit Structure 3. This interpretation accounts for the eroded condition of the Feature 2 specimens and the occurrence of the nonlocal genus *Abies* (fir), whose only other occurrence at the site is in the roof fall of Pit Structure 3.

Room Suite 3 yielded only 15 datable samples, with eight of the dates being in the A.D. 850s to early 870s (Figure 2.7). These rooms are spatially associated with Pit Structure 3, and their few dates have a distribution similar to that of the Pit Structure 3 dates. I interpret these dates as indicating construction in the late A.D. 850s and occupation into the mid–A.D. 870s.

## Pit Structure 4

The distribution of tree-ring dates from Pit Structure 4 closely approximates Ahlstrom's ideal. A stem-and-leaf plot of the dates (Figure 2.8) has a flat, extended left tail and an exaggerated terminal cluster formed by dates of A.D. 871 to 873 and two later dates of 874 and 875. This structure is believed to have been built in A.D. 873, and it was probably occupied for only a few years thereafter.

```
A.D.
680s  68  9
      **                   Key:  ** = break in scale of y-axis
800s  80  4                      underlined = cutting date
      81  12                     unmarked = noncutting date
820s  82  269
      83  28
840s  84  15
      85  22788
860s  86  11122456688999
      87  00111111111111111222222222222222222222222222222222233333345
```

**Figure 2.8.**
*Stem-and-leaf plot of the tree-ring dates for Pit Structure 4. Each numeric digit in the bars of the histogram represents the third digit of one tree-ring date.*

Pit Structure 4 apparently is an exception to the rule stated previously that pit structures and room suites were built together. Tree-ring dates confirm that Pit Structure 4 was a late addition to the site, and the placement of the structure in what had previously been a courtyard gave its occupants access to existing rooms in the roomblock. Interestingly, the latest dates from the roomblock come from rooms roughly north of Pit Structure 4: Room 10 (A.D. 873), Room 11 (A.D. 871 and 872), and Room 6 (A.D. 873). Room 10 was remodeled from a domestic room to a storage room sometime during the occupation of the site, and this change may have been concurrent with the construction of Pit Structure 4.

# Using Tree-Rings to Date Abandonment

Hantman (1983:111–123) considered the relationship between the abandonment of a site and its latest tree-ring date. He suggested that if construction and remodeling took place continually, then we can assume that the site was abandoned around the time of the latest tree-ring date from the site. Hantman noted that an "adequate sample" of dates is necessary for the principle to be applied. In response to Hantman, Ahlstrom noted that two aspects of an "adequate sample" merit attention:

> First, tree-ring dates must be available from portions of the site inhabited, though not necessarily built, late in the occupation. Second, use of the principle makes sense *only* if the site's tree-ring date distribution is continuous, particularly toward the end. Otherwise, there is no basis for arguing that the tree-ring record reflects the sort of recurrent architectural change that underlies the principle [Ahlstrom 1985:79; emphasis in original].

Hantman probably intended the "adequate sample" to mean that one needs a sufficient number of dated samples to represent the length of occupation and the diversity of wood-collecting practices at a site. By all three criteria, the Duckfoot sample of tree-ring dates should be adequate for inferring the approximate date of abandonment. There is an almost continuous sequence of dates from the early A.D. 820s to A.D. 876, with 69 percent of the dates occurring after A.D. 850. The years A.D. 875 and 876 are represented by one and two samples, respectively, and these are the latest dates for the site. The distribution of dates is consistent for most of the individual pit structures and room suites and for the site as a whole (Figure 2.2). The final episode of construction—the building of Pit Structure 4—was in the early A.D. 870s, and the few dates that fall after this strong terminal cluster are in the mid–A.D. 870s. It is reasonable to infer that the Duckfoot site was abandoned around A.D. 876, or at least between 876 and 880.

Stratigraphic evidence suggests that none of the structures collapsed any substantial length of time before abandonment of the remainder of the site. Assemblages of floor artifacts and features indicate that the primary uses (for example, domestic vs. storage) of several rooms changed during the occupation of the site, but none were destroyed before the site was abandoned. None of the structures were filled with trash, although Room 15 and Pit Structure 2 had secondary refuse on their floors. An intensive pottery-refitting study demonstrated that sherds from many of the broken vessels on the floors of these structures were still being used as containers on the floors of other structures (see Chapter 6).

Tree-ring dates also support the argument that all three architectural suites were built and occupied at about the same time, although absolute contemporaneity cannot be established. The latest dates in Architectural Suite 1 are A.D. 872 and 873, from Pit Structure 1. In Architectural Suite 2, the latest dates—also A.D. 872 and 873—come from the rooms. In Architectural Suite 3, there is a date of A.D. 873 from a room, but the latest dates on the entire site come from Pit Structure 3, with two dates of A.D. 876. The latest date from Pit Structure 4 is A.D. 875. The latest dates are quite consistent across the entire site, with the exception of the rooms in Room Suite 1, which have a latest date of A.D. 858.

## Summary and Conclusions

Architectural data from the roomblock suggest that construction at Duckfoot began with Architectural Suite 2 and continued with Architectural Suites 1 and 3. The meager assemblage of tree-ring dates from the rooms neither refutes nor strongly supports this sequence. Room Suite 2, the best-dated room suite at the site, was probably built during the late A.D. 850s—possibly about A.D. 857—and occupied into the A.D. 870s. On the basis of a lack of cutting dates and any data to the contrary, I infer that Pit Structure 2 was constructed at the same time as Room Suite 2. The dates from Room Suite 3 provide only very general evidence that suggests that construction took place in the A.D. 850s or 860s. However, on the basis of tree-ring dates obtained for samples from Pit Structure 3, I infer that the entire architectural suite was probably constructed in the late A.D. 850s—possibly A.D. 859—and that Pit Structure 3 was remodeled or rebuilt after A.D. 870. Room Suite 1 is interpreted as having been constructed in the mid- to late A.D. 850s; a small cluster of dates ending in A.D. 858 suggests that construction may have taken place in that year. Pit Structure 1 has a strong terminal cluster of dates in the mid–A.D. 860s and a smaller, but still substantial, cluster of dates in the A.D. 850s. On the basis of the association between Room Suite 1 and Pit Structure 1, it is possible to argue that all of Architectural Suite 1 was built in the A.D. 860s, but I do not favor this interpretation. Rather, the lack of A.D. 860s dates in Room Suite 1 and the presence of an A.D. 850s date cluster in Pit Structure 1 support an argument that all of Architectural Suite 1 was built in the late A.D. 850s and that the pit structure was extensively remodeled or rebuilt in the A.D. 860s. (Another possibility, though I think it remote, is that Room Suite 1 was built in the late A.D. 850s and remained without an associated pit structure for seven or eight years until Pit Structure 1 was built.) Finally, Pit Structure 4 was built around A.D. 873, and Room 10 may have been remodeled at the same time.

The tree-ring dates from pit structures at Duckfoot provide data that are relevant to the discussion of pit structure use life. The proposition that the number of pit features in the floor of a pit structure provides a relative measure of the length of occupation is clearly not true at Duckfoot. Pit Structure 4 is securely dated to A.D. 873, whereas Pit Structure 1 was built either in the mid- to late 850s or the mid-860s. There is no doubt that Pit Structure 1 was in use longer than Pit Structure 4, yet the latter has over twice as many pit features as the former. These data alone are enough to indicate that the abundance of pit features in a pit structure does not increase at a constant rate through time. I have presented a strong argument that Pit Structure 2 was built earlier than, but occupied as late as, Pit Structure 4, yet the two have about the same number of pit features. Variation in the number of pit features may relate to differences in the range of activities in the structure, as well as to differences in the duration of structure use. Cross-cultural data suggest that mud-walled buildings have an effective use life of four to 10 years, after which they need to be substantially rebuilt. The span of date clusters from Pit Structures 1 and 3 is consistent with such a short use life. If Pit Structure 1 was built in the mid– to late A.D. 850s, as suggested by its early date cluster, it probably needed to be rebuilt by the mid– A.D. 860s. I infer that Pit Structure 3 was most likely built in A.D. 859, after which the timbers may have been replaced several times, as indicated by a long string of cutting dates in the 860s and 870s.

The tree-ring dates strongly support the argument that Pit Structure 4 was a late addition to the site. I considered the possibility that Pit Structure 4 might have replaced Pit Structure 2, which is poorly dated but interpreted as having been built relatively early in the site-construction sequence. Furthermore, in Pit Structure 2, the roof apparently was dismantled, the support posts were removed, and trash was deposited on the floor. It seemed plausible that Pit Structure 4 was built as a replacement for Pit Structure 2 and that salvageable beams were recovered from the aging structure for use in the new one. Several lines of evidence suggest that this was not the case. First, the dates from Pit Structure 4 (Figure 2.8) do not indicate that any beams were reused. Second, there were no trash strata in the fill of Pit Structure 2; that is, the only refuse in the structure was on the floor and therefore associated with the abandonment of the structure and not with postabandonment filling by later site residents. Third, sherds from the floor of Pit Structure 2 were found to fit with sherds on the floors of several other structures (see Chapter 6), which suggests that Pit Structure 2 could not have been abandoned long before the rest of the site. These data indicate that all of the structures were in use until the entire site was abandoned, although the nature of the use of some structures changed. The date of site abandonment was not earlier than A.D. 876 and could have been as late as A.D. 880.

# 3

# Assemblage-Formation Processes

An understanding of how archaeological assemblages form is essential to making inferences about prehistoric activities and social organization. Archaeologists must address the question, What combination of natural and cultural processes produced the assemblage being studied? There is a relationship between human activities and the material residues they produce, but the archaeological record does not always directly reflect the particular activities we are interested in studying. For example, if an abandoned living room was used as a trash dump, an archaeologist would be incorrect in using the artifacts in the room as evidence of how it had been used as a living room. Domestic activities, such as cooking and food preparation, and maintenance activities, such as housecleaning and refuse disposal, are part of the normal pattern of activities at a site. There is much that we can learn about the organization of activities and social groups in prehistoric settlements, precisely because we can distinguish between different kinds of deposits resulting from different kinds of activities. In this chapter, I examine the factors and processes that affect the formation of archaeological assemblages, and I pay particular attention to the effect that these processes have had on artifact distributions at Duckfoot. An understanding of assemblage-formation processes is prerequisite to using artifact associations and distributions as evidence of household activities and household organization. The general problems discussed here are problems that all archaeologists face when using the archaeological record to address questions of anthropological interest.

The need to explain the natural and cultural processes by which the archaeological record forms was recognized as a part of the "new

archaeology" beginning in the 1960s. The development of new theoretical paradigms and new methods resulted in a flurry of research
into anthropological problems—such as social organization—that had
seldom, or never before, been addressed (Binford 1962; Clarke 1968;
Hill 1970a, 1970b). Much of this research was stimulated by a con-
viction that archaeological assemblages constituted "a 'fossil' record
of the actual operation of an extinct society" (Binford 1964:425).
Thompson and Longacre (1966:270), for example, asserted that "all
of the material remains in an archaeological site are highly patterned
or structured directly as a result of the ways in which the extinct
society was organized and the patterned ways in which the people
behaved." In reaction to such characterizations, Schiffer (1972:156)
identified a need for "explaining how the archaeological record is
produced in terms of explicit models, theories, and laws of how
cultural systems operate." Schiffer (1972:156) distinguished between
the *systemic context,* which describes artifacts as they are used in a
behavioral system, and the *archaeological context,* which describes materials that have passed through a cultural system and are now simply
a part of the natural environment (Schiffer 1987:4).

## Archaeological Recovery Processes

The assemblages that we study archaeologically are only a small
subset of the original systemic inventory of the artifacts used and
discarded by people. An archaeologist's conceptual framework and
problem orientation will influence what is perceived to be important
and even what is perceived to be data. Decomposition, deterioration,
and natural disturbance take their toll on the materials originally
deposited (Wood and Johnson 1978; Schiffer 1987), and the methods
we use to excavate, sample, collect, and analyze materials from sites
influence the "record" that we actually study. The use of analytic
systems, classifications, typologies, and attribute definitions always
involves making assumptions and generalizations about archaeological materials. The transformation from physical objects to qualitative
and quantitative data influences the way we think about the archaeological record and the prehistoric contexts we study.

Fieldwork at the Duckfoot site was conducted with the aid of lay
participants who had only minimal training before assisting with
excavation. Participant-excavators were closely supervised by professional staff whose own notes and records were supplemented by
those of the participants. With the exception of natural deposits in
the upper fill of pit structures and deposits in several exploratory
trenches in the courtyard and midden areas, all sediments were excavated with hand tools and sieved through ¼-in-mesh screens. The

upper fill strata in pit structures contained very few artifacts, which led to the decision to screen only a sample. Half of the upper fill of Pit Structure 3 and approximately three-quarters of the fill above the roof fall deposit in Pit Structure 4 were excavated with a backhoe. All structures and courtyard areas were excavated, including some structures that were not visible on the modern ground surface. The boundaries of the midden deposit were determined by excavating outward from the approximate center of the midden area to the point where artifact densities diminished sharply. Only in the southwestern corner of the midden did we fail to reach a marked decline in artifact density. About 16 m$^2$ (approximately 3 m$^3$) of midden deposits were left unexcavated. Around most habitation sites there is a peripheral zone that contains few artifacts. There was little excavation in this zone at Duckfoot, but, given the low artifact densities in the peripheral areas that *were* excavated and the paucity of artifacts observed on the modern ground surface, this should have little effect on the study results presented here. One area east of Pit Structure 3 (Figure 1.2) was excavated because a cluster of artifacts was observed on the modern ground surface. In addition, several trenches to the east, south, and west were excavated with a backhoe to make sure that we had not missed any pit structures.

The procedures used in the basic analysis of artifacts and samples from the Duckfoot site are described in Volume 1 (Lightfoot and Etzkorn 1993). In addition, several special analyses were conducted for specific problem-oriented studies. These include pottery-refitting and rim-arc and diameter analyses. The pottery-refitting procedure involved the reconstruction of vessels from the floors, features, and roof fall deposits of structures. In addition to refitting sherds within individual structures, we also attempted to find matches between parts of vessels recovered from different structures. The resulting data were useful in evaluating preabandonment and abandonment site-formation processes and in making inferences about the contemporaneity of abandonment of structures and features. The pottery rim-arc and diameter analysis was performed on rim sherds from the midden deposits, and the results of this study were extended to other deposits in order to estimate the total number of vessels discarded at the site. The purpose of this study, the details of which are discussed in Chapter 4, was to evaluate the model of social-group interaction that was developed on the basis of architectural patterns.

# Postabandonment Processes

Archaeological assemblages are subject to a variety of natural and cultural postabandonment processes and transformations before be-

ing investigated by archaeologists. For the most part, postabandonment processes have a destructive and disorganizing influence on
archaeological deposits. This entropy-driven trend (Ascher 1961) con-
trasts with the organizing and pattern-producing trends of preabandonment processes. It is important to consider postabandonment
processes because they affect the preservation and spatial distribution
of material remains in the archaeological record.

## Natural Processes

A number of natural processes—erosion, soil formation, and bioturbation (the action of roots, rodents, and burrowing insects)—affect
site deposits after abandonment. Of these, erosion has probably had
the least effect at Duckfoot. The site is located on the crest of a
ridge, and the modern ground surface slopes very gently to the
southeast. The sediments that fill the structures and cover the courtyards consist almost entirely of the decomposed and collapsed debris
of structure roofs and walls. The midden has a gentle slope of about
6 percent, and as a result, there has been very little erosion or
downslope movement of artifacts in this area.

Soil formation and bioturbation have been the dominant postabandonment environmental forces affecting the Duckfoot site. Because these processes are most active near the modern ground
surface, they primarily affect naturally deposited postabandonment
sediments. Soil formation and bioturbation cause the greatest damage to archaeologically meaningful contexts when such contexts are
buried only shallowly. For example, at Duckfoot, soil-formation
processes had largely obscured the jacal walls of Room 19 and
portions of the floor in Room 16. In addition, there were many
signs that burrowing rodents, which disturb stratigraphy and sometimes move artifacts and other materials both horizontally and verti-
cally, were active at the Duckfoot site.

## Cultural Processes

Once a site is abandoned, the processes that influence the content of
the archaeological assemblage can vary significantly depending on
the size of the population that remains in the settlement and in the
region. If people are still living in the area around a site when it is
abandoned, then the site is much more susceptible to scavenging
than if the surrounding area is also abandoned. If hostile neighbors
are still living nearby when a settlement is abandoned, and if the
distance to the new site is great, then the occupants would be more
likely to destroy buildings with their contents inside. Survey data
indicate that the area around Duckfoot was mostly abandoned from

about A.D. 900 to about A.D. 1000 or perhaps 1050. This hiatus is evidenced by the paucity of sites with Cortez Black-on-white pottery, which dates to the early Pueblo II period in the Montezuma Valley (Breternitz et al. 1974). The Dolores River valley, which was heavily populated during Pueblo I times, was also largely abandoned during the A.D. 900s. Habitation sites dating to the 900s apparently were more common in the southern and eastern portions of the Montezuma Valley and on Mesa Verde (Hayes 1964:91–93; Morris 1939). The area around Duckfoot may have remained important for hunting and foraging, but for more than 100 years after Duckfoot was abandoned, it apparently did not have a significant number of residential sites.

There was a substantial late Pueblo II occupation in the vicinity of Duckfoot, with one small roomblock within 100 m of the site and several large roomblocks within 1 km of the site. Pueblo II potters used crushed-sherd temper, so they might have collected some sherds from the surface of the Duckfoot site to use in pottery manufacture. Decorated white and red ware sherds also might have been collected as keepsakes or because they could be shaped into pendants. Finally, flakes or stone suitable for flaking may have been collected prehistorically simply because the Duckfoot midden provided an expedient source of raw material. However, the predominant stone material on the surfaces of the Pueblo II sites (chert) is different from that at Duckfoot (orthoquartzite), which suggests that there was a Pueblo II preference for better material and an established mechanism for obtaining it.

In Pit Structure 3, a deep, slab-lined pit (Feature 2) had been built into postabandonment fill along the north wall of the structure. The pit contained abundant charcoal and ash, and the sides were sooted and burned. The fire in this feature had also reddened the north wall of the pit structure, making it clear that the structure was less than half filled with sediment when the feature was built. The use surface associated with this feature, although never defined in the field, had to have been near the top of the collapsed roof. This suggests that the structure was reused very soon after the roof burned; the vertical-walled pit structure probably filled very quickly once the roof no longer covered it (cf. Petersen et al. 1987:157–179). The base of the feature stopped short of the pit structure floor, and therefore its construction had no effect on the floor assemblage.

A second example of reuse of the site is in Room 15. A rectangular, slab-lined bin (Feature 1) had been built in the partly filled room. The bottom of the bin was flush with the floor of the room, but the fill of a deep cist (Feature 5) was discovered beneath the sandstone slab that formed the bin's base. Pottery sherds from the lower fill of Feature 5 fit with sherds that were scattered across the floor of the room and with sherds in the fill of other pits in the room. This suggests that Feature 5 was open when the sherds were deposited in the various contexts in the room. Furthermore, Feature 5 had to have filled and the room itself had to have collapsed and filled to near its modern depth before Feature 1 was built because the sandstone slabs forming the walls of the bin had to have been supported by the sediments filling the room. No temporally diagnostic artifacts were found in the slab-lined bin, so there is no indication of when this reuse of the site occurred.

Many sites in the area around Duckfoot have been looted in the recent past, including several Pueblo II sites on private land that were destroyed in 1986 with bulldozers. Recent looting and collecting at Duckfoot have been much less severe. Two looter's pits could be seen on the modern ground surface at Duckfoot, one along the east wall of Room 10 and the other in Room 2. The looter's pit in Room 10 extended to the floor, but the one in Room 2 was confined to postabandonment deposits. The area around Duckfoot was used more intensively from the 1930s to the 1950s than it has been since; the remains of a historic homestead are only a few hundred meters southwest of Duckfoot. We know from verbal accounts of landowners that artifacts were collected from the surface of Duckfoot during this period, but the collections have not been examined by archaeologists. Among the pieces reportedly collected is a pottery "duck," which *could* be the vessel that stood on the two pottery feet recovered during Crow Canyon's excavations, including the one for which the site was named.

Postabandonment looting and collecting at Duckfoot probably did not affect the floor assemblages in the pit structures, because the massive roofs had collapsed onto the floors, effectively sealing the contents of each structure. Most of the domestic rooms in the roomblock burned to some extent but apparently did not collapse as rapidly as the pit structures. Therefore, it is possible that some usable artifacts were removed from the rooms after the site was abandoned as a residence. None of the structures at Duckfoot contained trash or secondary refuse in their postabandonment deposits, which suggests that none of the structures were abandoned long before the others. However, the use of some structures did change, and refuse was discarded or allowed to accumulate on the floors of other structures before abandonment.

## Abandonment Processes

The types of artifacts found in association with structure floors and roofs—and the distributions of those artifacts—are likely to be influenced by the conditions under which a site is abandoned. The archaeological record does not lend itself well to studies of events and moments from the past (Binford 1981). Abandonment—whether it be of a structure, a site, or a region—is best thought of not as a *moment in* time but as a *period of* time. Abandonment is not an event; it is a process involving people leaving a settlement, and the process may be slow and gradual or it may be abrupt. To a large extent, the abandonment process may be determined, directed, or constrained by internal and external conditions or factors. For example, the cause of abandonment, the distance to the new site, the available means of transport, the season of abandonment, and the size of the remnant population will influence how a site is abandoned, what is taken away, and what is left behind.

Abandonment processes are of interest for two reasons. First, understanding abandonment processes may help us explain much of the content and distribution of portable materials at sites, especially usable tools and containers. In other words, certain circumstances and conditions that prevailed during the abandonment period may have dictated why prehistoric residents took what they took to their new residences and why they left what they left at the old site. The second, and, in the context of this study, perhaps the most important, reason for studying abandonment processes is to be able to separate the effects of abandonment and preabandonment processes on the structure of archaeological assemblages. If the content and patterning of floor assemblages are to be used to make inferences about preabandonment activities and social organization at Duckfoot, the effects of abandonment processes must be filtered out.

## Burning of Structures

At the Duckfoot site, three of the four pit structures, six of nine front rooms, and one of 10 back rooms were burned (Figure 3.1) in what is interpreted to have been an intentional act of destruction, not a catastrophic accident. The burned roof debris lay directly on the floors of these structures or on top of fuel used to ignite the roofs, with no intervening layer of naturally deposited sediment. This stratigraphic sequence indicates that the structures burned during, not after, abandonment. The intentional destruction of buildings is seen as a clear sign that there was no anticipation of returning to the site or of reusing the structures or buried artifacts after the site was abandoned. The pit structure roofs apparently were destroyed in fires that involved very intense heat. Adams described evidence of this in Pit Structure 1:

> Many vegetal items had vitrified, becoming shiny and glasslike in appearance. Sides of rounded stems were swollen and had bubbled out in blisters. Some specimens believed to be resin globs had

become so hot that they turned liquid, then resolidified with drip tails pointing in one direction [Adams 1993:209].

Other evidence, including reddening of the structure walls, also indicated intense heat. Occasionally the sherds of a single vessel were unevenly sooted or reddened, so that, once reconstructed, the vessel had a "patchwork" appearance caused by the presence of buff, gray, and black sherds (Figure 3.2).

Wilshusen (1984, 1986) presented arguments and data showing that it is unlikely that Pueblo I earthen structures burned accidentally. For a pit structure to have burned with the intensity represented archaeologically at Duckfoot, large amounts of fuel would had to have been ignited within the structure, and at least some of the sediment would had to have been removed from the roof to allow a sufficient flow of oxygen. An experimental burning of an earth-and-wood structure showed such structures to be difficult to ignite and slow to burn (Glennie and Lipe 1984). These data contradict the intuitive view that is common in the American Southwest that these early pueblos were always at risk of a catastrophic conflagration (e.g., Cassells 1983:132–133). Data from human remains in Pit Structures 1, 3, and 4 at Duckfoot also indicate that these pit structures did not burn accidentally. In Pit Structures 1 and 4, a skeleton lay across an ash-filled hearth, but the bones were burned

**Figure 3.1.** *Plan of the Duckfoot site showing the structures that burned at abandonment.*

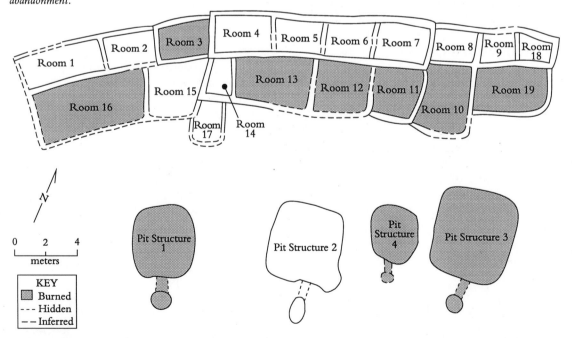

**Figure 3.2.** *Gray ware vessel reconstructed from burned and unburned sherds. Because sherd color cannot be used as a clue in such cases, vessel reconstruction is made even more difficult. This particular jar (Vessel 9) was found in pieces on the floor of Pit Structure 1. Height = 22.0 cm.*

on their top, not bottom, surfaces. In Pit Structure 3, the knees of Burial 4 overlapped the hearth, yet they were not burned at all. This pattern clearly demonstrates that when bones burned it was the result of exposure to something other than a hearth fire; that is, the bones burned as a result of coming into contact with burning roof debris or fuel that was placed on the floors to deliberately ignite the structures.

The practice of burning structures, especially pit structures, was common in the region during the late Pueblo I period. Wilshusen (1986) found that 22 of 44 excavated structures at Dolores that were occupied between A.D. 860 and 900 had burned at abandonment, and another five had their roofs dismantled but not burned. He also found a significant association between the burning of pit structures and the presence of ceremonial vaults, which are features that he interprets as occurring in structures with the greatest intensity of ritual use. Furthermore, Wilshusen found a significant relationship between the intentional dismantling of roofs without burning and the use of those structures as tombs. The burning of pit structures is not random in the Mesa Verde region, because it does not occur in a similar proportion of structures through time. Schlanger and Wilshusen (1993) showed that, during the A.D. 800s in the Dolores River valley, there was a significant relationship between periods of drought and site abandonment involving the burning of structures. From a practical standpoint, there is no need to burn structures when departing a residential site, and in most sites at most times, they are not burned at abandonment. The fact that all four pit structures at Duckfoot had human interments and all four were destroyed either by burning (three cases) or intentional dismantling (one case) suggests that the destruction of the buildings was an integral part of the abandonment process. A number of circumstances, ranging from mortuary rituals to acts of violence, could have led to the destruction of the pit structures as a part of the abandonment process. An important consideration here is that these circumstances could have had a significant effect on what was taken and what was left behind when the abandonment process was complete.

## Abandonment Mortuary Practices

All four pit structures at Duckfoot had one or more human skeletons on their floors, for a total of seven burials. These individuals had to have been interred about the time that the structures were abandoned, as the presence of bodies on the floors certainly would have hindered routine residential activity, and in each case, the skeletons were covered directly by collapsed roof debris. In Pit Structures 1, 3, and 4, the roofs were burned at abandonment, and the skeletal material was charred where it had come in contact with burning material inside the structures. Two children (sexes unknown), three adult males, and two adult females were interred on the floors of pit structures. The interments include both single individuals (Pit Structures 2 and 3) and multiple individuals (Pit Structures 1 and 4). An analysis by Hoffman (1993:265–266) showed no significant differences in the age and sex distributions of the seven individuals interred on the floors of pit structures vs. the seven buried in the midden.

Pit Structure 1 contained two adult male skeletons. Burial 1 was lying supine across the ash-filled hearth, with the legs slightly flexed and one knee up. The only burning was on the top of one knee, where it protruded into the burned roof fall stratum. Even though the torso of the skeleton lay across the hearth, there was no burning on the undersides of any of the bones. Therefore, it is unlikely that there was a fire burning in the hearth when the body was deposited. If there was no fire in the hearth, then the fire that burned the roof could not have been started accidentally by a spark from the hearth. Rather, the fire was probably deliberately ignited as part of a funerary ritual associated with the interment of Burial 1 and the abandonment of the site.

Burial 2 was found near the north wall of Pit Structure 1 and, in terms of its context, was the most enigmatic burial at the site. The skeleton rested mostly on the floor, although several burned beams were found under the torso. The skeleton was burned in several places, probably as the result of having come in contact with burning timbers. The left half of the cranium and surrounding facial bones were broken, either as a result of prolonged exposure to intense heat or as a result of the bones having been crushed by the collapsing roof (Hoffman 1993:257). Although the body might have been on the roof when the structure was burned, the majority of the roof fall deposits were above, not below, Burial 2. If the structure was intentionally burned, the body could have been positioned in the structure at the same time that fuel was being placed on the floor to ignite the fire. The charred timbers under the torso could have been pieces of fuel used to burn the structure rather than part of the fallen roof. If the body was still in the flesh before the roof came down, the heat could have caused the muscles to contract, resulting in the contorted position of the skeleton. Such postmortem movement could also account for some charred beams being under the skeleton even though most of the burned debris was above it.

Pit Structure 3 also contained an adult male skeleton (Burial 4) lying supine on the floor, with the lower legs flexed across the rim of the hearth. Signs of burning on the skeleton were confined primarily to the right side of the face and surrounding cranium, which was broken and incomplete. Charred beams lying on and above the burned area of the face and skull account for the condition of the bones. Even though the knees were over the ash of the hearth, they were not burned, which suggests that the hearth was not the source of the fire that ignited the roof. The fire that burned the roof was probably built elsewhere inside the structure, with the intention of destroying the roof to entomb Burial 4.

Pit Structure 4 contained the remains of an older adult female (Burial 12) and two children (Burials 11 and 14). The skeletons of the children were so thoroughly burned that the surviving bone fragments were almost unrecognizable. The head and upper torso of the adult female skeleton lay across the top of the ash in the hearth, and the back of the cranium was slightly imbedded in the ash. The skeleton was surrounded and partly covered by deliberately arranged sandstone rocks. The only burning on the bones of Burial 12 was on the portions of the upper surfaces that were not covered by the sandstone rocks. None of the bones that lay on the hearth ash were burned on their lower surfaces, demonstrating once again that the fire that burned the roof had to have been ignited by a source other than the hearth—probably a fire built elsewhere inside the structure with the intention of burning it. The destruction of the roof was probably a part of the funerary ritual that was associated with the abandonment of the site.

Pit Structure 2 is the only pit structure that did not have burned roof debris on the floor, yet it too contained a human skeleton

(Burial 3), in this case, that of an adult female. The condition and context of the Pit Structure 2 interment suggest that the individual died in some other location, was left exposed for some time after death, and finally was intentionally buried in Pit Structure 2. First, all the limb bones, including those of the hands and feet, were missing, which Hoffman (1993:258) attributed to carnivore activity because of the tooth puncture marks observed on the remaining skeletal elements. This physical evidence strongly suggests that the individual died somewhere other than in the pit structure and was not buried immediately after death. Second, Burial 3 was surrounded and partly covered by deliberately placed sandstone rocks, which indicates that the interment was a deliberate mortuary act and not a casual dumping of a body. Several lines of evidence, including features and stratigraphy, indicate that the roof was then dismantled and collapsed without having been burned.

The skeletons of the two children on the floor of Pit Structure 4 had been almost completely consumed by fire. The adults interred in Pit Structures 1, 3, and 4 all showed evidence of burning on the parts of the skeletons that were uppermost, and two of these had skulls that were crushed, apparently by collapsed roof debris. I have argued that the fires were set intentionally and that the apparent intensity of the heat is consistent with the interpretation that fuel was ignited inside the structures to burn the wooden parts of the roofs. There are several ethnographic accounts in which the content and structure of the abandonment assemblage were strongly influenced by mortuary practices that involved immediate abandonment of structures in which a death had occurred (Brooks 1993; Kent 1984:139–141; Deal 1985:275). If such practices were employed in prehistoric Pueblo times, one might expect that entire household inventories would have been abandoned as a result of taboos (e.g., Kent 1984). On the other hand, it is possible that the people performing funerary ritual activities might have introduced new items into the household inventory, items that were not there during the normal use of the structures.

## Season of Abandonment

Although the season in which a site is abandoned cannot be considered a "process," it *does* affect the content of the abandonment assemblage and therefore warrants consideration in this discussion. For example, if a site is abandoned in the spring, when there are few stored foods to transport, there might be less emphasis on transporting containers. The opposite might be true in the fall, when the need to transport harvests of corn and other foods would result in the removal of more containers.

Botanical remains from the Duckfoot site are the best source of information with regard to the season of abandonment (Adams 1993:219). Charred remains of immature flower heads of *Artemisia tridentata* (big sagebrush) were found in abundance on the floors of Pit Structures 1 and 3 and in limited amounts on the floor of Room 12. Flowering heads of modern sagebrush reach a comparable stage of maturity in September. There are three reasonable explanations for the presence of these immature flower parts: (1) They were part of the closing material used in roof construction; (2) they were collected and stored in the structures just before abandonment; or (3) they were brought into the structures as fuel to burn the roofs at abandonment.

If these structures were built in the fall and if sagebrush was used as closing material in the roofs, then the immature flower heads might have been fortuitously incorporated into the construction material. However, the flower heads of sagebrush would have made very weak and porous closing material, and they would have deteriorated very quickly. Also, there were no impressions of sagebrush parts in any of the pieces of burned mud from the roofs. The ubiquity of the immature sagebrush flowers on the floor and in vessels on the floor of Pit Structure 1, in particular, suggests that large amounts of the plant material were brought inside this structure at abandonment. If the structure was intentionally burned, the use of large quantities of sagebrush as fuel to ignite the roof is plausible. However, for the sake of this argument, it is not essential to know the reason that the sagebrush was inside the structures. It is only necessary to establish that it was inside the structures when they burned and that it was not incorporated in the materials used to build the roofs. This would place the likely time of abandonment in the early fall. An interpretation of winter, spring, or summer abandonment would require one to argue that the fragile, immature sagebrush flowers were harvested and stored without damage before the structure was burned. An interpretation of fall abandonment is also supported by the presence of *Zea mays* (corn) kernels and *Physalis longifolia* (groundcherry) and cheno-am (goosefoot or pigweed)[1] seeds in hearths and other features containing primary food-processing refuse (Adams 1993:219). The potential for these seeds to be stored beyond the season of harvest weakens their utility as seasonal indicators, however.

---

1. *Chenopodium* (goosefoot) and *Amaranthus* (pigweed) seeds are difficult to distinguish, particularly when burned. Throughout this volume, seeds that could be from plants in either genus are placed in the combined "cheno-am" category.

## Accumulation of De Facto Refuse

De facto refuse (Schiffer 1972, 1976, 1987) consists of the tools, facilities, and other cultural materials that, although still usable, were abandoned with a site or activity area. By definition then, de facto refuse is deposited only during abandonment, and the accumulation of de facto refuse reflects decisions to leave behind still-usable materials rather than to move them to a new settlement. These decisions may be affected by the length of time that abandonment was anticipated, the distance to the new site, the mode of transportation, and the immediate, long-term, or personal value of each item. Unusable debris or discard that, due to a reduction in housekeeping, is allowed to accumulate within an activity area or structure during abandonment should be considered abandonment refuse. Many structures at Duckfoot contained complete tools and reconstructible pottery vessels on their floors. Complete or nearly complete vessels are also interpreted as usable items that were abandoned as de facto refuse when the site or structure was abandoned. These items, although still usable, were not taken from the site for some reason. Three possible explanations are offered: (1) The distance to the new habitation was great, and there was a limited transport capability (for example, no wagons or beasts of burden); (2) ritual events (such as the burning of structures and the interment of the dead) might have involved the use of a certain number of tools or containers, which were left behind as part of the ritual inventory; and (3) the deaths of the individuals interred in pit structures might have reduced the population enough to reduce the number of vessels needed or the number that could reasonably be carried. If this last explanation were true, one might expect the number of de facto artifacts to be directly related to the number of individuals interred. At least on a structure-by-structure basis, this is not the case at Duckfoot.

## Discussion

Burning and dismantling structures was only one of several possible ways that settlements might be abandoned. If the buildings at Duckfoot were deliberately destroyed by the residents of the site, as I have suggested, then the implication is that these residents had no intention of returning and reoccupying the settlement. The destruction of potentially usable building materials suggests that the departing residents moved a considerable distance away so that salvaging materials was not feasible. Abandonment of rich inventories of still-usable tools and containers supports the notion that the residents moved far enough away or under hasty-enough conditions that they did not have the opportunity to make repeated trips to transport these items to their new residence. Early Pueblo sites with burned structures tend to cluster in time (Schlanger and Wilshusen 1993), and I propose that the burning of structures and abandonment of rich inventories of artifacts in or near the locations in which the items were used were associated with long-distance abandonments in which there was no anticipation of returning or no opportunity to return. Schlanger and Wilshusen (1993) documented four such events in the Dolores area between A.D. 680 and A.D. 910, which they associate with periods of drought. The period in which Duckfoot was occupied was one of favorable climatic conditions, whereas the abandonment of Duckfoot coincided with the beginning of a period of drought (A.D. 880–910) during which the Dolores area was also abandoned.

I have argued that all the structures at Duckfoot were abandoned at about the same time, that three of the pit structures and most of the living rooms were burned intentionally, and that the skeletons on the floors of the pit structures were intentionally interred. These circumstances strongly suggest that the site inhabitants departed the site relatively quickly, with no intention of returning. What is not explained in these arguments is why so many people died in such a short time, coincident with the rapid abandonment of the site. Although one cannot rule out other explanations, I address three general abandonment scenarios that seem plausible: disease, famine, and violence. An adequate explanation should take into account the similarities in mortuary practices and abandonment modes at contemporaneous sites in the region.

Disease is difficult to rule out as a possibility, although the skeletal remains do not show any signs of serious disease-related pathology (Hoffman 1993). The problem is that most diseases that may cause death do not cause damage to the skeleton. The mortuary population in pit structures at Duckfoot includes adult males, adult females, and children. Thus, the cause of death was something that did not discriminate with respect to age or sex. Infections, periodontal abscesses, intestinal parasites, and the like could have caused many deaths prehistorically (Merbs 1989), but it is unlikely that they would have caused a large number of simultaneous deaths. Tuberculosis is known to have been present in the Southwest prehistorically, with one of the earliest cases being from a Pueblo I site in the Kayenta area of northeastern Arizona (Merbs 1989:48–49). An infectious disease could have spread quickly through the population of a small hamlet and resulted in a number of deaths. If such an outbreak of disease occurred in a small hamlet, the survivors might have decided to bury the dead, destroy the structures, and abandon the site quickly to end the suffering they and their loved ones had experienced.

Indicators that might suggest that famine was a cause of abandonment at Duckfoot are mixed. Physical anthropological data indicate that the population was reasonably healthy, but climatic indicators suggest that there was a significant deterioration in agricultural conditions after A.D. 875. The human skeletal remains from Duckfoot reflect a generally healthy population, and manifestations of dietary stress (for example, anemia, periostitis, cribra orbitalia, and porotic hyperostosis) are infrequent and mildly expressed (Hoffman 1993). The most significant health-related problems that are apparent in the skeletal remains are dental caries and abscesses. The rate of occurrence of these dental problems is much higher (about 2.5 times) than among contemporaneous populations at Dolores (Hoffman 1993:295). A high incidence of dental caries and abscesses is typical of populations with high-carbohydrate diets. The relative difference in dental caries between Duckfoot and Dolores could be interpreted as indicating a greater reliance on corn at Duckfoot. Although heavy reliance on corn could have made the population more susceptible to dietary stress in the event of crop failure, it probably also suggests that, in general, the Duckfoot farmers had reliable yields of corn and regular surpluses, thus requiring less reliance on hunting and foraging.

Skeletal evidence is useful as an indicator of long-term nutritional heath, but it would not necessarily indicate a severe terminal episode of drought and famine. Petersen's (1989:122–125) climatic reconstruction for southwestern Colorado indicates that there was a period of severe drought from approximately A.D. 875 to 880 followed by a period of cooler-than-normal temperatures. Because Duckfoot is at a lower elevation than the Dolores area, the drought may have affected the residents of the Duckfoot area more than it affected those of the Dolores area and could have caused the abandonment of the area around Duckfoot by A.D. 880. Because of its higher elevation, the Dolores area would have been more severely affected by the period of cooler-than-normal temperatures that followed. Cooler temperatures at higher elevations would have resulted in shortened growing seasons and an increased risk of crop failure due to killing frosts.

Crop failure and subsequent nutritional stress also could have contributed to an increase in hostilities between communities during the abandonment period. Hostile neighbors could have raided small hamlets, like Duckfoot, to steal food. Although the skeletal remains from Duckfoot do not indicate that any of the individuals died as a result of trauma (Hoffman 1993:282–283, 290), an environment of violence and raiding might have caused the residents of small hamlets like Duckfoot to move to larger settlements. Larger villages were common at Dolores during the late A.D. 800s, and apparently there was an influx of settlers into some villages in the Dolores area (for example, Grass Mesa Village [Lipe, Kohler, Varien,

Morris, and Lightfoot 1988]) in the A.D. 880s. The period of drought from A.D. 875 to 880 could have encouraged the Duckfoot residents to move to higher elevations, where the effects of the drought would have been less severe. These migrants could not have foreseen that a subsequent period of cooler temperatures and shorter growing seasons would soon drive people out of the higher-elevation settlements as well.

# Preabandonment Processes

Preabandonment formation processes are those processes that take place in the systemic, or behavioral, context during the occupation of a settlement. The principal cultural activities that lead to deposition during this period include discard, loss, caching, and mortuary practices. In addition, reuse and recycling of artifacts can alter the form and location of materials as they enter the archaeological context. In this section, I focus on the cultural deposition processes at Duckfoot.

## Accumulation of De Facto Refuse

The de facto refuse assemblage consists of all the complete tools and containers that were abandoned in their use or storage contexts. Earlier in this chapter, I described the accumulation of de facto refuse as an *abandonment* process, but this does not mean that the content and distribution of de facto refuse assemblages are entirely the product of abandonment events. On the contrary, de facto refuse may consist largely of the remains of a systemic inventory after it has been altered by abandonment events. The assemblage of de facto refuse is particularly important because it existed in both preabandonment and abandonment contexts, and it still exists in the archaeological context that we study today. To the extent that the assemblage of de facto refuse has been protected from postabandonment disturbance, it offers an important avenue of investigation into preabandonment and abandonment activities. It is essential that we determine whether the de facto assemblage is representative of the normal systemic inventory of artifacts or whether it has been seriously altered by abandonment-period processes.

## Accumulation of Secondary Refuse

Secondary refuse accumulates as a result of discard, including the discard of manufacturing debris, broken or worn-out tools and containers, or even expediently used and discarded tools such as edge-damaged flakes. It also includes hearth debris, floor sweepings, and food waste, such as animal bones and plant remains. With the exception of those items that are charred, most perishable materials have decomposed and are not found. Middens contain accumulated debris representing a broad range of activities conducted over a long period of time. The contents of a midden are not influenced by abandonment processes to the extent that floor assemblages are. Midden deposits at the Duckfoot site are located south of the pit structures and cover approximately 350 m². The boundaries of the midden were determined by excavating contiguous squares to a point at which artifact frequency diminished sharply; in Figure 3.3, sherd

**Figure 3.3.** *Sherd density in the midden area.*

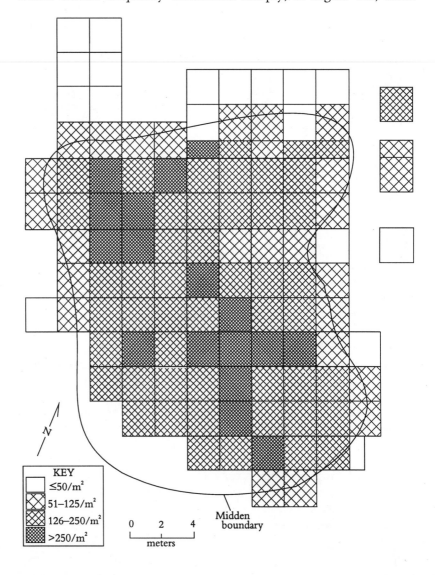

KEY

≤50/m²

51–125/m²

126–250/m²

>250/m²

Midden boundary

0    2    4

meters

density is used as a proxy for total artifact density. As seen in this figure, only in the southwestern corner of the midden did excavations fail to reach this "drop-off" point, but I estimate that approximately 96 percent of the midden deposits were excavated.

The midden contained the densest accumulation of debris at the site, but the items recovered from it do not make up the total assemblage of discarded materials (for the remainder of this chapter, referred to as the "total discard assemblage") from the site. The total discard assemblage also includes miscellaneous debris found in the postabandonment strata of structures and features, in the sediments excavated in the courtyard area, and on the modern ground surface. Some materials recovered from the floors of structures are secondary refuse and abandonment refuse (trash that accumulated during abandonment) and therefore are also part of the total discard assemblage. For example, Room 15 and Pit Structure 2 had large numbers of sherds on their floors that could not be incorporated into reconstructible vessels. These "orphan" sherds could be interpreted as (1) refuse dumped from nearby structures, (2) abandonment refuse that accumulated as routine housekeeping declined during the abandonment process, (3) sherds that were incorporated into the construction dirt of the walls and roofs, or (4) sherds that washed into the structures soon after abandonment. Figure 3.4 is a scatterplot that shows the number of floor-associated sherds that refit into vessels along one axis and the number of floor-associated orphan sherds along the other. Only sherds from front rooms and pit structures are included; sherds from back rooms are excluded because the assemblages from back rooms were not included in the systematic refitting process. Because of the bias in the sample, our knowledge of the proportion of vessel sherds to orphan sherds in back rooms is not comparable to that in front rooms and pit structures. The graph gives a good visual representation of the relationship between de facto and secondary or abandonment refuse. The axis labeled "Number of Vessel Sherds" can be read as depicting the abundance of de facto refuse sherds, which are those that could be refit into restorable or partly restorable vessels. The axis labeled "Number of Orphan Sherds" can be read as representing the frequency of primary, secondary, and abandonment refuse sherds, which I will refer to simply as "trash." Rooms 10, 11, 12, and 13 cluster in the lower left corner of the graph along the $x$-axis. The floor assemblage of Room 12 contains no restorable vessels, and the floor assemblages of the other three rooms contain only a few sherds that refit into partial vessels. In addition, with the exception of Room 13, relatively small amounts of trash—probably accounted for by primary refuse and sherds that were incorporated into construction sediments—were recovered from the floors of these structures. In Pit Structure 4 and

**Figure 3.4.** *Scatterplot comparing the frequencies of floor-associated "orphan" sherds and floor-associated sherds that were incorporated into reconstructed vessels. Increases in the number of vessel sherds are interpreted as indicating more de facto refuse; increases in the number of orphan sherds are interpreted as indicating more secondary or abandonment refuse.*

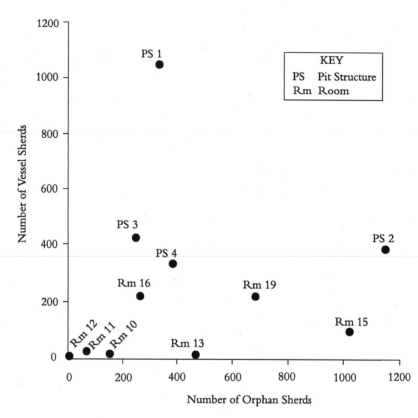

Room 16, about equal numbers of sherds are accounted for by reconstructible vessels and trash. In Pit Structures 1 and 3, a significant majority of the sherds consist of de facto refuse (vessel sherds), and the accumulation of trash (orphan sherds) is roughly equivalent to that in Room 16 and Pit Structure 4. Rooms 15 and 19 and Pit Structure 2 fall into the opposite corner of the graph, with the vast majority of the sherds recovered from the floors of these structures representing trash. These three structures have three to 10 times as many orphan sherds as reconstructible-vessel sherds on their floors. Certainly some secondary refuse had been dumped on the floors of these structures near the time of abandonment.

## Preabandonment Mortuary Practices

The treatment and disposal of the dead involve activities that affect the archaeological record in at least two ways. First, the skeletal remains themselves are often found in the archaeological record, and second, mortuary rituals frequently involve the burial of grave goods. In early reports of ancestral Pueblo ruins, the concentrations of refuse to the south of the kiva depressions—what, today, are referred to as midden areas—were commonly described as burial mounds (Prudden 1903). Burials are often found in the midden areas in later sites, but only about 25 percent of the burials from excavated Pueblo I sites in the Dolores River valley were from midden deposits (Stodder 1987:351–353). The low frequency of burials in many sites may result, however, from nearly a century of looting the midden areas of sites in search of burials and their associated grave goods. Seven human burials were found in the midden area at Duckfoot, and none of these had been disturbed by looters, although most showed evidence of rodent activity. The seven individuals buried in the midden consist of three adults—two males and one female—and four children (under 16 years of age). Three individuals were found in supine positions, two were on their left sides, one was on its right side, and the position of one could not be determined, because it had been so severely disturbed. Three of the skeletons were fully flexed, three were partly flexed, and the position of one could not be determined. None of the midden burials were found with grave goods.

## The Duckfoot Artifact Assemblage

In this section, I briefly discuss the artifacts recovered from Duckfoot and summarize the general archaeological contexts in which they were found. More detailed discussions of artifacts, including definitions of artifact types and descriptions of the analytic procedures used for the Duckfoot project, are presented in Volume 1 (Lightfoot and Etzkorn 1993).

In the sherd and general artifact tables in this section, proveniences are grouped into three categories: structure floors, midden deposits, and other fill. These categories were selected because they reflect differences in the natural and cultural formation processes that produce archaeological assemblages. For instance, items found on structure floors most likely are there as the result of actual human deposition. In other words, when you find something on a structure floor, there is a good chance it is there because someone put it there prehistorically. Although it is possible for artifacts on the roof to fall onto the floor as a structure collapses, it is more likely that such artifacts will be incorporated into the sediments above the floor. An item that ends up on the floor at abandonment could have been used, stored, or discarded in that location. Complete tools and containers found on a structure floor are more likely to be items that were used or stored in that structure than are broken or partial artifacts. On the other hand, a certain number of broken tools, sherds, flakes, and other miscellaneous items may accumulate as primary refuse on a floor during the use of the structure.

The midden deposits at Duckfoot are concentrated in an area south of the pit structures. Although most of the items recovered from this area, as one would expect, are broken or "used-up" artifacts that were intentionally discarded, there are a certain number of complete, usable items as well. Some of these complete items, especially the smaller ones, might have been lost, or they might have been thrown away as a component of something else that was being discarded. For example, a small arrow point might have been accidentally dropped in the midden and not found, or it could have been imbedded in an animal carcass that was discarded in this area. Other tools in the midden may represent activities that actually took place there. After a period of accumulation, the midden would have been a good source of materials for recycling. Also, any work done prehistorically in the midden area would have required little cleanup, because the debris or by-products would have already been in the discard area.

The provenience category "other fill" refers to a variety of other deposits that make up a substantial portion of any site. This category includes materials from deposits such as the sediments above the floors of pit structures (including roof fall), the collapsed and "melted" mud walls of rooms, and the sediments in the courtyard areas and elsewhere that have been heavily altered by bioturbation and soil formation. Many of the artifacts in these contexts are likely to be materials that were lost or discarded and then incorporated into the site deposits in a variety of ways. Some artifacts might have been incorporated into the construction materials used to build and maintain walls and roofs. There are several examples of whole and broken metates, manos, peckingstones, and other stone tools that were used in wall construction or maintenance at Duckfoot (see Lightfoot, Etzkorn, and Varien 1993:Figure 2.37). Smaller items, such as sherds and flakes, might have been accidentally or intentionally mixed into the mud that was used to construct or repair walls and roofs. Materials that were discarded, lost, or abandoned in the courtyard area or elsewhere at the site might have washed into a pit structure or been displaced by the various natural processes already discussed.

In the tables summarizing the pottery vessel assemblage from Duckfoot, different provenience groupings are used. Because the vessel-reconstruction (refitting) study was limited to specific contexts in selected structures, the proveniences in these tables are grouped into only two broad categories: structure floors and structure fill, the latter consisting primarily of deposits specifically identified as roof fall.

## The Sherd Assemblage

Three pottery ware categories—gray ware, white ware, and red ware—are represented in the 112,197 sherds recovered from Duckfoot. Each ware represents a different production technology, and each is represented by multiple types. Ware and type descriptions, as well as an explanation of the analytic system used for the Duckfoot project, are provided in Volume 1 (Etzkorn 1993b). In general, the gray, white, and red ware types from Duckfoot are typical of the Pueblo I period, and they occur in approximately the same percentages as in late Pueblo I assemblages in the Dolores River valley and elsewhere in the region (Blinman 1988a, 1988b).

### Early Pueblo Pottery

Gray ware, which is the locally made, unpolished, unpainted utilitarian ware, accounts for about 90 percent of the total Duckfoot sherd assemblage by count (Table 3.1). Most gray ware vessels are jars,

Table 3.1. Summary of Sherds by Ware and Form

| Pottery Ware and Form | Structure Floors | | Midden | | Other Fill | | Total | |
|---|---|---|---|---|---|---|---|---|
| | Count | Weight (gm) | Count | Weight (gm) | Count | Weight (gm) | Count | Weight (gm) |
| Gray Ware | | | | | | | | |
| Jar | 6,946 | — | 58,929 | — | 33,118 | — | 98,993 | — |
| Bowl | 28 | — | 221 | — | 417 | — | 666 | — |
| Other | 49 | — | 256 | — | 566 | — | 871 | — |
| Corrugated jar | 2 | — | 69 | — | 167 | — | 238 | — |
| SUBTOTAL | 7,025 | 101,062 | 59,475 | 325,695 | 34,268 | 230,175 | 100,768 | 656,932 |
| White Ware | | | | | | | | |
| Jar | 103 | — | 1,042 | — | 513 | — | 1,658 | — |
| Bowl | 141 | — | 2,731 | — | 1,013 | — | 3,885 | — |
| Other | 13 | — | 33 | — | 32 | — | 78 | — |
| SUBTOTAL | 257 | 4,233 | 3,806 | 15,208 | 1,558 | 8,774 | 5,621 | 28,215 |
| Red Ware | | | | | | | | |
| Jar | 87 | — | 1,223 | — | 397 | — | 1,707 | — |
| Bowl | 185 | — | 2,757 | — | 1,075 | — | 4,017 | — |
| Other | 6 | — | 33 | — | 32 | — | 71 | — |
| SUBTOTAL | 278 | 1,967 | 4,013 | 14,379 | 1,504 | 6,081 | 5,795 | 22,427 |
| Other[a] | 0 | — | 6 | — | 7 | — | 13 | — |
| SUBTOTAL | 0 | — | 6 | — | 7 | — | 13 | — |
| TOTAL | 7,560 | 107,262 | 67,300 | 355,282 | 37,337 | 245,030 | 112,197 | 707,574 |

NOTE: Weights were recorded only at the level of ware (gray, white, and red) and were not subdivided by pottery form.

[a] Includes mudware.

although bowls, effigies, and other forms do occur. During sherd analysis, the default form category for gray ware sherds was jar. That is, all gray ware sherds were classified as jars unless a particular sherd was from the rim of a vessel and was curved in such a way that it could *not* have been from a jar. As a result, the number of gray ware jar sherds reported in Table 3.1 is inflated with body sherds from other gray ware vessel forms that could not be distinguished from jar sherds. Early gray ware is represented in the Duckfoot assemblage by three formal Pueblo I types—Chapin Gray (1,225 sherds), Moccasin Gray (4,883 sherds), and Mancos Gray (1,086 sherds).

White ware is polished, slipped with a film of white or gray clay, painted, or subjected to some combination of these three surface treatments. White ware vessels were also made locally, although they represent only about 5 percent of the Duckfoot sherd assemblage by count (Table 3.1). The early formal types present in the Duckfoot assemblage are Piedra Black-on-white (1,175 sherds) and Chapin Black-on-white (348 sherds).

Red ware pottery found at Duckfoot and at other Pueblo I sites in the region is thought to have been made in southeastern Utah, with the core production area located approximately 55 km west of Duckfoot (Hegmon et al. 1991). Red ware vessels were made with red-firing clays that do not occur locally. They are polished, usually painted, and sometimes slipped. Red ware makes up about 5 percent of the total Duckfoot sherd assemblage by count (Table 3.1). Bluff Black-on-red was the dominant formal type during the late Pueblo I period; it accounts for all the red ware vessels from Duckfoot that could be identified to formal type, and it is the dominant red ware type in the sherd assemblage as well (2,023 sherds). Abajo Red-on-orange and Deadmans Black-on-red, pottery types that generally were made earlier and later than Bluff Black-on-red, respectively, are also present but in much smaller quantities (45 Abajo sherds, 39 Deadmans sherds).

### Late Pueblo Pottery

Pottery styles changed significantly during the late A.D. 800s and early 900s, and a few sherds of later pottery types are present in the Duckfoot assemblage. These include 238 corrugated gray sherds and 94 late (Pueblo II and/or Pueblo III) white ware sherds. The assemblage of late white ware that could be identified to formal type consists of 37 Cortez Black-on-white, 51 Mancos Black-on-white, four McElmo Black-on-white, and two Mesa Verde Black-on-white sherds. Combined, the corrugated sherds and identifiable late white ware sherds represent less than one-third of one percent of the total collection.

## The Vessel Assemblage

After the sherd analysis was complete, an attempt was made to systematically refit sherds into vessels. Most of the sherds included in this special study are from front rooms and pit structures, primarily floor and roof fall proveniences. Although assemblages from back rooms were not examined systematically, a few distinctive sherds that were easily recognized as belonging to particular vessels were also included. The reconstruction of pottery vessels involved an attempt to refit every sherd from the floor or roof fall stratum of a structure to every other sherd from those same contexts in that structure. In addition, an attempt was made to match partial vessels between structures. By examining all the sherds from the floors and roofs of each structure, it was possible to determine the combination of vessels and orphan sherds present in these assemblages. The reconstruction of pottery vessels resulted in a wealth of data that is used throughout this volume to study formation processes, as well as to infer the distribution of activities and social interactions across the site. Vessel reconstruction provided a wide range of data useful in quantifying the relationship between whole vessels and sherds, which was an essential complement to the sherd-based analysis.

Standardized observations were recorded for each reconstructed vessel, including information about vessel form, pottery type, volume, rim diameter, modification, and evidence of use (before and after modification). A variety of other measurements and observations were made relating to the form and completeness of each vessel. The basic form classes identified are listed in Table 3.2. In addition to the 11 manufactured vessel forms shown in this table,

Table 3.2. Specific Form Classes in the Reconstructed-Vessel Assemblage

| Vessel Form | Description |
| --- | --- |
| Wide-mouth jar | jar with spheroid base and cylindrical neck |
| Pitcher | small wide-mouth jar with vertical strap handle on neck |
| Olla | narrow-necked jar with large volume |
| Gourd jar | jar with bottle-gourd shape |
| Seed jar | spheroid, neckless jar with constricted orifice |
| Beaker | straight-sided, nearly cylindrical container without handle |
| Bowl | container that has hemispheric shape; orifice is largest diameter |
| Double bowl | two bowls joined together |
| Ladle | small bowl with long, straight handle |
| Dipper | bowl with "handle" that is shallow extension of the bowl |
| Effigy | stylized zoomorphic container |
| Sherd container | large sherd recycled for use as a shallow, platter- or saucerlike container |

"sherd containers," which are large sherds that were recycled for continued use as platterlike receptacles after the original vessels broke, are also included, to bring the total number of forms recognized to 12.

### Jar Size Classes

Gray ware jars occur in a wide range of sizes. The Duckfoot assemblage includes everything from miniatures, with volumes as small as 36 ml, to ollas, with volumes of up to nearly 24 liters. The size distribution is almost continuous; however, for the study presented in Chapter 4, it was desirable to define size classes rather than treat size as a continuous variable. Furthermore, it was desirable to define size classes that could be determined from the rim diameter of the vessel (in cases in which the rim diameter could not be measured, the orifice diameter—which for necked vessels is usually very similar to rim diameter—was substituted). The ability to estimate vessel size or volume based on rim diameter is contingent on there being a significant relationship between the two (Fitting and Halsey 1966; Whallon 1969). For Pueblo I pottery, Blinman (1988a) showed that rim diameter is strongly correlated with vessel volume in some vessel forms (for example, bowls and wide-mouth jars) but not in others (for example, ollas). Blinman demonstrated that there is a significant nonlinear relationship between rim diameter and *effective volume* (the volume when the vessel is filled to the point of inflection [Hally 1986:279]) for cooking jars made between A.D. 720 and 920 in the Dolores River valley. In Blinman's study, the relationship became approximately linear when a logarithmic transformation was applied to the effective volume (Blinman 1988a:169–177). The strongest relationship occurred during the A.D. 840–880 period, which is contemporaneous with the occupation of Duckfoot.

An analysis similar to Blinman's was performed on the reconstructed-vessel assemblage from Duckfoot, which includes 46 gray ware jars (wide-mouth jars, pitchers, gourd jars, and ollas) sufficiently intact for the analyst to measure both rim (or orifice) diameter and effective volume. As in the Dolores vessel assemblage, there is a strong positive relationship between rim diameter and effective volume for all necked jars except ollas. The relationship between rim diameter and effective volume in the Duckfoot assemblage of gray ware jars (excluding ollas) also becomes approximately linear when a logarithmic transformation is applied to the effective volume. A scatterplot showing the relationship between rim diameter and effective vessel volume for the 46 gray ware vessels included in the analysis was used to define size classes. The classes were defined by marking lines perpendicular to the rim-diameter axis of the scatterplot that would result in the best separation of vessels into distinct volume classes. The results are shown in Figure 3.5. As expected, the miniature jars formed a distinct cluster, as did the ollas. The remaining jars were separated into three size classes: small, medium, and large. The rim-diameter and volume classes are almost identical to those defined independently by Blinman (1988a:175) using gray ware jar data from the Dolores Archaeological Program. The two classes of gray ware jars that do not separate on the basis of rim diameter are small jars and ollas, which have almost identical rim and neck sizes but very different volumes.

## Complete Vessels

Thirty-five vessels from the Duckfoot site are classified as *complete* or *nearly complete, reconstructible;* their distribution with respect to form and general context is presented in Table 3.3. Note that some of the vessel-form categories are subdivided by size. Three vessels in the Duckfoot assemblage—two miniature gourd jars and one miniature pitcher—are actually complete and unbroken. Two vessels—a small pitcher and a seed jar—are complete after reconstruction. Thirty vessels that are treated as complete in this discussion and in the chapters that follow are classified as *nearly complete, reconstructible.* Two kinds of vessels are included in this category: vessels whose missing

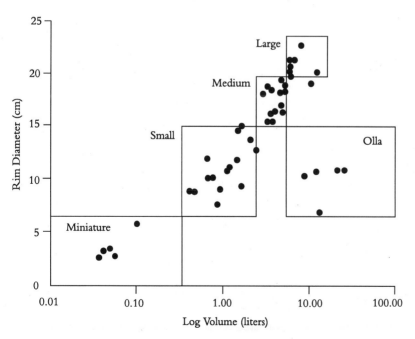

**Figure 3.5.** *Scatterplot comparing rim diameter and effective volume for gray ware jars (wide-mouth jars, pitchers, gourd jars, and ollas). The x-axis shows effective volume on a logarithmic scale.*

Table 3.3. Complete and Nearly Complete Vessels by Context

| Vessel Condition | Vessel Form | Floors | Fill | Total |
|---|---|---|---|---|
| Complete, unbroken | miniature pitcher | 1 | | 1 |
| | miniature gourd jar | 2 | | 2 |
| Complete, reconstructible | small pitcher | 1 | | 1 |
| | seed jar | 1 | | 1 |
| Nearly complete, reconstructible | small wide-mouth jar | 7 | | 7 |
| | medium wide-mouth jar | 8 | | 8 |
| | large wide-mouth jar | 2 | 2 | 4 |
| | miniature pitcher | 1 | | 1 |
| | small pitcher | 1 | | 1 |
| | olla | 3 | | 3 |
| | beaker | | 1 | 1 |
| | bowl | 2 | 1 | 3 |
| | dipper | 1 | | 1 |
| | effigy | 1 | | 1 |
| TOTAL | | 31 | 4 | 35 |

pieces were probably lost during archaeological recovery and vessels whose missing pieces may well have been lost while the vessel was still in use prehistorically. It is known that certain vessels were intact, though cracked, in the field. However, after these same vessels were collected, washed, reconstructed, and glued, random sherds were missing. It is not unusual for a few sherds to be lost during recovery and processing; it is also possible that some sherds were simply too small to be processed and refit. The Duckfoot assemblage also contains vessels that were probably missing pieces prehistorically, but the gaps would not have significantly hampered vessel function. For example, an olla that is missing a portion of its rim can still be used to store corn or water with a very minor reduction in performance.

### Partial Vessels

*Partial* vessels are vessels that were not sufficiently intact to have been used as whole containers. Generally, partial vessels are less than 80 percent present, and the missing pieces are believed to have been lost or discarded prehistorically. In addition, partial vessels do not appear to have been reshaped or used after they broke. Partial vessels could have been stored in structures as provisional discard. *Provisional discard* refers to the accumulation or storage of broken tools or containers that are thought to have some potential reuse or recycling value (Hayden and Cannon 1983). The site residents may have saved larger pieces of broken vessels for recycling as sherd containers, scoops, or other sherd tools. Alternatively, partial vessels associated with other

Table 3.4. Partial Vessels by Context

| Vessel Form | Floors | Fill | Total |
|---|---|---|---|
| Small wide-mouth jar | 7 | 1 | 8 |
| Medium wide-mouth jar | 3 | 2 | 5 |
| Large wide-mouth jar | 2 | 1 | 3 |
| Miniature pitcher | 1 | | 1 |
| Small pitcher | 1 | | 1 |
| Olla | 2 | 2 | 4 |
| Gourd jar | 1 | | 1 |
| Seed jar | 1 | | 1 |
| Bowl | 9 | 5 | 14 |
| Double bowl | | 1 | 1 |
| Ladle | 1 | | 1 |
| Dipper | 1 | | 1 |
| TOTAL | 29 | 12 | 41 |

broken or depleted artifacts may be part of a discard, or secondary refuse, assemblage. The partial-vessel assemblage from Duckfoot is summarized in Table 3.4.

### Sherd Containers

A number of sherds on structure floors at Duckfoot show evidence of modification or use after breakage. Forty-nine of these are *sherd containers*, that is, large fragments of broken vessels that continued to be used as containers after the original, or parent, vessels broke. The evidence of continued use includes sooting and staining patterns and edge modification (both intentional shaping and edge wear). Distinctive sooting and staining patterns are the clearest evidence of use: The soot or other stain on a sherd container is centered at the bottom of the container, which was not necessarily the bottom of the original parent vessel (Figure 3.6). Context played a role in the identification of sherd containers: Items discovered on structure floors were more likely to be recognized and reconstructed than were items found in other contexts. In addition, when these items were found on floors with other, more obvious, de facto refuse, they were more likely to be interpreted as being in a use-associated context rather than in a discard context. In Pit Structure 1, for example, sherd containers found on the floor were associated with clusters of whole cooking vessels. Of the 49 sherd containers recognized in the Duckfoot assemblage, 30 are defined on the basis of sooting or staining patterns, four on the basis of edge modification, and the remaining 15 were identified only on the basis of size, shape, and context (Table 3.5).

**Figure 3.6.** *Sherd containers identified primarily on the basis of staining or sooting, the location of which suggests that the stains were acquired after the original vessels broke and the sherds were recycled for use as shallow cooking containers. Vessel 46, left, was found on the floor of Pit Structure 3; Vessel 52, right, was found on the floor and in the roof fall deposits of the same structure. Maximum dimension, both pieces = 16.0 cm.*

Table 3.5. Sherd Containers by Context

| Sherd Container Type | Floors | Fill | Total |
|---|---|---|---|
| Sooted, stained | 28 | 2 | 30 |
| Edge modified | 4 | 0 | 4 |
| Other | 14 | 1 | 15 |
| TOTAL | 46 | 3 | 49 |

Each sherd container from Duckfoot was treated as a distinct vessel apart from the original, or parent, vessel from which it was derived. Although information about the parent vessel was recorded, the final use of each sherd container as a shallow bowl or platter is what is being considered here. Sherd containers are not included in any of the previously discussed categories (for instance, a sherd container that was once part of a wide-mouth jar is counted as a sherd container only), and the distinction between sherd containers and all other vessel forms is maintained throughout the studies that follow.

## Other Artifacts

Other artifacts from use and discard contexts at Duckfoot are summarized in Table 3.6. The midden category most clearly contains materials that represent secondary refuse disposal. The structure-floors category includes several different kinds of refuse, as was demonstrated above with the sherd data. When evaluating a floor context that has a mixture of primary, secondary, and de facto refuse, it is often impossible to determine the process that led to any individual item making its way onto that floor. This is especially true of expedi-

Table 3.6. Summary of Selected Artifacts by Context

| Artifact Type | Structure Floors | | Midden | | Other Fill | | Total |
|---|---|---|---|---|---|---|---|
| | Complete[a] | Fragment | Complete[a] | Fragment | Complete[a] | Fragment | |
| Trough metate | 19 | 8 | 0 | 0 | 9 | 0 | 36 |
| Slab metate | 2 | 0 | 0 | 0 | 4 | 0 | 6 |
| Metate[b] | 1 | 0 | 0 | 0 | 0 | 28 | 29 |
| One-hand mano | 3 | 0 | 1 | 2 | 3 | 0 | 9 |
| Two-hand mano | 72 | 10 | 2 | 18 | 58 | 35 | 195 |
| Mano[b] | 0 | 0 | 0 | 5 | 0 | 3 | 8 |
| Abrader | 7 | 7 | 9 | 18 | 5 | 31 | 77 |
| Hammerstone | 9 | 1 | 8 | 3 | 10 | 2 | 33 |
| Polishing stone, polishing/hammerstone | 2 | 0 | 13 | 3 | 13 | 0 | 31 |
| Axe, maul, axe/maul | 11 | 1 | 1 | 1 | 8 | 3 | 25 |
| Stone disk | 2 | 0 | 7 | 0 | 6 | 0 | 15 |
| Modified cobble | 28 | 9 | 6 | 15 | 14 | 13 | 85 |
| Core[c] | 17 | — | 238 | — | 85 | — | 340 |
| Modified core | 1 | 0 | 1 | 1 | 3 | 0 | 6 |
| Flake | 411 | 691 | 10,281 | 5,569 | 3,201 | 1,583 | 21,736 |
| Edge-damaged flake[c] | 30 | — | 608 | — | 205 | — | 843 |
| Other chipped-stone debris[c] | 71 | — | 321 | — | 101 | — | 493 |
| Peckingstone | 82 | 6 | 231 | 19 | 121 | 10 | 469 |
| Biface | 0 | 0 | 4 | 18 | 2 | 6 | 30 |
| Projectile point | 5 | 1 | 26 | 12 | 16 | 5 | 65 |
| Drill | 2 | 0 | 7 | 0 | 1 | 1 | 11 |
| Modified flake | 11 | 1 | 229 | 45 | 86 | 16 | 388 |
| Other chipped-stone tool | 2 | 0 | 14 | 4 | 5 | 2 | 27 |
| Other modified stone/mineral | 12 | 3 | 8 | 21 | 20 | 21 | 85 |
| Modified or shaped sherd[d] | 13 | 14 | 47 | 88 | 37 | 38 | 237 |
| Pottery effigy | 0 | 0 | 0 | 2 | 0 | 0 | 2 |
| Pendant (stone, bone, shell) | 3 | 0 | 2 | 0 | 6 | 0 | 11 |
| Bead (stone, bone, shell) | 1 | 0 | 4 | 0 | 4 | 0 | 9 |
| Shell bracelet | 0 | 5 | 0 | 1 | 0 | 4 | 10 |
| Awl | 8 | 15 | 4 | 0 | 13 | 11 | 51 |
| Gaming piece | 1 | 0 | 5 | 0 | 2 | 0 | 8 |
| Other bone artifact | 0 | 7 | 2 | 8 | 5 | 8 | 30 |
| TOTAL | 826 | 779 | 12,079 | 5,853 | 4,043 | 1,820 | 25,400 |

NOTE: Artifact types are defined in Volume 1 (Lightfoot and Etzkorn 1993).

[a] The "Complete" category includes all items coded as complete, incomplete, and condition unknown.

[b] More specific type designations cannot be made because the items are too fragmentary or their forms too ambiguous to allow determination of type.

[c] Condition was not recorded for cores, edge-damaged flakes, or chipped-stone debris.

[d] The total number of modified and shaped sherds reported here (237) differs from that reported in Volume 1 (228) (Etzkorn 1993:148). The discrepancy is caused by the different treatment of modified sherds that were incorporated into reconstructed vessels: nine such sherds were excluded from consideration in Volume 1 but are included here.

ent tools, such as edge-damaged flakes, which were probably collected, used, and discarded on a continual basis. It is easier to make the argument that larger items (for example, metates), which are difficult to transport, probably were not moved very far when discarded at abandonment. The "Other Fill" column in Table 3.6 includes items found on the modern ground surface, in the fill strata of structures (including roof fall deposits), in the fill above the courtyard area, in deposits outside the north wall of the roomblock, and in other miscellaneous areas that were not on floors or in the midden area. Most of the artifacts recovered are discarded items that made their way into the various contexts as a result of natural and cultural postabandonment processes.

# 4

# Pottery Discard and Systemic Inventories

In this chapter, I apply the general principles of site formation discussed in Chapter 3 in an analysis of the effects of abandonment behavior on the de facto refuse assemblage from Duckfoot. The basic question is, How can we use the archaeological assemblage of discarded and de facto refuse to learn more about the original systemic inventory from which it was derived? There is an ongoing and sometimes heated debate in archaeology over what kind of record the archaeological record is and how we can legitimately use it to learn about the past (Ascher 1961; Schiffer 1976, 1985; Binford 1981). Specifically, there have been many accusations that archaeologists misuse the archaeological record by erroneously assuming that all archaeological assemblages can be interpreted as being the result of Pompeii-like abandonment scenarios. The term *Pompeii premise* was coined by Ascher (1961:324) to refer to the perception that archaeological deposits may be interpreted as "the remains of a once living community, stopped as it were, at a point in time." Schiffer (1985) criticized Southwestern archaeologists for failing to adequately evaluate the effects that formation processes have on floor assemblages. He argued that "the real Pompeii premise is that the archaeologist can treat house-floor assemblages at any site *as if* they were Pompeii-like systemic inventories" (Schiffer 1985:18; emphasis in original). One alternative advocated by Schiffer is to evaluate what has been removed from the inventory of tools and containers that were originally in use at the site. Cordell et al. (1987:573) criticized this approach because Schiffer had offered no means of scientifically evaluating his results. They concluded that "we can discern no strategy for determining or even evaluating how many of what kinds of objects should be found in any location or context" (Cordell et al. 1987:574). This chapter offers one approach to addressing this problem.

Archaeologists often equate a rich floor assemblage in a burned structure with a complete systemic inventory (e.g., Montgomery and Reid 1990:93–94; Pauketat 1989:299–300). This type of inference is tempting and, in some cases, may be justified, but it is rarely tested. In this chapter, I use the assemblage of discarded pottery (the "discard assemblage") from Duckfoot to construct a simulated systemic inventory. The discard assemblage is composed largely of secondary refuse generated during the occupation of the site, and it represents the breakage of pottery vessels used in the systemic context during the entire span of occupation. Assemblages from structure floors can be compared with the simulated systemic inventory to determine what items might have been added or removed during abandonment. The results tell us something about abandonment behavior, and they allow us to better determine the relationship between preabandonment activities and the archaeological assemblages they produce.

One principle that underlies the logic of this study is that things made of similar material and similar construction, used in similar ways, will wear out in a similar amount of time. This principle underlies any study of artifact discard or accumulation rates. We are seeing contemporary examples of this phenomenon as an increasing number of aging commercial jets built in the 1960s begin to "wear out" (that is, become increasingly susceptible to crashing). They wear out because of the stresses induced by repeated cycles of takeoff and landing, which result in expansion and contraction of the bodies of the jets. The same principle can be applied to pottery cooking pots. Cooking pots wear out (that is, become increasingly susceptible to breakage) as a result of "thermal shock," that is, the stress induced by repeated cycles of heating and cooling, which result in expansion and contraction of the bodies of the pots.

Pottery vessels are used for a variety of tasks, including cooking, storage, transporting water, and so forth. All other things being equal, the rate at which vessels break is related to the ways in which they are used. Thus, if we know the length of occupation and the size and composition of the total assemblage of discarded pottery, we should be able to calculate a basic rate of accumulation. However, the rate of total accumulation is not precisely what we want to know; we want to know what was in the systemic inventory. For example, a rate of discard of eight widgets a year for a site with two households could be achieved either by each household having one widget at a time that wears out or breaks every three months or by each household having eight widgets, half of which wear out every year. To calculate an average momentary population of widgets, we need to know something about how long an individual widget lasts under normal circumstances. Different types of artifacts in a systemic inventory wear out or break at different rates, and therefore the proportions of types in the discard assemblage will not be the same as their proportions in the systemic inventory.

Schiffer (1987:54) presented a formula for calculating the total discard assemblage that involves the number of items of a particular type in the systemic inventory and the use life of an artifact of that type:

$$T_D = \frac{St}{L}, \tag{1}$$

where $T_D$ = the total number of discarded artifacts of a given type, $S$ = the average number of artifacts of that type typically in use (this is the systemic number), $t$ = the length of occupation, and $L$ = the use life of an artifact of the given type. Therefore, if we are interested in solving for $S$ (the number of items in the systemic inventory), we can rearrange the formula as follows:

$$S = \frac{T_D L}{t}. \tag{2}$$

However, even if we can use tree-ring dates to accurately estimate the length of occupation, there are still two unknowns: artifact use life and the number of artifacts of the specified type in the total discard assemblage. We know the size of the discard assemblage in terms of sherds, but we need to be able to estimate the number of vessels of various types in the discard assemblage. If we can estimate the number of vessels discarded at the site, we can calculate the number of pottery vessels in the systemic inventory ($S$).

# Estimating Vessel Use Life

Archaeologists have long recognized that there is a consistent relationship between vessel morphology and use, a relationship that has also been confirmed with ethnological and ethnoarchaeological data (Henrickson and McDonald 1983; Smith 1985). The morphological attributes that make vessels suitable for particular uses can be specified on the basis of mechanical properties and vessel performance (Ericson et al. 1972). It is also possible, as other researchers have shown (e.g., Blinman 1988a; DeBoer 1985), to develop some expectations about the relative use lives of different vessel classes on the basis of their uses. Blinman (1988a) used four functional categories—cooking jar, bowl, olla, and seed jar—in his study of Pueblo I pottery from the Dolores area.

Wide-mouth jars were commonly used for cooking, as evidenced by sooting (Blinman 1988a), and the category *cooking jar*, as it is used in this volume, refers to gray ware wide-mouth jars and pitchers. Cooking jars are expected to have had the highest rate of breakage and the shortest use lives of all the vessel-use classes because they were used frequently, they were exposed to accidental impacts, and they were exposed to repeated thermal shock, or thermal fatigue (Steponaitis 1983:97–98; Bronitsky and Hamer 1986). Bowls, ladles, and dippers in the Duckfoot assemblage are combined into a single *bowl* category, and all are interpreted as having been used for serving and perhaps eating. Bowls would have had little exposure to heat shock but a relatively high exposure to impact and abrasion. *Ollas* are large jars with necks that are narrow both in absolute terms and in proportion to vessel girth. Ollas are thought to have been used primarily for storage and transport of liquids (Blinman 1988a:131–137); therefore, they would not have been subjected to heat shock, and their exposure to impact and abrasion would have been far less than that of cooking jars. *Seed jars* have small or restricted orifices and no necks. Blinman (1988a:160) suggests that seed jars were best suited for long-term storage of dry, granular materials. Therefore, seed jars would not have been exposed to heat shock, and their exposure to impact or abrasion would have been minimal. In the Duckfoot study, both ollas and seed jars are recognized as distinct use classes, although in some analyses, I chose to include seed jars in a more general "other" category.

The uses of other vessel forms, such as gourd jars, beakers, effigies, and miniatures, are not specified, but these vessels occur in relatively low frequencies in the Duckfoot assemblage. Although miniatures can occur in a variety of vessel forms, all those found at Duckfoot were jars. Despite the fact that they are shaped the same as vessels in other form classes, such as cooking jars or ollas, miniatures are too small to have been used in the same ways as these other vessels, and therefore they constitute a use class distinct from those already mentioned. Sherd containers are not included in the discussions and tables in this chapter because they are recycled vessels that were modified from their original vessel forms.

White and red ware vessels occur in low frequencies in the Duckfoot assemblage, and, as decorated wares, they had a higher production cost than did gray ware vessels. White and red wares were rarely, if ever, used for cooking. Because of their painted designs, low frequencies, and high production costs relative to gray ware vessels, it is likely that red and white ware vessels had a lower frequency of use and longer use lives than did gray ware vessels.

For calibrating the various vessel-use classes into actual use-life values, I consulted the ethnoarchaeological literature. Mills (1989:Table 4) summarized data from nine different ethnographic groups and calculated average vessel use lives for four functional vessel categories: cooking, storage, serving, and "other." I used these average values as a starting point to estimate the use lives of vessels at Duckfoot. Cooking vessels in Mills's study had an average use life of 2.2 years, a figure that appears to have been somewhat inflated by the long use lives of Kalinga cooking vessels. Without the Kalinga vessels, the average use life of the remaining cooking vessels was 1.5 years. In all cases, except for the Kalinga, the use lives of serving vessels were approximately the same as for cooking vessels, or approximately 1.5 years. Storage vessels had a cross-cultural average of 5.4 years, and other vessel forms had an average use life of 6.4 years. These cross-cultural averages were used as proxies for the use lives of medium cooking jars, bowls, ollas, and "other" vessel forms in the Duckfoot assemblage (Table 4.1). The use-life estimates for the remaining vessel forms (also shown in Table 4.1) were based partly on the cross-cultural averages and partly on the general principle demonstrated by DeBoer (1985) that vessel use life is directly proportional to vessel weight. The estimated use-life values ($L$) shown in Table 4.1 were used in the discard equation to solve for the content of the systemic vessel inventory ($S$). We can use tree-ring dates to estimate a 25-year occupation of Duckfoot, and now we have an estimate of vessel use lives, derived from ethnographic data. The vessel component of the total discard assemblage ($T_D$) is the only remaining variable that needs to be calculated in order to use the discard equation to simulate the systemic vessel inventory.

Table 4.1. Use-Life Estimates for Vessels from Duckfoot

| Vessel Form | Estimated Use Life (years) |
| --- | --- |
| Small cooking jar | 1.2 |
| Medium cooking jar | 1.5 |
| Large cooking jar | 3.0 |
| Olla | 5.4 |
| Bowl | 1.5 |
| Other[a] | 6.4 |

[a] "Other" consists of gourd jars, beakers, seed jars, miniature jars, effigy vessels, and all red and white ware jars.

## Estimating the Total Discard of Vessels

The total assemblage of discarded vessels consists of all the vessels that were broken and discarded throughout the occupation of the site. The initial problem, of course, is how to make the transformation from sherd counts to estimated number of vessels. The procedure I used is explained in detail below, but first I will briefly describe the logic that underlies the process. In the previous chapter, I demonstrated, as Blinman (1988a) did, that there is a significant relationship between vessel volume and rim diameter. Therefore, it should be possible to analyze rim sherds from discard contexts and, on the basis of the curvature of each sherd, determine the rim diameter of the parent vessel and the proportion of the rim (in degrees of arc) that is present. Each sherd can then be assigned to a size class (on the basis of curvature as an indicator of rim diameter). The degrees of arc represented by the sherds can be summed for each class and divided by 360 degrees (the number of degrees of arc in a full circle). The result is an estimate of the minimum number of vessels in each form and size class discarded during the occupation of Duckfoot. As one might imagine, the process in real life is not quite that simple.

## Rim–Arc Analysis

### The Sample

It was not possible to analyze all the rim sherds from the Duckfoot site, but it was possible to study a large sample. Gray ware sherds account for about 90 percent of the sherd collection, and therefore only gray ware rim sherds were included in the rim-arc analysis. All the sherds included in the analysis—what I refer to as the *rim-arc sample*—were recovered from a 388-m² area within and around the midden, which contained refuse that accumulated during the entire span of occupation at the Duckfoot site. The excavation units selected for sampling yielded over 65,000 sherds (more than half of the total assemblage of discarded sherds from the site), and 57,703 of those are gray ware. Of these, 3,616 are gray ware rim sherds, and all but 14 could be assigned to a vessel-form class, for a total of 3,602 sherds in the rim-arc sample. On the basis of the 3,602 rim sherds analyzed, I estimated the number of vessels discarded in the sampled midden contexts and evaluated the estimate by comparing the weight of sherds in sampled contexts to the expected weight of the simulated sample assemblage.

### Methods

The rim-arc analysis, which was based on a method described by Egloff (1973), involved the use of a polar coordinate graph, which has graduated concentric circles and radial lines that mark angles from a 0-vector starting point. During analysis, each rim sherd was moved in or out along the concentric circles until a circle was found that best matched the curvature of the sherd. The diameter of that circle was the estimated diameter of the rim of the sherd's parent vessel. The proportion of the circle represented by the sherd was estimated (in degrees) using the graduated radial lines. The analyst recorded the form of the parent vessel as accurately as possible. Small sherds were assigned only to a general form category such as jar or bowl, but larger sherds were often assigned to a more specific form category such as olla or cooking jar. If a sherd was very small—say 1 cm or less along the rim—or very straight, it was not possible to measure its curvature. The lack of measurable curvature meant that the diameter of the rim and, consequently, the size of the parent vessel was unknown. If the rim diameter was unknown, it was also impossible to measure the proportion of the rim present (degrees of arc). In such cases, the length of the sherd along the rim was measured. Diameter-arc and sherd length were mutually exclusive observations. If a sherd's diameter could be measured, then so could its arc, but its length would not be measured. If the diameter could not be measured, then only the length was recorded. Of the 3,602 rim sherds analyzed, rim diameter and arc were measured for 2,348 (65 percent); length only was recorded for the remaining 1,254 (35 percent) sherds.

I wrote a simple computer program that used a set of counting and accumulating variables for each form and size class to compile the rim-arc data. The program read a line of data and, on the basis of the form class recorded for that sherd, moved to a segment of code that determined whether the diameter measurement was greater than zero; if so, the sherd was assigned, on the basis of its diameter, to a size subclass, where it was counted and its arc measurement added to the current total for that form and size class. If the diameter was not recorded, the sherd was counted by a different counter variable, and its length was added to the current total length for that form class (with no size subclass). After all the sherd data were read, counted, and accumulated, the arc totals for each form and size class were divided by 360 and printed in a table along with sherd counts for each class. Finally, the length totals for each form class were summed and then divided by the average rim circumference for that form class, as calculated for the reconstructed-vessel assemblage from Duckfoot.

### Separating Olla and Small-Cooking-Jar Rims

The range of rim diameters is exactly the same for ollas and small cooking jars, which makes it difficult to estimate the total assemblage of discarded vessels from rim sherds alone. Unless a rim sherd is unusually large, it cannot be assigned confidently to a vessel-form class more specific than jar. This is not a trivial problem, because an olla and a small cooking jar, when broken, contribute vastly different numbers and weights of sherds to the total assemblage of discarded sherds. In the whole-vessel collection from Duckfoot, the rim diameters of ollas are entirely within the size range of rim diameters of small cooking jars. Therefore, if it were possible to derive a typical ratio of ollas to small cooking jars, one could assume that this ratio would apply to the Duckfoot discard assemblage and simply assign the appropriate proportions of rim sherds to the two categories. In the Duckfoot reconstructed-vessel assemblage, the ratio of ollas (5) to small cooking jars (15) is 1:3.

Because this estimate of the discard assemblage ultimately will serve as the standard for comparing the composition of floor assemblages, it would be better to estimate the ratio of ollas to small cooking jars independently of the floor assemblages. In the analysis of rim sherds from the midden, I assigned all rim sherds to the most specific form class possible, including one class called "olla or small cooking jar." Most sherds could not be assigned to a form class more specific than bowl, jar, or other. The ability to distinguish the rim of an olla from the rim of a small cooking jar depended on the sherd being large enough to include part of the shoulder or body of the vessel. Because the necks of ollas and small cooking jars are similar in thickness, diameter, and height, they are equally likely to produce identifiable neck sherds when broken. Therefore, the rate of occurrence of identifiable neck sherds for ollas and small cooking jars should be proportional to the rate of occurrence of these vessel forms in the discard assemblage. In the rim-arc sample, 18 rim sherds were confidently identified as olla sherds and 52 were identified as sherds from small cooking jars. Therefore, the ratio of olla rim sherds to small-cooking-jar rim sherds is 1 to 2.9. I used this ratio to assign the estimated 64.5 vessels in the combined category of "olla or small cooking jar" to one of the two form classes.

### The Rim-Arc Vessel Estimate

The 2,348 rim sherds for which rim diameter and degree of arc were measured produced an estimate of 159.1 vessels (Table 4.2). The 1,254 sherds for which only length was recorded produced an estimate of an additional 36.4 vessels (Table 4.3). Size and use classes

Table 4.2. Estimated Number of Gray Ware Vessels in the Sampled Portion of the Midden, Calculated on the Basis of Sherds With Measurable Diameters and Degrees of Arc

| Vessel Form | Number of Sherds | Estimated Number of Vessels |
|---|---|---|
| Small cooking jar | 52 | 5.8 |
| Medium cooking jar | 791 | 49.0 |
| Large cooking jar | 434 | 19.5 |
| Olla | 18 | 3.0 |
| Olla or small cooking jar | 852 | 64.5 |
| Miniature jar | 41 | 7.2 |
| Seed jar | 19 | 1.5 |
| Bowl | 141 | 8.6 |
| TOTAL | 2,348 | 159.1 |

NOTE: The sum of arcs in each class was divided by 360 degrees.

Table 4.3. Estimated Number of Gray Ware Vessels in the Sampled Portion of the Midden,
Calculated on the Basis of Sherds Without Measurable Diameters or Degrees of Arc

| Vessel Form | Number of Sherds | Sum of Lengths (cm) | Average Circumference (cm) | Estimated Number of Vessels |
|---|---|---|---|---|
| Jar, unknown size | 1,220 | 1,652.5 | 46.5 | 35.5 |
| Bowl, ladle, dipper | 34 | 56.3 | 60.8 | .9 |
| TOTAL | 1,254 | 1,708.8 | — | 36.4 |

NOTE: Estimates are based on sherds for which length, rather than diameter, was measured. The sum of sherd lengths was divided by the average rim circumference for that class of vessels in the reconstructed-vessel assemblage.

are not included in Table 4.3, because the rim diameters of the sherds could not be determined. Combined, the results presented in Tables 4.2 and 4.3 give us a total estimate of 195.5 vessels for the 388 m² of midden that were included in the rim-arc sample.

One vessel measurement that does not change when a vessel breaks, regardless of sherd size, is weight. Therefore, it is possible to use the weights of gray ware sherds from the same contexts as the sherds included in the rim-arc sample to evaluate the accuracy of the vessel estimates derived from the rim-arc analysis. I used the reconstructed-vessel assemblage from the Duckfoot site to estimate the average weight for each vessel-form class. Not every reconstructed vessel was complete, but during vessel analysis, an assessment was made of what proportion of each vessel was present. I added a weight-correction factor for incomplete vessels to account for the missing portions. Table 4.4 lists the number of vessels represented in the rim-arc sample and the average weight of vessels in that form

Table 4.4. Values Used to Calculate the Expected Weight of
Gray Ware Sherds in the Rim-Arc Sample

| Vessel Form | Estimated No. of Vessels | Average Weight of Reconstructed Vessels (g)[a] | Expected Weight of Sherds (g)[b] |
|---|---|---|---|
| Small cooking jar | 53.7 | 583 | 31,307 |
| Medium cooking jar | 49.0 | 1,635 | 80,115 |
| Large cooking jar | 19.5 | 2,551 | 49,745 |
| Olla | 19.6 | 4,083 | 80,027 |
| Miniature jar | 7.2 | 126 | 907 |
| Jar, unknown size | 35.5 | 1,655 | 58,753 |
| Seed jar | 1.5 | 681 | 1,022 |
| Bowl | 9.5 | 1,818 | 17,271 |
| TOTAL | 195.5 | — | 319,147 |

[a] Calculated from the actual weight of reconstructed vessels with a weight-correction factor added to account for the missing proportion of each vessel.
[b] Calculated by multiplying the values in the preceding columns.

class in the reconstructed-vessel assemblage. By multiplying these two values for each form class and summing the results, I derived a value of 319,147 g, which is the expected weight of gray ware sherds from the portion of the midden from which the rim-arc sample was recovered. The actual weight of gray ware sherds from these excavation units is 317,765 g, which is remarkably close to the value given above. The difference in weight (1,382 g) is less than that of an average cooking jar of medium size. These results indicate that the number of vessels estimated to be present on the basis of the rim-arc analysis is accurate.

## Estimating the Total Discard of Gray Ware Vessels

Only gray ware sherds from midden-area deposits were included in the rim-arc analysis, and these represent only a part of the total assemblage of discarded gray ware. The remaining portion of the assemblage is represented by sherds from other contexts around the site that contain primary and secondary refuse, as well as postabandonment deposits.

There are 317,765 g of gray ware sherds (57,703 sherds) from the proveniences that were included in the rim-arc analysis. These sherds represent more than half (55 percent) of the 581,647 g of sherds (97,622 sherds) in the total assemblage of discarded gray ware, which I define as all gray ware sherds recovered from the Duckfoot site except those incorporated into reconstructed vessels (complete vessels, partial vessels, or sherd containers). I added an additional 10 percent (58,165 g) to the total weight of discarded gray ware sherds to account for sherds missing as a result of postabandonment processes or our failure to recover every last sherd from the site. The result is an adjusted total discard assemblage of 639,812 g of gray ware sherds. The sherds from contexts included in the rim-arc sample represent approximately 50 percent of the adjusted total discard assemblage, and therefore the total discard of vessels in each category should be equivalent to twice the number derived in the rim-arc sample (Table 4.5). However, it is necessary to account for the 35.5 jars of unknown size in the rim-arc sample, which would represent 71 jars in the total assemblage of discarded vessels. These 71 jars were probably derived from the same range of vessel forms represented in the reconstructed-vessel assemblage, and they are likely to have occurred in the same proportions as these vessels in the rim-arc sample. Therefore, in Table 4.5, the values in the column labeled "Total No. of Discarded Gray Ware Vessels" were calculated by doubling the number of vessels estimated in the rim-arc sample and proportionally distributing the 71 jars of unknown size among the other necked-jar categories (that is, all jar forms except seed jar).

Table 4.5. Estimate of the Total Number of Gray Ware Vessels Discarded at Duckfoot

| Vessel Form | Estimated No. of Vessels in Rim-Arc Sample | Estimated No. of Vessels in Other Fill | No. of Jars of Unknown Size Distributed Proportionally[a] | Total No. of Discarded Gray Ware Vessels |
|---|---|---|---|---|
| Small cooking jar | 53.7 | 53.7 | 26.9 | 134.3 |
| Medium cooking jar | 49.0 | 49.0 | 24.5 | 122.5 |
| Large cooking jar | 19.5 | 19.5 | 9.8 | 48.8 |
| Olla | 19.6 | 19.6 | 9.8 | 49.0 |
| Miniature jar | 7.2 | 7.2 | — | 14.4 |
| Jar, unknown size | 35.5 | 35.5 | — | — |
| Seed jar | 1.5 | 1.5 | — | 3.0 |
| Bowl | 9.5 | 9.5 | — | 19.0 |
| TOTAL | 195.5 | 195.5 | (71.0) | 391.0 |

[a] The total number of all cooking jars and ollas in the rim-arc sample and other fill is estimated to be 283.6. To determine how many vessels had to be added to each vessel-form class in order to proportionally distribute the 71 vessels of unknown size, the combined count in each form class was divided by 283, and the resulting values were multiplied by 71.

## Estimating the Total Discard of White and Red Ware Vessels

The rim–arc analysis was applied only to gray ware sherds and therefore cannot be used to estimate the number of white and red ware vessels discarded at Duckfoot. White and red wares occur in low frequencies at Duckfoot, with the two combined representing only about 7 percent of the sherd assemblage by weight and 10 percent by count. Unlike plain gray ware sherds, white and red ware sherds may be polished, painted, or slipped. These decorative treatments are generally applied to the inside surfaces of bowls, dippers, and ladles and to the outside surfaces of jars and other forms. Therefore, individual white and red ware sherds can be assigned more consistently than gray ware sherds to a general form class, such as bowl, jar, or other. Bowl forms (which include dippers and ladles) are by far the most common vessel forms in the white and red ware assemblages; this is true in the reconstructed-vessel assemblage, as well as in the sherd assemblage. Six of 15 reconstructed white ware vessels and 13 of 15 red ware vessels are bowl forms.

A total of 5,621 white ware sherds was recovered from Duckfoot, with a total weight of 28,215 g and an average weight of 5.0 g per sherd. Of the 5,464 orphan sherds (those that were not refit into vessels), 1,613 (30 percent) are jar sherds, 3,783 (69 percent) are bowl sherds, and 68 (1 percent) are from other vessel forms. A total of 5,795 red ware sherds was recovered, with a total weight of 22,427 g and an average weight of 3.9 g per sherd. Of the 5,452 orphan sherds, 1,635 (30 percent) are jar sherds, 3,752 (69 percent) are bowl sherds, and the remaining 65 (1 percent) are sherds from other vessel forms.

When using sherd frequencies and weights to estimate the number of vessels discarded at Duckfoot, it is necessary to account for sherds that were not recovered (see the discussion of postabandonment and archaeological recovery processes in Chapter 3). With this in mind, an adjusted total discard value was derived by increasing the sherd frequencies by 10 percent, as was done for gray ware sherds. This adjusted total sherd-discard value for each form class was then multiplied by the average sherd weight for that ware (5.0 g for white ware and 3.9 g for red ware) to produce an adjusted total discard weight. The adjusted total discard weight for each form class was then divided by the average weight of vessels in that form class to calculate the estimated total vessel discard. The results of these calculations and the values used in computing them are shown in Table 4.6.

## The Systemic Inventory

Having derived plausible use-life values for different vessel forms, an estimate of the number of vessels in the discard assemblage, and an estimate of the total length of site occupation (from tree-ring dates), we can now calculate the composition of the expected systemic inventory. The systemic inventory calculations are based on formula (2), presented earlier in this chapter, and the results are shown in Table 4.7. The results are used to address questions involving the relationship between the systemic inventory of vessels and the assemblage of de facto refuse recovered archaeologically.

Table 4.6. Estimate of the Total Number of White and Red Ware Vessels Discarded at Duckfoot

| Pottery Ware and Form | Orphan Sherd Count | Adjusted Total Sherd Discard | Adjusted Total Discard Weight (g) | Average Vessel Weight (g) | Total No. of Discarded Vessels |
|---|---|---|---|---|---|
| White Ware | | | | | |
| Jar | 1,613 | 1,774 | 8,870 | 1,250 | 7.1 |
| Bowl | 3,783 | 4,161 | 20,805 | 575 | 36.2 |
| Other | 68 | 75 | 375 | 416 | .9 |
| Red Ware | | | | | |
| Jar | 1,635 | 1,799 | 7,016 | 1,400 | 5.0 |
| Bowl | 3,752 | 4,127 | 16,095 | 495 | 32.5 |
| Other | 65 | 72 | 281 | 150 | 1.9 |

NOTE: Orphan sherds are those not included in reconstructed vessels. Adjusted Total Sherd Discard = Orphan Sherd Count + 10 percent; Adjusted Total Discard Weight = Adjusted Total Sherd Discard × average sherd weight (5.0 g for white ware and 3.9 g for red ware); Average Vessel Weight is derived from the projected whole weights of reconstructed vessels in each form class at Duckfoot; Total No. of Discarded Vessels = Adjusted Total Discard Weight ÷ Average Vessel Weight for each form class.

Table 4.7. Estimate of the Momentary Systemic Inventory of Vessels

| Vessel Form | Total Vessel Discard $(T_D)$ | Estimated Use Life $(L)$ | Systemic Frequency $(S)$ |
|---|---|---|---|
| Small cooking jar | 134.3 | 1.2 | 6.4 |
| Medium cooking jar | 122.5 | 1.5 | 7.4 |
| Large cooking jar | 48.8 | 3.0 | 5.9 |
| Olla | 49.0 | 5.4 | 10.6 |
| Bowl | 87.7 | 1.5 | 5.3 |
| Other[a] | 32.3 | 6.4 | 8.3 |
| TOTAL | 474.6 | — | 43.9 |

NOTE: On the basis of tree-ring sample results, the length of occupation is inferred to have been 25 years.

[a] "Other" consists of gourd jars, beakers, seed jars, miniature jars, effigy vessels, and all red and white ware jars.

## The Systemic Inventory and Site Abandonment

What can the difference between the archaeological vessel assemblage on structure floors and the expected systemic inventory tell us about abandonment behavior? Figure 4.1 compares the actual assemblage of complete or nearly complete vessels from the floors of structures at Duckfoot with the expected systemic inventory derived from the discard calculations. For the site as a whole, the count of medium cooking jars is very near the expected frequency. Small cooking jars are 50 percent more abundant and "other" vessels forms are about 25 percent more abundant than expected. Large cooking jars and bowls occur in only about one-third the expected frequencies, and there are only about one-fourth as many ollas on structure floors as expected.

Large cooking jars, ollas, and bowls are the most depleted vessels in the Duckfoot floor assemblages, and it is probably not coincidental that these items are the most valuable in terms of replacement cost. Large vessels require more manufacturing time and materials than do small vessels, and large vessels would have been useful as containers for carrying food or other loose materials when moving to a new site. Decorated vessels, although small, have a higher production cost than do gray ware vessels because of the additional manufacturing steps of polishing, slipping, and preparing and applying paint. Decorated bowls may have been taken from the site at abandonment, not only because they had a greater replacement cost, but also because they had greater intrinsic value than did the plain gray vessels. Decorated vessels are more beautiful than plain gray vessels, and the designs probably gave the vessels greater symbolic meaning and value compared with undecorated vessels. Because of how they were used, decorated vessels had longer use lives and hence were more likely to have become treasured heirlooms. Small, undecorated vessels had the shortest expected use life and the lowest

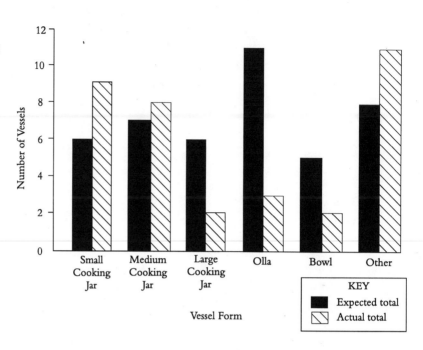

**Figure 4.1.** *Histogram comparing the expected vessel inventory and the actual vessel assemblage from floor and roof fall contexts in pit structures and front rooms (excluding Rooms 14 and 17). Expected values are derived from Table 4.7 and are rounded to the nearest whole vessel.*

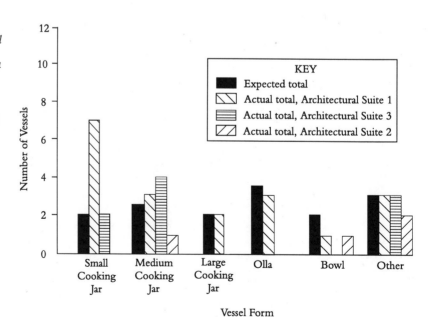

**Figure 4.2.** *Histogram comparing the expected vessel inventory and the actual vessel assemblage from floor and roof fall contexts in pit structures and front rooms (excluding Rooms 14 and 17), by architectural suite. Pit Structure 4 is included with Architectural Suite 2. Expected values for each suite are one-third the whole-site expected values (from Table 4.7) rounded to the nearest half vessel.*

replacement cost, so they had the lowest priority for transport to the new site. Thus, replacement cost and intrinsic value seem to be reasonably good explanations for why certain vessels were taken to the new site rather than left behind when Duckfoot was abandoned. If abandonment was rapid and there was no opportunity to make multiple trips, materials would have been selected for transport on an immediate-priority basis. Items that would have been needed immediately upon arrival, heirlooms, and containers for carrying goods to the new site would have had a higher priority than items that would not have been immediately essential or those that could have been most easily replaced.

## Systemic Inventories of Individual Architectural Suites

What do the abandonment assemblages of individual architectural suites tell us about abandonment behavior? Assemblages from the three architectural suites at Duckfoot may be compared individually with an expected assemblage for an architectural suite, which I postulate as being one-third of the whole-site inventory. Some variation is expected commensurate with household size, but dividing the whole-site assemblage equally gives a simple standard for comparison. Do individual architectural suites have abandonment assemblages that approximate the expected systemic inventory? Figure 4.2 shows the actual abandonment vessel assemblage for each architectural suite compared with the expected vessel inventory for an architectural suite. Pit Structure 4 is grouped with Architectural Suite 2 in Figure 4.2. The vessel forms that appeared to be depleted in the whole-site comparison (large cooking jars, ollas, and bowls) appear to be depleted mainly in Architectural Suites 2 and 3. Architectural Suite 1 has an abandonment vessel inventory that closely approximates the expected inventory, with one exception: small cooking jars are more than three times more abundant than expected.

Architectural Suite 3 has the expected number of small cooking jars (two) and other forms (three miniature jars), but it has more than the expected number of medium cooking jars and no large cooking jars, ollas, or bowls. The volume of one of the medium cooking jars on the floor of Pit Structure 3 is only slightly smaller than that defined for large jars. If the larger "medium jar" had been classified as a "large jar," then the assemblage of cooking jars would be very close to the expected. The overabundance of medium jars and the lack of large jars may also indicate that, late in the occupation, the size of the household occupying Architectural Suite 3 was smaller than normal. Turner and Lofgren (1966) used the sizes of bowls and cooking jars to estimate household size, arguing that there should be a direct positive relationship between vessel volume and household size. If this were true, then the cooking-vessel assemblage in Architectural Suite 3 could indicate that large jars were not needed as much as medium jars, because the size of the group occupying the suite had declined. The population could have declined as a result of the normal progression of the domestic cycle, such as older residents dying or grown children moving away. The reconstructed vessels in Architectural Suite 3 were all from Pit Structure 3 and Room 19.

Architectural Suite 2 has the most depleted vessel assemblage of all the suites, even though it consists of two pit structures and more rooms than either of the other two suites. The assemblage of complete or nearly complete vessels consists of two miniature jars from the floor of Pit Structure 2 and a bowl and a medium cooking jar from the floor of Pit Structure 4. All the other reconstructed vessels in Architectural Suite 2 are partial vessels and sherd containers. Pit Structure 2 was the only pit structure that did not burn, and it had the largest quantity of orphan sherds on its floor of any structure at the site. Pit Structure 2 was the only pit structure that did not appear to have been rapidly abandoned. There was secondary refuse on the floor, whole vessels had been salvaged or scavenged, a partial skeleton had been placed on the floor and covered with rocks, and then the roof had been dismantled and deposited on the floor. The depleted vessel assemblage in Architectural Suite 2 is consistent with the interpretation that at least Pit Structure 2, if not the entire architectural suite, was abandoned more gradually than the remainder of site. Architectural evidence, tree-ring dates, and stratigraphy all suggest that Pit Structure 4 did not replace Pit Structure 2 but, rather, that the two were both in use during the last years of occupation. Pit Structure 2 seems to have been gradually abandoned, and it appears that many usable artifacts were removed and trash was allowed to accumulate on the floor, at least during the final season of use.

The expected vessel inventory, derived from the discard assemblage, provides a standard for evaluating the number of vessels in the systemic inventory for the site as a whole or for an individual suite of structures. The diversity of abandonment assemblages from one architectural suite to another probably reflects differences in abandonment processes between architectural suites. The abandonment inventory of Architectural Suite 1 approximates the expected systemic assemblage, although the relatively large number of small cooking jars may be the result of lateral cycling (receiving vessels from residents of other architectural suites as gifts or through exchange) or scavenging from the other architectural suites after they were abandoned. Architectural Suite 2 has a depleted vessel inventory, which suggests that its systemic inventory may have been depleted by curation, scavenging, or lateral cycling. That is, some of the vessels that ended up in other structures could have been taken from Architectural Suite 2, indicating that it was abandoned more gradually.

The floor assemblages in Architectural Suites 1 and 3 and in Pit Structure 4 meet many of the expectations of rapid abandonment (Stevenson 1982): (1) presence of abundant de facto refuse in the living area, (2) presence of many items that one would normally expect to have been taken to the new residence, and (3) little secondary refuse (or abandonment refuse) in the living area. Architectural Suite 2, and Pit Structure 2 in particular, fits the material conditions expected for a more gradual abandonment: The suite contains abundant secondary refuse on floors, very little de facto refuse, and few heirlooms or other items of high intrinsic value.

## Abandonment Inventory Enrichment?

Most of the processes that deplete de facto refuse inventories in one location may also enrich assemblages in other structures and sites. Of particular concern at the Duckfoot site was the effect that funerary ritual may have had on the content and distribution of the floor assemblages. It is common to find vessels and other funerary offerings in graves in prehistoric Pueblo sites. Therefore, if the pit structures at Duckfoot were being used as tombs, it is possible that the floor assemblages had been enriched as a part of the funerary events associated with the abandonment of the structures.

The only evidence of inventory enrichment associated with abandonment at Duckfoot is the larger-than-expected number of small cooking jars in Pit Structure 1; however, this enrichment is not believed to be related to the interment of the two individuals on the structure floor. The absence of these and other vessel forms in Architectural Suite 2 suggests that abandonment might have begun earlier in Architectural Suite 2 than it did in the other two architectural suites. If so, the abandonment would have been more gradual, allowing more opportunities for lateral cycling of materials out of Architectural Suite 2 and into Architectural Suites 1 and 3. These events would have resulted in a surplus of certain vessel forms in the latter two architectural suites at abandonment. When Architectural Suites 1 and 3 were abandoned, they were abandoned rapidly, and vessels were taken away on an immediate-priority basis. Vessels that were not immediately necessary or were not of high intrinsic value were simply abandoned on the floors of structures. The conditions that stimulated a rapid abandonment were probably also the conditions that caused the death and interment of at least the six individuals interred in Pit Structures 1, 3, and 4.

# 5

# The Use of Structures

One goal of this study is to understand the organization of household groups at the Duckfoot site. We cannot observe the cultural behaviors and human interactions that are of interest, but we can make inferences about such behaviors and interactions on the basis of the physical traces of activities that were performed in structures. Vernacular architecture reflects a culturally prescribed set of design principles for organizing space and for structuring social interactions. Buildings provide shelter, but they also contribute to structuring and maintaining social order. Architectural arrangements reflect a cultural conception of how the social environment is, or should be, organized. Once built, structures serve to constrain activities and certain social interactions. However, the use of structures can change through time as a result of changes in group size, composition, or organization.

Architecture can be an important source of information about how prehistoric societies thought about and organized space. A question remains as to how well architectural patterns reflect the way specific spaces were actually used. Data presented in Chapter 2 suggest that structures might have been remodeled at intervals of 10 years or less. Changes in the use of structures could have occurred on a shorter-term basis in response to the developmental cycle of domestic groups or changes in resource-procurement strategies. Although the walls of a structure were relatively static, other parts of a structure may have been modified to accommodate changes in the way it was used or changes in the social group that used it. For example, the distribution of artifacts and features on structure floors probably responded more quickly to changes in activity organization and structure use than did the walls of those structures. The distribution of artifacts and features on floors may be used to make inferences about activity organization at or near the time of structure abandonment.

My ultimate goal in studying the use of structures is not to identify single activities but, rather, to identify what Rapoport (1990:11) calls "systems of activities and systems of settings." In his discussion of domestic architecture and the use of space, Rapoport summarizes some important points:

> Activity *systems* are inevitably organized in space and time. It follows that one cannot look at single activities but one must consider activity systems. It also follows that one cannot merely consider a particular building because people do not live in, or act exclusively in, single buildings; they use various buildings, a variety of outdoor spaces, settlements, and whole regions: they inhabit cultural landscapes [Rapoport 1990:12; emphasis in original].

Although the focus of this chapter is not the entire Pueblo I cultural landscape, I do attempt to define the organization of certain activities or activity systems at the Duckfoot site. First, I identify and discuss the evidence for certain activities within structures. Then I address the redundancy and complementarity of activities between architectural suites and between rooms and pit structures.

Structures are bounded spaces where a variety of activities took place and where artifacts relating to those activities are likely to have been deposited as primary or de facto refuse. A problem, of course, is that artifact distributions do not always reflect the locations where activities were performed when the site or structure was occupied. To a large extent, the archaeological record is a record of where things were stored or discarded. Seymour and Schiffer, for example, note that structures may be repositories for artifacts that were not actually used in them:

> Other artifacts that were not actually used within the structure but were essential to activities carried out elsewhere by members of the household may have been stored within the structure. . . . In other words, structures are a kind of focal point for a residential or activity group where various belongings are stored, used, and removed according to different schedules [Seymour and Schiffer 1987:576].

Refuse discarded within abandoned structures can further contribute to the background noise that needs to be filtered out before any attempt to identify the activities that may have taken place in the structure. The sherds of a reconstructible cooking pot on the floor of a structure may indicate the location in which the vessel was used, stored, maintained, or discarded. The argument for an artifact's use in a particular location is made on the basis of context. That is, the location of an artifact with respect to other artifacts and features may support a reasonable inference that the item was used in that location in association with other functionally related items. The argument for inferring activities and activity locations from the spatial associations among artifacts and features is strengthened by understanding the formation processes likely to have produced the observed patterns. Specific studies of abandonment and preabandonment formation processes were presented in Chapters 3 and 4. These studies demonstrated that we cannot assume that artifacts were always deposited in the locations in which they were used.

## Objectives and Methods

In this chapter, I use artifact and feature data from Duckfoot to address three basic questions: (1) What activities took place in the various structures at Duckfoot? (2) Are structure size and location good indicators of the types of activities that took place in structures? (3) Do patterns of activity redundancy and complementarity at Duckfoot support the model of a nested hierarchy of social groups?

In this chapter, *floor-associated* refers to artifacts that were lying either directly on a floor or within 5 cm of a floor. Every item used and abandoned on a floor will not end up being on the floor in the archaeological context. For example, if a complete vessel resting on the floor before abandonment is broken into pieces by the falling roof, some sherds from that vessel almost certainly will come to rest in the fill above the floor. At the same time, sherds that were incorporated into the mud used to build the roof, or sherds from a vessel that was on the roof, may fall and land on or near the floor as the roof collapses. If the definition of *floor-associated* were limited to include only those items that were directly and demonstrably in contact with the floor, many items that were in fact a part of the systemic floor inventory would be excluded. Conversely, the more artifacts from the fill above the floor that one includes with the floor-associated assemblage, the more likely the assemblage is to include items that were *not* a part of the systemic floor inventory. Defining *floor-associated* to include items found in contact with the floor and within 5 cm of the floor is a compromise that at least is consistent from one context to the next.

## Analysis of Activity Areas

At the Duckfoot site, the locations where certain household activities were performed are discernible because of the presence of features and primary and de facto refuse left behind on floors and living surfaces. In this volume, I use the term *domestic activities* to refer to those activities associated with food preparation and consumption, such as short-term storage, food grinding, cooking, serving, and eating. These domestic activities are of particular interest because of their universal biological necessity and because their demand for tools and facilities makes them well suited to archaeological analysis. In addition, there are many nondomestic activities, such as tool and pottery manufacture, building construction, and mortuary practices, that leave distinctive physical traces, which— when found in context—can be used to make inferences about activity location and organization. Other activities, such as certain rituals, may leave physical residues, but the arguments that link the physical remains with the performance of the activities are more problematic. And finally, there are activities, such as sleeping and long-term storage, that either leave no trace or leave only perishable traces, such as baskets, mats, or seeds, that often do not survive in the archaeological record. Such activities do require space, however, and some of them may be inferred from the presence of available space within a facility and the lack of evidence of other activities.

## Grinding

Grinding areas are defined by the presence of manos and metates, which were used to grind food, especially corn. Metates are heavy (up to 45 kg at Duckfoot) and relatively immovable. When metates are found on floors in association with other food-preparation items, such as manos or sherd containers, one can infer that they are in or near their prehistoric use locations. Unmodified cobbles or chunks of sandstone were often used to prop up the ends of metates to support them in the proper position for grinding. Peckingstones, abraders, and cobbles with evidence of abrasion and pecking are also commonly associated with grinding areas and were probably used in a variety of food-preparation tasks. Wright (1990) studied various aspects of grinding-tool wear by experimentally replicating and using manos and metates similar to those found at Duckfoot. Her corn-grinding experiments showed that the grinding surfaces of the tools had to be refurbished (roughened) regularly by pecking in order to maintain an effective grinding surface. Peckingstones have evidence of the kind of battering that one would expect to see on a tool used to peck a smooth sandstone surface, and they are interpreted as being the tools that were used for refurbishing the grinding surfaces of manos and metates. At Duckfoot, peckingstones were often found in association with manos and metates on structure floors. In several instances, manos and peckingstones were found together on the floors of structures that did not have metates. Fourteen of the 16 structures that had manos on their floors also had peckingstones on their floors ($\chi^2$ = 8.0, $df$ = 1, p < .01). This significant association supports the argument that peckingstones were used to peck the surfaces of grinding tools and that the pecking-stones and grinding tools were stored together.

## Cooking

Cooking activity areas are defined by the presence of hearths, fire pits, or burned spots, and sometimes cooking pots, which usually have sooted outer surfaces. Sherd containers also appear to be a common, if not standard, piece of equipment for cooking, serving, and eating (Hally 1986; Mills 1989). In addition to providing heat for cooking, an open fire in the hearth would have provided light and heat for the living space at night and during the winter months. The artifacts associated with cooking are portable and could have been moved easily from their use locations to storage locations or to different use locations. When a site or structure was abandoned, the artifacts could have been moved to a different structure or even to a different site. Therefore, the presence of a hearth, fire pit, or burned spot in association with primary cooking refuse, such as carbonized food remains, is considered adequate to support an inference of cooking. Hearths and fire pits, both of which are formally con-structed pits that were excavated into structure floors or other sur-faces, are believed to have been used repeatedly over a long period of time; burned spots, which indicate where small fires were built di-rectly on surfaces rather than in excavated pits, are inferred to have been used expediently over a shorter period of time.

## Storage

There are two distinct types of storage facilities: storage rooms and storage features. Storage rooms are interpreted as *long-term storage* facilities, an interpretation that most often is made because of a lack of evidence of other activities. A successful agricultural strategy re-quires storing surplus food, at least for a winter and more likely for longer, to buffer against unpredictability in food production. Access to long-term storage rooms at Pueblo I sites may have been re-stricted in an attempt to improve food preservation and control food distribution (Gross 1987; Hegmon 1991). Storage features such as bins (small, slab-lined enclosures) and cists (large-volume pits) are interpreted as *short-term storage* facilities, and they are common in Pueblo I rooms that have cooking and food-processing activity areas. The wing walls in Pueblo I pit structures performed essentially the same function as storage bins by separating an area within each structure that could have been used for short-term storage. Fewer goods could have been kept in storage features than in long-term storage rooms, but the stored goods would have been in more accessible locations.

When tools, containers, and cooking vessels are not actually being used, they are, for all practical purposes, in storage. If a modern house were abandoned with dirty dinner dishes left on the table and dirty pots on the stove, one would consider these implements to be in their use locations. In most modern households, dishes are washed and put into cabinets until they are needed again for preparation or consumption of another meal. I introduce the term *active storage* to refer to the locations where cooking vessels or other implements are kept near their location of use. For example, if a sooted pot were found in a hearth, a good argument could be made not only for its use as a cooking jar but also for its location of use. If that same cooking pot were recovered from a structure without a hearth, we might infer it to be in a storage context. A pot found in the low-traffic area along the interior wall of a pit structure just a few feet from the hearth might be considered to be in active storage.

## Manufacturing

Tool-manufacturing and pottery-making areas may be recognized archaeologically because tool and pottery manufacture often leave physical traces. An area where chipped-stone tools were manufactured might be marked by the presence of cores, flakes, and hammerstones. Areas where ground-stone and bone tools were manufactured, maintained, or repaired may be indicated by the presence of pecking-stones and abraders. Pottery-making areas may be marked by the presence of tempered clay and modified sherds; the latter were used to smooth the surfaces of pots and bond the coils of clay while the clay was in a plastic state. Sewing and hide working might be indicated by the presence of bone awls. In some cases, manufacturing activities may have taken place in the same locations as other activities, and at Duckfoot, manufacturing activity areas are often included within what are defined as multiple-use or active-storage areas.

## Ritual

Inferring ritual activities is difficult because we lack the theoretical tools we need to link ritual activities with specific physical traces. Even in our own culture, ceremonies and integrative rituals often involve food preparation and consumption. Thus, ritual and domestic activities are not necessarily in opposition, and they may not be mutually exclusive in a given space. Wilshusen (1988d, 1989b) ar-

gued that certain features in prehistoric Pueblo sites, including sipapus and sand-filled pits, were associated with ritual activities. These
features are common in Pueblo I pit structures but absent in surface
rooms (Varien and Lightfoot 1989). The occurrence of sipapus and
sand-filled pits at Duckfoot is interpreted as evidence of ritual activity.

## Mortuary

Mortuary practices often include a ritual aspect and therefore may
be considered a specific type of ritual behavior. Mortuary practices
typically leave physical traces, including at least a human skeleton
and possibly some grave goods.

## Multiple Use

There are many other essential individual and household activities,
such as sleeping and social gathering, that do not leave physical
traces but do require open space within structures. These activities
may be represented archaeologically by areas that are devoid of tools
and clutter in structures that also have evidence of other activities
such as food preparation or tool manufacture. The implication is that
these areas had to have been actively maintained as open areas. The
label given to this type of activity area should not be construed as
implying that other areas of the site were not multipurpose. Multiple-
use areas as defined here have few permanent features and were
cleaned up on a regular basis. The tools used in these activity areas
may have been stored along the walls around the perimeter of the
open space.

# Patterns of Structure Use

For more than a century, Southwestern archaeologists have relied on
ethnographic analogue as a means of understanding and interpreting
the use of prehistoric pueblos (Morgan 1965; Mindeleff 1891; see
also review by Lipe and Hegmon [1989]). Primarily on the basis of
nineteenth-century ethnography and studies of pueblo architecture,
archaeologists have traditionally classified individual rooms or structures as belonging to one of three categories: (1) domestic, or habitation, rooms; (2) storage rooms; and (3) religious, or ceremonial,
rooms. Hill (1966) analyzed a variety of artifact and ecofact data, in
addition to architecture, to evaluate the use of structures at Broken K
Pueblo in east-central Arizona and concluded that the structures
could be grouped into the three traditional functional types. Dean
(1969) added two other types of rooms—granary and grinding

room—in his study of room use in the Kayenta area. Jorgensen (1975) conducted one of the most systematic studies of its time, using factor analysis and implicational analysis of artifact and feature assemblages to interpret room use at Table Rock Pueblo in eastern Arizona.

Adams (1983) used architectural data (including internal features but not artifacts) and information gathered from living informants at the modern Hopi village of Walpi to interpret room use. He defined six room types: (1) storage, (2) habitation, (3) religious, (4) piki house, (5) granary, and (6) religious storage. He could not distinguish storage rooms from religious storage rooms on the basis of architectural features but noted that religious storage rooms were adjacent to religious rooms and kivas. He found significant differences in size, location, and doorway access to different types of rooms, although he combined storage, granary, and religious storage rooms in each of his subsequent comparisons. Adams (1983:51) found that room size was a good predictor of room use. The relationship between room use and size had also been noted by Hill (1966, 1970a) at Broken K Pueblo and by Sullivan (1974) at Grasshopper Pueblo. Adams (1983) found that religious rooms were significantly larger than habitation rooms, which were significantly larger than storage rooms. He then tested these empirical generalizations on prehistoric sites and found that they held true for Betatakin in the Kayenta area (Dean 1969), and for Badger House Community at Mesa Verde National Park (Hayes and Lancaster 1975). However, he did not explain how he determined room use in these archaeological sites in order to test the relationship between size and use. Adams also found that room location was a good predictor of room use at Walpi. Habitation rooms were almost exclusively located on the upper stories, with access from the outside, whereas storage rooms were significantly more likely to be located on lower floors, with access only through other rooms owned by the clan or lineage segment.

Ciolek-Torrello (1978, 1985) argued against the use of these historic Southwestern analogues in his typological analysis of rooms. He instead used a multivariate approach, similar to that used by Jorgensen (1975), involving factor analysis of artifact and feature distributions in rooms occupied at about the same time at Grasshopper Pueblo. Ciolek-Torrello used factor analysis of artifact and feature associations in structures to define six classes, or types, of structures. He then looked at the factors that were most important in defining the class and from these assigned functional, or use, types to each group of structures. The six room types defined by Ciolek-Torrello (1985:53) are (1) limited activity, (2) habitation, (3) domestic storage, (4) multifunctional habitation, (5) manufacturing, and (6) storage/manufacturing.

The approaches used by Jorgensen (1975) and Ciolek-Torrello (1978, 1985) are of interest because they objectively consider a broad range of feature and assemblage associations. Their use classes were essentially computer-generated on the basis of factors derived from similarities in feature and artifact assemblages. Furthermore, the typology created groups that could be explained after the fact because one could see the underlying patterns in the data that caused the computer to assign rooms to each group. These quantitative approaches allow one to take into account a large number of variables in a large number of rooms.

## Use of Structures at Duckfoot

A multivariate analysis of structure use at Duckfoot is presented here, but using a visual analysis of the distributions of floor-associated artifacts and features. Because the number of rooms at Duckfoot is small, the data are manageable without the use of multivariate statistics. Table 5.1 is a matrix in which selected artifact and feature types are listed in rows, and each structure (except for Room 20) is represented by a column. Some abundant artifact types, such as orphan sherds and unmodified flakes, were eliminated from this matrix. Other artifact and feature types with extremely low frequencies were either eliminated or combined into more general types. Capped features—that is, features that were deliberately filled and sealed before abandonment—are not included in Table 5.1; uncapped ("in use") features and features whose status is not known *are* included. The cells in the matrix display the frequency of artifact and feature types by structure. The columns in the matrix are arranged such that structures with similar clusters of attributes are grouped together, and the shading draws attention to the combinations of attributes that are judged to be most important in defining the similarity of structures and therefore in assigning use classes. Structures are grouped on the basis of the presence or absence of certain variables or clusters of variables rather than on differences in frequency. Differences in artifact frequency are likely to result from differences in formation processes, as well as from differences in structure use. For example, Room 15 has a rich assemblage of artifacts, but a study presented in Chapter 3 demonstrated that secondary refuse was discarded on its floor. In general, features are given more emphasis than artifacts. For example, the occurrence of a fire pit in Room 5 is given more emphasis than the occurrence of six peckingstones in Room 6 (Table 5.1) in assigning the respective structures to a use class. In viewing Table 5.1, one can see that the artifact and feature diversity generally increases across the page from left to right.

Table 5.1. Frequencies of Selected Floor Artifacts and Features by Structure

Use Class

| Variable ↓ | Long-Term Storage | | | | | | | | | | | Specialized Storage | | Domestic | | | | | | Pit Structure | | | |
|---|---|---|---|---|---|---|---|---|---|---|---|---|---|---|---|---|---|---|---|---|---|---|---|
| Structure No. → | 1 | 2 | 3 | 6 | 7 | 8 | 9 | 14 | 17 | 18 | 4 | 10 | 15 | 5 | 11 | 12 | 13 | 16 | 19 | 1 | 2 | 3 | 4 |
| Hearth or fire pit | | | | | | | | | | | | | | 1 | 1 | 1 | 1 | 1 | 1 | 1 | 1 | 1 | 1 |
| Bin | | | | | | | | | | | | 3 | | 1 | 2 | 2 | 1 | | | | | | |
| Cist | | | | | | | | | | | | 2 | 2 | 1 | | | | 1 | 2 | | | | |
| Pit, post hole | 1 | 2 | | | | | 4 | | | 1 | 2 | 10 | 3 | 1 | 5 | 10 | 4 | 13 | 25 | 7 | 5 | 13 | 12 |
| Sand-filled pit | | | | | | | | | | | | | | | | | | | | | 11 | 12 | 5 |
| Ash pit | | | | | | | | | | | | | | | | | | | | 1 | 1 | 1 | 1 |
| Wing wall, vent | | | | | | | | | | | | | | | | | | | | 2 | 2 | 1 | 2 |
| Cooking jar | | | | | | | | | | | | | | | | | | 1 | 2 | 10 | | 4 | 1 |
| Olla | | | | | | | | | | | | | | | | | | | | 3 | | | |
| Partial vessel | | | | | | | | | | | | | 3 | | | | | 2 | 3 | 7 | 7 | 2 | 4 |
| Sherd container | | | | | | | | | 1 | | | | | | | | 1 | | 1 | 14 | 7 | 11 | 8 |
| Other vessel | | | | | | | | | | | | | 2 | | | | | | 1 | 1 | 2 | 3 | 1 |
| Modified, shaped sherd | | | | | | 1 | | | | | | 1 | 1 | 1 | | | | | | 1 | 7 | 4 | 6 |
| Metate (all types) | | | | | | | | | | | | | | | | 3 | 2 | 3 | | 4 | 3 | 8 | 5 |
| Mano (all types) | | | 2 | | 2 | 1 | | | | 1 | 3 | | 2 | 5 | 1 | 5 | 8 | 4 | 7 | 10 | 4 | 13 | 14 |
| Peckingstone | | | 6 | 2 | 1 | | 1 | | | | | 1 | 2 | 2 | 5[a] | 10 | 7 | 2 | 1 | 4 | 26 | 1 | 8 |
| Abrader | | | | | | | | | | | 1 | | | | | 1 | 1 | | 1 | 1 | 3 | 2 | 1 |
| Modified cobble | | | | | | | | | | | 1 | 1 | | 1 | 1[a] | 1 | 4 | | 2 | 6 | 4 | 7 | 7 |
| Projectile point | | | | | | | | | | | | | | | | | | | 1 | 2 | | 1 | 1 |
| Axe, maul | | | 1 | | | | | | | | | | | | 1 | | | | 1 | 3 | 2 | 1 | 3 |
| Modified flake | | | | | | | | | | | | | | 1 | | | | | | | 3 | | 2 |
| Core | | | 1 | | | 3 | | | | | | | 1 | | | 2 | 1 | | | 3 | 3 | 1 | 2 |
| Hammerstone | | 1 | | | | | | | | | | | | 1 | | | | | | 2 | 1 | 2 | 3 |
| Awl | | | | | | | | | | | | | | 1 | | | | | 1 | 3 | 5 | 1 | 8 |

NOTE: Shading indicates variables emphasized in determining use classes. Use-class assignments reflect the status of structures during the abandonment period; capped features are not considered. Artifact types are defined in Volume 1 (Lightfoot and Etzkorn 1993).
[a] Includes artifacts found in Feature 3, a cist.

Four structure-use classes were assigned on the basis of the clustering of these variables. Again, these data patterns and associations were derived visually and not by a quantitative clustering program. The use classes are shown at the top of the matrix in Table 5.1. In order of increasing diversity, the use classes are (1) long-term storage, (2) specialized storage, (3) domestic, and (4) pit structure. Admittedly, the term *pit structure* does not describe a use category, but certainly this architectural class of structures forms a distinct use class. Pit structures might well fall into the category that Ciolek-Torrello (1985:53) defined as "multifunctional habitation." The activities represented in structures of each of these classes is discussed in the following section.

# Activities in Structures at Duckfoot

Figure 5.1 summarizes the distribution of activity areas in structures at Duckfoot at abandonment. In the following sections, I describe the features and artifacts used to define not only these activity areas but also several that existed, or are inferred to have existed, earlier in the occupation of the site. Maps showing the distribution of artifacts and features in individual structures are included in Volume 1 (Lightfoot, Etzkorn, and Varien 1993).

## Long-Term Storage Rooms

Long-term storage rooms were probably used primarily for food storage. Gross (1987) studied storage facilities in the Dolores area and inferred that corn was probably stored much as it is in modern pueblos, dried and stacked on the cob. Tools and other materials also could have been stored in these long-term storage rooms. When the

**Figure 5.1.** *Activity areas in structures at abandonment. In pit structures, the numbers following the activity area abbreviations correspond to the activity area numbers used in text. Multiple-use activity areas are not shown.*

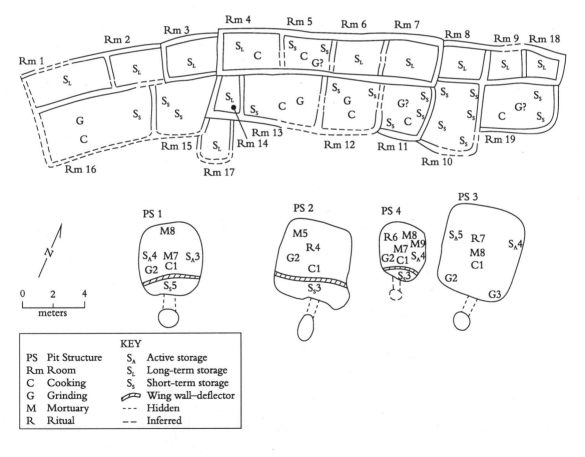

supply of stored food ran low, some of these rooms could have been used for other activities as well.

### Rooms 1–3, 6–9, and 18

Rooms 1, 2, 3, 6, 7, 8, 9, and 18 are small rooms in the northern (back) row in the roomblock. They are interpreted as long-term storage rooms because they generally lack evidence of other activities. Few artifacts were found on the floors of these rooms, and those that were found might have been stored in those locations. Manos and peckingstones were found together in two of the back storage rooms and separately in two others (Table 5.1). Features are also uncommon in these long-term storage rooms, with a total of only eight pits or post holes in four of the eight rooms.

### Rooms 14 and 17

Room 14 is in the front (southern) row of rooms, and Room 17 was added to the front of the roomblock in an area that had previously been the courtyard. A mano, a peckingstone, and a modified sherd were found on the floor of Room 14; no artifacts were found on the floor of Room 17. In terms of their small size, lack of floor features, and paucity or absence of floor artifacts, Rooms 14 and 17 more closely resemble the back rooms than they do the other front rooms at Duckfoot. Consequently, Rooms 14 and 17 are interpreted as long-term storage rooms.

### Room 4

Room 4 is a back room that is similar in size and shape to the other long-term storage rooms; however, it differs from the others in that a burned spot, consisting of burned sediments and a layer of ash, was found on its floor. Burned and broken small-mammal bones (mostly *Lepus* [jackrabbit] and *Sylvilagus* [cottontail]) were recovered from the ash and the floor surrounding the feature. Flotation samples collected from the ash associated with the burned spot contained seeds of cheno-am (goosefoot or pigweed) and *Stipa hymenoides* (Indian rice grass) but no cultigens (Table 5.2). Artifacts recovered from the floor include three manos, an abrader, and a modified cobble. Room 4 contains no formal features, such as a hearth or bin, that are typical of domestic rooms. The burned spot and associated remains reflect a brief use of the structure at, or soon after, abandonment. It appears that Room 4 was used for cooking one or maybe a few meals consisting mostly of rabbits and wild plants. Except for this

Table 5.2. Summary of Food Taxa in Structure Hearths

| Taxon | Rm 4 | Rm 5 | Rm 11 | Rm 12 | Rm 13 | Rm 16 | Rm 19 | PS 1 | PS 2 | PS 3 | PS 4 |
|---|---|---|---|---|---|---|---|---|---|---|---|
| Cheno-am | + | | + | + | + | + | + | + | + | + | + |
| *Zea mays* | | + | | + | + | + | | + | + | + | |
| *Physalis longifolia* | | | + | + | + | + | | | | + | + |
| *Stipa hymenoides* | + | | + | + | + | + | | | | | |
| *Juniperus* | | | | + | | + | | + | | + | |
| *Opuntia* | | | + | | | + | | | | | |
| *Portulaca retusa* | | | | | + | + | | | | | |
| *Descurainia* | | | | | + | | | | | | |
| Gramineae | | | | + | | | | | | | |
| Malvaceae | | | | + | | | | | | | |
| *Yucca baccata* | | | | | | + | | | | | |

SOURCE: Adapted from Adams (1993:Table 6.15).
NOTE: Taxa listed in order of ubiquity.
Rm = Room; PS = Pit Structure.

brief use near the time of abandonment, Room 4 is similar to the other long-term storage rooms.

## Specialized Storage Rooms

Rooms 10 and 15 have in common that they are in the front, or southern, row of rooms and were used as storage structures late in the occupation of the site. They differ from long-term storage rooms in having internal storage features. Long-term storage rooms are thought have been used for stacking stored goods, such as corn, without containers (Gross 1987), and they usually lack internal storage features. Specialized storage rooms, on the other hand, have bins and cists, which suggests that different kinds of things were stored or that the storage strategy was different. Specialized and long-term storage rooms also differ in terms of access. Most long-term storage rooms have more restricted access; that is, one would had to have passed through a domestic room in order to gain access to a back-row room. In contrast, Rooms 10 and 15 probably were accessible from the courtyard, although the remodeling of the rooms to convert them to storage facilities might have included modification of their entrances.

### Room 10

Room 10 is a front-row room that apparently was originally used as a domestic room and later was changed to a storage room. The position of Room 10 in the front row of rooms and the presence of a hearth early in the occupation suggest that it probably was built as a domestic room. At some time during the occupation, however, the hearth was capped and then truncated by the construction of a large, subfloor cist. The final feature assemblage included three slab-walled bins and two subfloor cists, which suggests that Room 10 was used for compartmentalized storage. Although some of these features might have been in the room from the beginning, it is unlikely that they all were, because they take up a substantial amount of the floor space. In addition, there were few artifacts on the floor, which is consistent with the interpretation that Room 10 was used predominantly for storage in the final stages of the occupation.

### Room 15

Room 15 is a front room with a deep, centrally located cist, similar to that in Room 10, and a shallower cist near the west wall, similar to the one in Room 11. It is not clear if Room 15 originally was used as a domestic structure, but the presence of two cists in the room at abandonment suggests that it was predominantly used for storage at least toward the end of the occupation. Several partial vessels were refit from sherds found on the floor and in the fill of the two cists. These refits indicate that the cists were open at abandonment, when trash was being discarded onto the floor of Room 15. The floor and lower fill of Room 15 contained abundant refuse, particularly sherds that produced few reconstructible vessels. This is significant because a slab-walled bin had been built over the fill of the large, central cist. The base of the slab-walled bin was at floor level, making it appear to be contemporaneous with the late use of the room. However, the results of the refitting analysis refute that interpretation, suggesting instead that the cist was open at abandonment and that the slab-walled bin represented a postabandonment reuse of the room, probably after the walls and roof had collapsed and the structure had filled.

## Domestic Rooms

Rooms 12, 13, and 16 have feature and artifact assemblages that indicate their use as domestic structures at abandonment (Table 5.1). The presence of a hearth, one or more short-term storage features, metates, manos, and peckingstones in each of these rooms supports this interpretation. Rooms 5, 11, and 19 contain the same kinds of features and artifacts, with the exception of metates, and therefore are also interpreted as domestic rooms. It is likely that the metates were removed from these rooms during abandonment. Rooms 16 and 19 contain cooking jars, as well as other vessels. The floors of all six domestic rooms were littered with sherds that may represent the primary refuse of vessels that were in use during the period of abandonment. Flotation samples from the hearths of the domestic rooms contained a greater diversity of possible food remains than did the hearths of pit structures (Table 5.2). *Zea mays* (corn) kernels were present in four of the six samples from domestic-room hearths. In addition, hearths in domestic rooms yielded the charred remains of a variety of wild plants, including cheno-am (goosefoot or pigweed), *Physalis longifolia* (groundcherry), *Stipa hymenoides* (Indian rice grass), and others (Table 5.2). The five domestic rooms in the front, or southern, row of rooms burned at abandonment, but the fires were apparently not as intense as those that burned the pit structures.

### Room 5

Room 5 is a small room in the back row of the roomblock. A shallow, ash-filled fire pit had been excavated into the floor, and a slab-walled bin was located in the northeast corner. The presence of these features suggests that Room 5 served as a domestic structure, and this interpretation is supported by the artifact assemblage as well. Artifacts found on the floor include five manos, two peckingstones, a modified cobble, a bone awl, a modified flake, and a hammerstone. Together, the artifacts and features suggest that a broad range of activities, including grinding, cooking, and possibly tool manufacturing, tool maintenance, and hide working, took place in Room 5. This broad range of activities is typical of domestic rooms rather than of long-term storage rooms. The assemblage lacks a metate, but this is also true of the assemblage from Room 11, which, like Room 5, is interpreted as a domestic room. Several metates were found in postabandonment deposits in other rooms, including those in Room 17. It is possible that metates were used in Room 5 and later removed. Although this structure originally may have been used for long-term storage, by the end of the occupation it was being used predominantly for domestic activities.

### Room 11

Room 11 has two corner bins, a subfloor cist, a hearth, and a warming pit, which leads to the interpretation that this was a domestic room. The structure had been cleaned at abandonment, and no reconstructible vessels or complete tools were found on the open floor. Artifacts associated with the use of the room were recovered from storage features; these include five peckingstones, one mano, one modified cobble, and a modified sherd, all interpreted as having been stored in the features.

A cooking area is defined on the basis of the hearth and warming pit and the edible-plant remains found in both these features. Short-term storage is indicated by the presence of bins and a cist. The artifact assemblage is also generally typical of domestic rooms; how-ever, metates are notably absent, and the single mano recovered from the room was from a storage context. The absence of metates might best be explained as a result of abandonment or postabandonment processes. At Duckfoot, seven out of 10 structures with a formal hearth or fire pit in use at abandonment also had metates on their floors; there are no structures with metates (on their floors) that do not also have hearths. The probability of such a sample being drawn by chance from a theoretical population in which there is no rela-tionship between hearths and metates is .0029 (Fisher's exact test). A set of grinding tools was found in the postabandonment fill about 10 cm above the floor of Room 7, which is the adjacent storage room to the north of Room 11. The set includes four metates, five manos, five modified cobbles, and three peckingstones. Room 7 has no features, and the grinding implements and associated artifacts were found in the fill above the floor rather than on the floor itself, which suggests that these tools were not used in Room 7. Other tools that are rare in storage rooms but more common in domestic structures were also found at the same level in the lower fill of Room 7. These include two projectile points, a shaped sherd, a bone awl, a bone pendant, and a modified flake (although only the pen-dant was mapped). This assemblage of items probably was removed from Room 11 and discarded or cached in Room 7 at abandonment or shortly thereafter. The artifacts were found in the unburned roof fall and lower wall fall of Room 7. The fill separating the artifacts from the floor in Room 7 might have been deposited during aban-donment, when pit structures and front rooms were being destroyed. Clearly, the large, heavy grinding tools did not move by themselves, so the only plausible explanations are that the implements were on the roof of Room 7 at abandonment or were pulled from some-where else on the site and dumped into Room 7. No source of surplus grinding tools is more likely than Room 11.

### Room 12

Room 12 has a hearth and two corner bins. Three metates, five manos, an axe or maul fragment, an abrader, and 10 peckingstones were found on its floor. On the basis of these features and artifacts, the room is interpreted as a domestic structure. No complete or nearly complete reconstructible vessels were found in Room 12, and only 10 sherds were recorded as being associated with the floor. The grinding implements were scattered throughout the room and were not situated in a clear in situ activity area (see Lightfoot, Etzkorn, and Varien 1993:Figure 2.20), but the presence of the hearth, metates, manos, and peckingstones suggests that food was processed and cooked in Room 12. The presence of the two corner bins suggests that food was stored on a short-term basis.

## Room 13

Room 13 has a hearth, a large corner bin, and a variety of floor artifacts, which leads to the interpretation that it served as a domestic room. The artifacts recovered from the floor include two metates, eight manos, an abrader, four modified cobbles, and seven peckingstones. Several other artifacts, including four manos, a maul, three peckingstones, a biface, and a projectile point, were found just above the floor in the burned roof fall stratum; however, it is possible that these were not actually associated with the use of Room 13. North and west of the hearth, large cooking-jar sherds were scattered across the floor and within the postabandonment fill immediately above the floor. However, a sherd container was the only reconstructible vessel. The two metates were stacked, grinding surfaces down, to the east of the hearth, and manos were scattered across the central portion of the room. The features and artifacts offer evidence of grinding, cooking, and short-term storage, which supports the interpretation of Room 13 as a domestic room. Apparently, any vessels that might have been used in the room (with the exception of the sherd container) were removed at abandonment.

## Room 16

Room 16 is interpreted as having been a domestic room at abandonment on the basis of the hearth, three metates, four manos, and two peckingstones found on its floor (Surface 2). These features and artifacts are evidence of grinding and cooking. A cist provided short-term storage in Room 16, and there apparently was access to ample long-term storage space in adjacent rooms, including Room 15.

The floor of Room 16 was covered by a 5-cm-thick layer of burned sediment, ash, and twigs. The twigs could have been placed on the floor as fuel in a deliberate attempt to burn the room by igniting brush and sticks inside. Artifacts were found on top of this burned layer, and even though it was not a prepared floor, it was treated as a use surface (Surface 1). The artifacts on Surface 1 include a metate, four manos, a modified cobble, a peckingstone, a piece of a bone awl, and a modified cobble that might have been a fetish. These items might have been deposited after the room was abandoned. Alternatively, they could have been placed in the room as a part of the process of abandoning the structure. The artifacts were buried beneath collapsed wall debris and therefore must have been deposited during, or soon after, abandonment.

### Room 19

Room 19 contains more features and yielded a greater variety of de facto refuse than any other room at Duckfoot and is interpreted to be a domestic room. The abundance of features is due in part to the presence of a large number of post holes (11), most of which were incorporated into the southern and eastern walls. Two cists in Room 19, including one that is large and bell shaped, indicate that short-term storage took place in this room. Cooking is well represented by the presence of a hearth, two cooking jars, a sherd container, and three partial vessels; serving and eating probably also took place in Room 19. No metates were found on the floor of Room 19, but one was found in the burned roof fall deposits about 5 cm above the floor, and two others were found in the fill of an adjoining storage room (Room 9). These metates could have been removed from the floor of Room 19 and placed in these other contexts during abandonment. The recovery of seven manos, a peckingstone, an abrader, and two modified cobbles from the floor makes it reasonable to infer that a grinding area was present in Room 19. A projectile point, an axe, and a bone awl were also found on the floor. The bone awl and cobbles could have been used for hide working.

## Pit Structures

Pit structures have the greatest abundance and diversity of artifacts and features of any structures at the site. Three of the four pit structures burned, which resulted in floor assemblages that are remarkably intact, with many items found in use, active-storage, or short-term storage contexts. Hearths, grinding implements, short-term storage areas (in three out of four structures), and a variety of manufacturing tools reflect domestic activities such as cooking, grinding, tool manufacture, and tool maintenance. In addition, the occurrence of human burials and certain types of features unique to pit structures may indicate that these structures were used for mortuary and other ritual activities. The artifact assemblages in pit structures differ from those in the domestic rooms in the types and frequencies of the artifacts listed in Table 5.1, particularly those listed toward the bottom of the table. A variety of tools and containers apparently were used or stored in pit structures, including ollas (which may have been used to store food or water), cooking jars, bowls, seed jars, sherd containers, modified sherds, manos, metates, peckingstones, abraders, projectile points, axes, mauls, bone awls, modified flakes, cores, and hammerstones. Stone flakes and orphan sherds are common in the assemblages from the three burned structures, where many of them probably represent primary refuse. They are even more abundant in the assemblage from Pit Structure 2, where they most likely represent a combination of primary and secondary refuse. Eighteen modified or shaped sherds were recovered from the floors of the four pit structures, and some of these might have been used as scrapers for pottery manufacture (Waterworth and Blinman 1986). Projectile points, axes, mauls, bone awls, modified flakes, cores, and hammerstones occur primarily in pit structures. These tools may have been used for manufacturing and materials-processing (for example, hide working and preparing clay or temper for pottery) in the pit structures, or they may simply have been stored there. In either case, the presence of such artifacts suggests that the pit structures were focal points for using or storing many types of tools that are not well represented in the surface rooms. Hearths in pit structures yielded fewer plant types that could be interpreted as food than did hearths in domestic rooms (Table 5.2). Cheno-am (goosefoot or pigweed) seeds were present in the hearths of all four pit structures, and *Zea mays* (corn) kernels were present in all but the hearth of Pit Structure 4.

A number of feature types are unique to pit structures at Duckfoot: wing walls, deflectors, ventilation systems, sipapus, paho marks, ash pits, sand-filled pits, and sand piles. The presence of deflectors, wing walls, and ventilation systems solely in pit structures may be explained functionally because such features were needed to control air flow in underground chambers containing hearths. These features might have been unnecessary in surface rooms, which had doorways, roof hatches, and wall apertures to control air flow. The other features, predominantly pit features, that are so common in Pueblo I pit structures must certainly relate to activities that occurred with some regularity in pit structures but that did not occur in above-ground rooms. In Table 5.1, the category "sand-filled pit" is made up of sipapus, cylindrical pits, and basin-shaped pits that were filled with clean sand. Sand does not occur in the local soil profile; it had to have been imported, probably from nearby stream beds. There is a consistent association between sand-filled pits and pit structures; one does not find sand-filled pits in surface structures. Wilshusen (1989b) argued that sipapus and other sand-filled pits in pit structures were related to the ritual use of these structures. He also traced the occurrence of these types of features in pit structures from Basketmaker III through historic times and presented a strong argument that they were used for religious rituals and ceremonies. Part of his argument is based on the presence of small, conical pits filled with sand that surround or overlap these usually cylindrical pit features. These small pits may be the impressions of prayer sticks or other ritual paraphernalia and are sometimes called "paho marks." In fact, three of the four pit structures at Duckfoot have paho marks around their sipapus. Even if one rejects the significance of sipapus as ritual features and lumps them into the more generic, descriptive category of "cylindrical, sand-filled pit," they still exist as a feature type that is virtually always present in Pueblo I pit structures but is absent from above-ground rooms. One cannot easily explain them as being related to domestic activities. Wilshusen (1989b) argued that some cylindrical pits were used for setting up temporary altars within structures and that the pits were filled with sand when they were not being used. This could explain why piles of sand are sometimes found on the floors of pit structures, as they are in Pit Structure 2 at Duckfoot. The sand could have been stockpiled in low-traffic areas such as at the base of a post or along a wall, then reused to fill the pits as needed. Basin-shaped pits in pit structures are also commonly filled with sand, in contrast to those found in rooms, which are almost never filled with sand.

Ash pits are also unique to pit structures. Ash pits are defined on the basis of their association with hearths, as well as by their contents, which are almost always ash. Ash pits may have been used as warming pits (using hot coals from the hearth), as temporary refuse receptacles for ash removed from hearths (which would eventually be discarded in the midden), or as storage pits for ash being saved for use in cooking. Adams (1983) documented the occurrence of ash pits in Hopi piki houses, where piki bread (a traditional, paper-thin corn bread) is made.

### Pit Structure 1

Pit Structure 1 has the best-preserved floor assemblage of any structure at the Duckfoot site. The roof burned and collapsed at abandonment, sealing the contents in place. Eight activity areas are defined on the basis of the features and artifacts on the floor. (In the photographs in this section, artifacts from selected activity areas are shown from the perspective of someone in the center of the pit structure looking outward, toward the structure walls. Although actual spacing and exact orientations were not duplicated in the photographs, an attempt was made to approximate the general groupings and relative positions of the artifacts as they were discovered. Vessels found in pieces were reconstructed. Items found stacked one on top of the other were usually photographed side-by-side, particularly if a heavy item had been placed on top of a lighter one. For exact locations of all of the artifacts found on the floor of Pit Structure 1, refer to the floor map in Volume 1 [Lightfoot, Etzkorn, and Varien 1993:Figure 2.12].)

Activity Area 1 is a cooking and food-preparation area in the center of the structure. It is defined primarily by the presence of the hearth and ash pit. Items associated with this activity area are a small Chapin Gray cooking jar (Vessel 4), a small Chapin Gray pitcher (Vessel 3), a partial Moccasin Gray cooking jar (Vessel 14), three manos, an edge-damaged flake, and a peckingstone. These items are interpreted as belonging to a cooking and food-preparation tool set. Additional tools and vessels from activities that were conducted nearby may have also been used in Activity Area 1.

Activity Area 2 is a grinding and food-processing area located west of the hearth. The area is defined by an in situ metate that had been placed on stones so that the trough sloped in the proper position for grinding. In addition, two other metates had been leaned against the nearby western wing wall. A Moccasin Gray jar (Vessel 27), three sherd containers (Vessels 57, 103, and 104), two manos, two peckingstones, and four modified cobbles found on the floor surrounding the in situ metate also may have been associated with this activity area. Tool manufacturing may have taken place in this area as well, as evidenced by the presence of flakes and a hammerstone. Selected artifacts associated with Activity Area 2 are shown in Figure 5.2.

Activity Area 3 is an active-storage area defined by a variety of tools and whole and partial vessels along the east wall of the main chamber (Figure 5.3). The placement of these items along the wall made them readily accessible to anyone processing or cooking food in the activity areas surrounding the hearth (Activity Areas 1 and 2). No features are included in this activity area. A mano, four Moccasin Gray jars (Vessels 6, 8, 9, and 28), a Mancos Gray jar (Vessel 10), seven sherd containers (Vessels 5, 7, 98, 99, 100, 101, 102), a white ware sherd scoop (Vessel 123), a red ware sherd scoop (Vessel 114), and a modified sherd are included in Activity Area 3. Most of the vessels are sooted wide-mouth jars and sherd containers that are interpreted as having been used for preparing and cooking food. A bone awl, a modified cobble, a ball of unfired clay, and a cake of (unidentified) white powder also may have been kept in active storage in the same area. These items suggest that hide working and pottery production may have taken place in Pit Structure 1.

Activity Area 4 is an active-storage area near the center of the western edge of the structure. The items that make up Activity Area 4 are five complete or nearly complete pottery vessels (Vessels 11, 12, 13, 15, and 29; see Figure 5.4) that were clustered together near the west wall as if they had been set out of the way. Activity Area 4 is defined as an active-storage area because it appears that the vessels

**Figure 5.2.** *Selected artifacts found in Pit Structure 1, Activity Area 2, a grinding and food-processing area west of the hearth. The metate in the upper right corner was found in the position in which it was used, with several stones supporting it at the proper angle for grinding. The three large pottery fragments in the lower right corner are sherd containers, which were positioned at the open end of the metate trough, where they could have been used to hold meal as it was ground. The other two metates were found leaning against the wing wall, easily accessible to anyone working in this area. Also shown are manos, peckingstones, modified cobbles, a hammerstone, and a Moccasin Gray jar included in this activity area. Length of metate in upper left corner = 54.5 cm.*

**Figure 5.3.** *Selected artifacts found in Pit Structure 1, Activity Area 3, an active-storage area along the east wall of the structure. Most of the large pottery fragments are sherd containers and scoops; note the large modified sherd found inside the sherd container in the upper left corner. Most of the items shown in this photograph were probably used for preparing food in Activity Areas 1 and 2, although the awl and modified cobble may have been used for hide working. All of the vessels and tools appear to have been deliberately placed along the wall of the structure, where they would have been out of the way of foot traffic but easily accessible to individuals working elsewhere in the structure. Height of tallest vessel ("center" row, far left) = 28.5 cm.*

may have been used on a regular basis in the same general area for cooking or food preparation.

Activity Area 5, south of the wing wall, is interpreted as an area that was used predominantly for storage, and it has three subareas within it. Larger items, such as ollas and sandstone slabs, apparently were stored in the corners of the structure; smaller items were kept in the more open area in the center. Items found in the east end of Activity Area 5 include a large Chapin Gray olla (Vessel 17) and a mano. Items found in the west end include a large Chapin Gray olla (Vessel 25), two partial Moccasin Gray cooking jars (Vessels 16 and 19), a gray ware sherd container (Vessel 106), a Bluff Black-on-red bowl sherd (which fits with Vessel 37 from Room 16), a mano, three cores, several flakes, a maul, and a hammerstone. Smaller items, including a miniature seed jar, a bone awl, a projectile point, an edge-damaged flake, a grooved maul, an axe, and a shell pendant, were found in the central part of the area behind the wing wall. Activity Area 5 is interpreted as a tool-storage area, but tool manufacture and maintenance might have taken place there as well. The ollas and

**Figure 5.4.** *Artifacts found in Pit Structure 1, Activity Area 4, an active-storage area along the west wall of the structure. The three wide-mouth jars, one olla, and one seed jar were clustered together, out of the way of traffic but within easy reach of individuals working around the hearth (Activity Area 1) or in the food-processing area just north of the wing wall (Activity Area 2). Height of vessel in upper right corner = 26.5 cm.*

**Figure 5.5.** *Selected artifacts found in Pit Structure 1, Activity Area 5, a short-term storage area south of the wing wall. Many of the items found in this area—for instance, the axe, mauls, projectile point, mano, and pendant—were probably stored in this location for use elsewhere; others—including the cores and hammerstone—may have been used, as well as stored, in this area. Although the pottery artifacts may simply have been stored behind the wing wall when not in use, the two ollas and perhaps some of the other large vessels could have been used to hold food, water, or other substances. Height of tallest vessel = 45.1 cm. See Figure 5.6 for a close-up of the small artifacts in the lower left corner.*

other large vessels might have contained stored substances, such as food or water. Selected artifacts from Activity Area 5 are shown in Figures 5.5 and 5.6.

Activity Area 6 is a multiple-use area in the northern third of the structure where activities other than food preparation, cooking, or storage were performed. The area is generally defined by the absence of clutter on the floor, although a number of artifacts were found around the perimeter of this area, especially along the north wall of the pit structure. The artifacts included in Activity Area 6 are a sherd container (Vessel 105), a projectile point, two manos, a peckingstone, a flake, an edge-damaged flake, and a fragmentary bone awl. These artifacts do not appear to represent a single tool kit but, rather, are notable for the diversity of activities they may represent. Some of the artifacts along the north wall were probably stored or lost in Activity Area 6 rather than being used there. Two capped sipapus were recorded on the floor in Activity Area 6, and these suggest that ritual activities probably took place there before the final use of the pit structure. The area may have been used as a work area that was cleaned up regularly; it may have been a sleeping area; it may have

**Figure 5.6.** *Close-up of the seed jar, shell pendant, projectile point, maul, edge-damaged flake, bone awl, mano, and axe shown in Figure 5.5. Length of shell pendant = 33.7 mm.*

been a sitting and social-gathering area; or it may have served all these purposes and more.

Activity Areas 7 and 8 are mortuary activity areas represented by two skeletons (Burials 1 and 2). The individuals are believed to have been placed in the pit structure before it was intentionally destroyed. Thus, the mortuary activities do not represent the typical use of the pit structure but, rather, the final use. The mortuary activity areas are superimposed on Activity Areas 1 and 6, described above. The mortuary use of the structure may have been part of a ritual associated with the abandonment of both the structure and the site.

### Pit Structure 2

The roof of Pit Structure 2 did not burn, and the floor assemblage did not have the contextual integrity of the assemblage in Pit Structure 1. There were fewer complete tools and vessels on the floor, and the spatial arrangement of artifacts did not as clearly indicate the locations of activities. Secondary refuse had been deposited on the floor during abandonment. The roof of Pit Structure 2 had been intentionally dismantled, which probably resulted in the disturbance of any activity areas that existed before abandonment.

Only one nearly complete vessel—a miniature Chapin Gray bird-effigy vessel (Vessel 58)—was found on the floor of Pit Structure 2. Seven partial vessels were present, and five of these (Vessels 87, 88, 118, 125, and 130) were reconstructed from sherds scattered across the entire floor. Sherds from the other two partial vessels (Vessels 89 and 110) and five sherd containers (Vessels 91, 92, 93, 94, and 95) were recovered from somewhat more localized areas. Out of a total of 1,640 sherds found on the floor of Pit Structure 2 or in floor features, only 394 are parts of reconstructed vessels; the remaining 1,246 sherds are "orphans" that could not be assigned to vessels, partial vessels, or sherd containers. The implication is that far more of the pottery assemblage is refuse that was discarded at abandonment as opposed to de facto or primary refuse. If this is true of the pottery, then it is probably true of the other artifacts and materials as well. Some of the artifacts in Pit Structure 2 may well have been associated with the use of the structure, as were the features, but it would be difficult to demonstrate that a particular item was deposited as primary, rather than secondary, refuse. It is clear that the refuse was deposited during, rather than after, abandonment because it was on the floor, which had been sealed by the collapsed roof. If the secondary refuse had been associated with postabandonment use of the structure by people still living at the site, it would have been mixed in the sediments in and above the roof fall stratum, which was not the case.

Five activity areas are recognized in Pit Structure 2. Activity Area 1 is a cooking and food-preparation area defined by the presence of a hearth and ash pit, which were overflowing with ash. No artifacts were clearly associated with this activity area. The hearth probably would have been used for cooking, as well as for heating and lighting the living space in Pit Structure 2.

Activity Areas 2 and 3 are grinding and short-term storage areas, respectively. Although a specific grinding area could not be defined on the floor of Pit Structure 2, the presence of metates and manos suggests that there was such an activity area when the structure was being used. Three metates were found on the floor of Pit Structure 2: A complete metate lay flat on the floor northwest of the hearth, and two fragments were found north and east of the hearth. Two complete manos and one incomplete mano were found on the floor south of the wing wall. The presence of these tools suggests that there was a grinding area in the main chamber of Pit Structure 2 and a short-term storage area south of the wing wall. The implements may have been dispersed and mixed with secondary refuse at abandonment.

The presence of multiple sand-filled pits in various locations on the floor suggests that ritual activities were conducted in Pit Structure 2; although a specific area cannot be delineated, the evidence of such activities is collectively designated Activity Area 4. In addition, the presence of a capped sipapu and associated paho marks indicates that ritual activities involving these features took place earlier in the use of the structure, before the abandonment period.

Activity Area 5 is a mortuary activity area represented by a partial human skeleton (Burial 3) that was found face down on the floor and surrounded and partly covered by a pile of sandstone rocks. Eight peckingstones, two bone awls, and a mano fragment are among the rocks that surrounded the skeleton. It was not possible to determine if these artifacts were already on the floor or if they had been placed there along with the sandstone rocks that surrounded Burial 3. This burial represents a secondary interment and not an in situ death or primary burial. The body had to have partly decomposed in some other location before being brought to Pit Structure 2 for final deposition. The interment of this individual and the dismantling of the structure roof are interpreted to have been part of a ritual associated with abandonment.

### Pit Structure 3

Eight activity areas are defined on the floor of Pit Structure 3. Activity Area 1 is a cooking area defined by the presence of a hearth and ash pit. The hearth would have been used for cooking, and it would have provided heat and light in the structure. Artifacts found in the vicinity of the hearth and ash pit include a mano, two abraders, a modified cobble, a modified piece of orthoquartzite, and a metate fragment. These artifacts could have been used to prepare food, although they do not appear to have been used for cooking per se. The three pieces of animal bone found on the floor near the hearth may be the remains of a meal that was cooked in the hearth.

Activity Area 2 is a grinding area in the southwest corner of the pit structure defined by a metate that was found in the position in which it was used. Three stone metate rests supported the closed end of the metate so that the open end of the trough tilted slightly downward. Three manos were associated with this metate: one was on top of the metate, one was on the floor to the west, and one supported an edge of the metate. A grooved-and-polished axe was centered beneath the metate, but the metate did not rest on it. Other artifacts associated with the metate include a large, gray ware sherd container (Vessel 45) and a peckingstone. A stone disk was also found in this area. Two additional metates had been leaned against the western part of the south wall, and a mano was found beneath them. These tools were not found in the positions in which they were used, but they are considered part of Activity Area 2.

Activity Area 3 is a second grinding area in the southeast corner of Pit Structure 3. It, too, is defined by a metate found in its use position, with two sandstone blocks supporting the west end. Four manos were found near the metate, and a thin, ground-and-pecked cobble lay on the floor in front of the open end of the metate trough. A second metate had been leaned against the eastern part of the south wall, and a mano was found between it and the wall. A hammerstone, several flakes, and three nearly complete pottery vessels (two Moccasin Gray cooking jars [Vessels 40 and 44] and a small Mancos Gray jar [Vessel 43]) were also found in the southeastern quadrant of the structure. The vessels could have been in their use location or in an active-storage location. It is not unlikely that they were used in this area, because containers were needed to hold grain both before and after it was ground, and food grinding, mixing, and cooking are all related activities. Figure 5.7 shows selected vessels recovered from the floor of Pit Structure 3, including those found in Activity Area 3.

Activity Area 4 is an active-storage area along the east wall of the pit structure. Artifacts in Activity Area 4 include a complete Moccasin Gray jar (Vessel 26), a large gray ware sherd container (Vessel 48), and a small, burned fragment of a coiled basket. These containers may have been used for preparing and cooking food around the hearth. Activity Area 5 is an active storage area along the west wall of Pit Structure 3. It includes two gray ware sherd containers (Vessels 46 and 49) and half of a Moccasin Gray jar (Vessel 42), which was also used as a sherd container. As in Pit Structure 1, manufacturing tools were stored or used in the vicinity of the active-storage areas. Tools associated with manufacturing in Activity Areas 4 and 5 are a

**Figure 5.7.** *Selected pottery vessels from Pit Structure 3. The assemblage includes cooking jars, miniature vessels, and a number of sherd containers. Note the sooting on three of the sherd containers: In each case, the stain is on the side of what would have been the complete parent vessel but is on the bottom of the fragment that served as the sherd container. This indicates that the stains most likely were acquired after the parent vessels broke and the sherds were recycled for use over a cooking fire. Height of tallest vessel ("top" row, right) = 25.1 cm.*

bone awl, a modified cobble, two flakes, a core, a hammerstone, and several modified sherds. These tools could have been used for hide working, stone tool manufacture, and pottery making.

Activity Area 6 is a multiple-use area in the north half of the pit structure. The central portion of this area had few artifacts and was probably maintained deliberately as an uncluttered area for working, social gathering, eating, and sleeping. Several artifact clusters were found along the north wall of the pit structure, and clusters were found near each of the northern roof-support posts. These clusters probably represent active-storage areas that were located specifically to take advantage of low-traffic areas around the perimeter of the open work space. An artifact cluster near the northwest corner post includes a sherd container (Vessel 47) and a flat-bottomed miniature vessel that is missing its neck and rim (Vessel 50). Near the northeast corner post was another artifact cluster consisting of two miniature gray ware jars (Vessels 23 and 24), a partial small white ware jar (Vessel 97), a flake, a modified core, a mano with yellow pigment on its grinding surface, and a small clump of yellow ocher. Near the northeast corner of the structure was a clump of white mineral pigment that may have been associated with the yellow pigment and the pigment-covered mano. Several flakes were found on the floor near the northern corners, and a large, flat modified cobble lay in the northwest corner. Scattered along the north wall were one corner-notched, Basketmaker-style projectile point, a stone drill, two pottery pipe fragments, and two worked-bone fragments.

Activity Area 7 is a ritual activity area defined by the presence of numerous sand-filled pits, including one interpreted as a sipapu. The sipapu was surrounded by a cluster of small, sand-filled paho marks, which were probably used in rituals involving prayer sticks, and several cylindrical sand-filled pits may have served as sockets for temporary altars during ceremonies (cf. Wilshusen 1989b). A second sipapu had been capped with sediment, which indicates that it was intentionally taken out of use sometime before abandonment.

Activity Area 8 is a mortuary activity area defined on the basis of a human skeleton, Burial 4. This activity area is superimposed on the multiple-use and ritual areas (Activity Areas 6 and 7) in the central portion of the structure. Burial 4 did not appear to represent an in situ, accidental death but, rather, a deliberate interment in which the pit structure was used as a tomb.

### Pit Structure 4

Nine activity areas are defined in this small pit structure. Activity Area 1 is a cooking area defined by the hearth and ash pit in the central portion of the structure. A mano, several flakes, and clusters of sherds found nearby may have been related to cooking and food preparation. East of the hearth was a cluster of reconstructible vessels consisting of a nearly complete Moccasin Gray cooking jar (Vessel 74), a partial Moccasin Gray jar (Vessel 83), two gray ware sherd containers (Vessels 84 and 85), a white ware sherd container (Vessel 126), and a partial red ware bowl (Vessel 109). These and other selected vessels from the floor of Pit Structure 4 are shown in Figure 5.8. An unfired "pinch pot" was also found near the hearth.

Activity Area 2 is a grinding area and possibly a tool-manufacturing area in the southwest quadrant of the pit structure north of the wing wall. The grinding area is defined on the basis of a metate found in its use position and three manos. Also believed to be associated with the grinding area is a metate that had been leaned, upside down, against the wing wall; a grooved axe lay next to it on the floor. In the same area, a hammerstone, a core, and a flake were found. These items may indicate that stone tools were manufactured, refurbished, or repaired in the grinding area.

Activity Area 3 is a short-term storage area south of the wing wall that has three distinct subareas. In the southwest corner there were four shaped sandstone slabs stacked in a pile, a metate, the tips of two bone awls, a Moccasin Gray sherd container (Vessel 80), and a cluster of sherds that fit with other sherds in the structure to form a partial Mancos Gray jar (Vessel 75). In the central area south of the deflec-

**Figure 5.8.** *Selected pottery vessels from Pit Structure 4. The assemblage includes bowls, cooking jars, and several sherd containers. The light-colored spots on the interior surfaces of some vessels are labels that allowed analysts to track the proveniences of the individual sherds that were included in each reconstructed vessel. Height of vessel in upper left corner = 21.3 cm.*

tor was a cluster of five modified cobbles, a vent-cover slab, a partial Chapin Gray jar (Vessel 78), and several sherds that also fit with Vessel 75. In the eastern end of the area behind the wing wall were seven manos, two peckingstones, a hammerstone, and numerous sherds, some of which fit Vessels 75 and 82, the latter a Moccasin Gray sherd container. Many of these tools had been stacked one on top of the other, suggesting that they were being stored.

Activity Area 4 is an active-storage area and possibly a manufacturing area along the east side of the structure, north of the wing wall. Although tools are inferred to have been stored in this location, they would have been readily accessible and may have been used in this area as well. Half of a Bluff Black-on-red bowl (Vessel 59) and a portion of a partial Moccasin Gray jar (Vessel 83) rested on the floor adjacent to the wing wall in the east half of the pit structure. Manufacturing tools and debris found in this area include two peckingstones, a polishing/hammerstone, a modified cobble, several flakes, four bone awls, four modified sherds, and two unfired sherds.

Activity Area 5 is a multiple-use area in the north half of Pit Structure 4. As in similar activity areas in the other pit structures, the artifact density was low, suggesting that the area was kept clean for a variety of activities, perhaps including socializing, eating, sleeping, and tool manufacturing. There are two distinct artifact clusters within Activity Area 5. The recovery of a core, two flakes, a bone awl, and a modified cobble from the northwest quadrant of the structure may indicate that tool manufacturing and hide working took place in this activity area. Also found in the northwest quadrant were a bone gaming piece, a calcite pendant, a sherd container (Vessel 81), and the other half of Vessel 59, which is a Bluff Black-on-red bowl. Six additional sherds from Vessel 81 were found in Room 12. Artifacts clustered in the northeastern quadrant of Pit Structure 4 include a bone awl, a grooved axe, an abrader, a translucent chert or chalcedony flake, a clump of white mineral pigment, and a sliver of bone. These artifacts might represent tool-manufacturing activities.

Activity Area 6 is a ritual activity area defined on the basis of several sand-filled pits in various locations across the floor in Pit Structure 4. In addition, a sipapu and its associated cluster of paho marks were found north of the hearth. However, the sipapu and the paho marks had been capped with clean sediment, which indicates that they were no longer in use and probably were not even visible late in the occupation.

Activity Areas 7, 8, and 9 are mortuary activity areas defined by the skeletal remains of an adult female at least 50 years old (Burial 12), a child, aged five to six (Burial 14), and another child, aged three to four (Burial 11). Burials 11 and 14 were almost completely destroyed by burning.

# Structure Use, Size, and Location

In this section, I examine the proposition that structure size and location are good indicators of use. I use summaries of floor artifact and feature assemblages to address the general relationships between structure use, size, and location. By location, I am referring to the distinction between front-row rooms, back-row rooms, and pit structures.

First, let us examine the relationship between structure size and general location (surface room vs. pit structure). The floor areas of rooms range from 3.69 m$^2$ to 22.95 m$^2$; the floor areas of pit structures range from 8.90 m$^2$ to 23.95 m$^2$. Although there is considerable overlap in the range of sizes between rooms and pit structures, most of the overlap is created by a single very large room (Room 16) and a single very small pit structure (Pit Structure 4). If these two outliers are excluded, the remaining distribution falls into line, with pit structures being larger than rooms.

Next, let us consider only the surface rooms and address the question, What is the strength of the relationship between room size and use? The use categories applied here are the ones defined above for rooms: (1) long-term storage, (2) specialized storage, and (3) domestic (Table 5.1). If *size* is the independent variable and *use* the dependent variable, how much more likely are we to predict room use if we know the size of the room? The average floor area is 9.16 m$^2$, and the median floor area is 8.92 m$^2$. Therefore, I defined two size classes, with *small* being less than or equal to 9 m$^2$ and *large* being greater than 9 m$^2$. The relationship between room size and room use is shown in a contingency table (Table 5.3). One measure of the strength of the relationship between room size and room use is Goodman and Kruskal's tau (Blalock 1979:307–310), which measures the proportional reduction of errors. If the number of rooms in each use category were known, and if the 19 rooms were assigned randomly to the three use categories (dependent variable), one would expect to make 10.53 errors. If the number of rooms in each size category (independent variable) were also known, one would expect to make

Table 5.3. Contingency Table Showing the Relationship Between Room Size and Final Use

| Room Use | Room Size | | |
|---|---|---|---|
| | Small (≤9 m$^2$) | Large (>9 m$^2$) | Total |
| Long-term storage | 10 | 1 | 11 |
| Specialized storage | 0 | 2 | 2 |
| Domestic | 1 | 5 | 6 |
| TOTAL | 11 | 8 | 19 |

Table 5.4. Contingency Table Showing the Relationship Between
Room Location and Final Use

| Room Use | Room Location | | |
| --- | --- | --- | --- |
| | Front | Back | Total |
| Long-term storage | 2 | 9 | 11 |
| Specialized storage | 2 | 0 | 2 |
| Domestic | 5 | 1 | 6 |
| TOTAL | 9 | 10 | 19 |

only 1.82 errors in assigning rooms to each use category. Using Goodman and Kruskal's tau ($\tau_b$ = .827), there would be a proportional reduction of errors of 83 percent in predicting structure use, given that we know the number of structures in each size class. Thus, there is a very strong relationship between structure size and structure use.

Let us now consider the relationship between room use and location with respect to front (southern) row or back (northern) row of the roomblock. We can pose a question similar to the one above, with location as the independent variable and use as the dependent variable (Table 5.4). How much more likely are we to assign a room to the correct use class if we know how many front and back rooms there are? If the number of rooms in each use category were known, and if the 19 rooms were assigned randomly to each use class, then, again, one would expect to make 10.53 errors. If one also knew how many rooms were in each row of the roomblock, then one would expect to make only 5.33 errors in assigning rooms to each use class. The Goodman and Kruskal's tau ($\tau_b$ = .493) indicates that there would be a proportional reduction of errors of 49 percent. That is, one would cut the number of errors in half by knowing the number of rooms in each row of the roomblock. This measure indicates that there is a strong relationship between how a room is used and its location in the front or back row of the roomblock.

# Redundancy and Complementarity of Activities

Let us assume that comparable social segments, such as households, have about the same basic economic, subsistence, and ideological needs—for example, food production and storage, food preparation and cooking, tool manufacture, religious ritual, and so forth. If this is true, similar social units should have similar sets of tools and facilities to satisfy those needs. That is, the activities that are performed at the household level should be repetitive, or redundant, from one house-hold to the next. We should be able to use this generalization to evaluate the redundancy of activities represented in the archaeological record and infer social-group boundaries at sites. A corollary of the redundancy generalization is that when two rooms have traces of entirely different activities that fulfill different needs, the rooms are complementary, and both are essential to fulfilling basic economic, subsistence, and ideological needs of the social group that uses both rooms. On the contrary, activities that are shared at a suprahousehold level of organization should not be redundant at the same level as household activities.

If an activity is organized at the suprahousehold level, its physical expression should not occur in every household suite. In fact, one would not expect such activities to occur in spaces where access is restricted to a single household. Rather, one would expect supra-household activities to take place in facilities that are accessible to, and shared by, multiple households or even multiple roomblock groups. For example, in prehistoric Pueblo sites, suprahousehold ceremonial activities might have taken place in courtyards, oversize pit structures, or great kivas. If pottery production were organized at the level of the roomblock group, then one might expect one large kiln to have been associated with each roomblock cluster. There might have been instances in which a household-level structure, such as a pit structure, was used for social or ceremonial gatherings involving the entire roomblock group or at least involving some members of all the households. If responsibility for such gatherings rotated from one household to another, then any physical evidence of the activity would be redundant across households. However, certain structures in a roomblock cluster might have contained specialized features to accommodate specific suprahousehold ceremonies or gatherings; in that case, the occurrence of these features would be complementary across household-group boundaries.

## Patterns Within Architectural Suites

Do patterns of activity redundancy and complementarity at Duck-foot support the model of a nested hierarchy of social organization? The boundaries of the architectural suites were inferred from construction details, and each suite consists of a pit structure, two to five front rooms, and three to four back rooms. Architectural Suite 1 consists of Pit Structure 1 and Rooms 1, 2, 3, 15, and 16. Architectural Suite 2 consists of Pit Structure 2 and Rooms 4 through 7, 11 through 14, and 17. Architectural Suite 3 consists of Pit Structure 3 and Rooms 8, 9, 10, 18, and 19. In Chapter 4, I treated Pit Structure 4 as part of Architectural Suite 2 for the purpose of making assemblage comparisons, but here I have kept it separate in order to continue evaluating its relationship to each architectural suite.

### Architectural Suite 1

The presence of multiple long-term storage rooms (Rooms 1, 2, and 3) represents a redundancy in storage facilities in Architectural Suite 1. The domestic activities represented in Pit Structure 1 and Room 16 (cooking and food processing, or grinding) are redundant. Two nearly identical sets of vessels on the floor in the east and west halves of Pit Structure 1 are indicative of some redundancy even within this structure. There could well have been two infrahousehold social groups (nuclear families?) who shared Pit Structure 1 and Room 16. If so, these infrahousehold groups could not have occupied separate domestic rooms in the roomblock, because Room 16 is the only domestic room in this architectural suite. Room 16 (22.95 m$^2$) is one-and-a-half times larger than Pit Structure 1 (14.92 m$^2$). Clearly, if multiple groups could have shared Pit Structure 1, they also had ample room to share Room 16 and long-term storage space in Rooms 1, 2, 3, and 15 (combined floor area of 37 m$^2$).

Complementary relationships between structures are best represented in front-to-back (south-to-north) relationships. Long-term storage in Rooms 1, 2, and 3 would have been complementary to the domestic activities represented in Room 16 and Pit Structure 1. Room 15 would have been complementary to all the other structures in the suite by providing specialized storage space. In addition to being used for domestic purposes, Pit Structure 1 provided a facility for household-level rituals (including mortuary rituals), ceremonies, and social gatherings. The complementarity of activities within the architectural suite is evidence of the close social ties of the residents. A number of activities represented by tools and features in Pit Structure 1 are not represented in rooms, and those who used Pit Structure 1 would have needed access to long-term storage space in the roomblock. These relationships support the nested-hierarchy model, which interprets an architectural suite as the facilities used by a single household. Variations in the size and complexity of architectural suites may reflect variations in the size and complexity of the households that occupied them.

### Architectural Suite 2

There is substantial redundancy of activities represented in the domestic rooms in Architectural Suite 2. Each domestic room contains a cooking area; Rooms 12 and 13 each have a grinding, or food-processing, area; and Rooms 5 and 11 probably had grinding tools that were removed during abandonment. Cooking and grinding areas were defined in Pit Structure 2 as well, for a total of five different areas in which domestic activities are represented. Long-term storage was available in Rooms 4, 6, 7, 14, and 17; not including Room 17, there apparently was one storage room per domestic room. Short-term storage was available in all four domestic rooms (Rooms 5, 11, 12, and 13) and in the area behind the wing wall in Pit Structure 2. Room 5 was not directly accessible from the exterior of the pueblo but, rather, had to have been entered through Room 13. Therefore, even though Rooms 5 and 13 are both domestic rooms, they cannot be interpreted as having housed separate social groups. It is also likely that the residents of both rooms shared access to the same long-term storage rooms (Rooms 4 and 14).

Activity complementarity is best seen in comparisons of domestic rooms, storage rooms, and the pit structure. The pit structure was used for domestic activities, but it did not have its own long-term storage facilities. The pit structure provided space for activities that are not represented in the rooms, including ritual and ceremonial activities, and in that respect, its use was complementary to the rest of the architectural suite. The redundancy and complementarity of activities support the nested-hierarchy model for Architectural Suite 2. In light of the patterns discussed here, it seems unlikely that Pit Structure 4 was affiliated with Architectural Suite 2, because there would have been insufficient long-term storage space for the occupants of Pit Structure 4.

### Architectural Suite 3

Architectural Suite 3 consists of one domestic room (Room 19), three long-term storage rooms (Rooms 8, 9, and 18), a specialized storage room (Room 10), and a pit structure (Pit Structure 3). The three long-term storage rooms represent redundancy in long-term storage facilities and a relative abundance of storage space in an architectural suite with only one domestic room. There is redundancy in cooking activities between Room 19 and Pit Structure 3. There were manos but no metates on the floor of Room 19. There were metates in the roof fall strata of Rooms 9 and 19 that could have been used in Room 19. In Pit Structure 3, two grinding areas and two active-storage areas represent activity redundancy within a single pit structure. It is possible that two infrahousehold groups occupied the pit structure, even though there is only one domestic room in the architectural suite.

Room 10 is classified as a specialized storage room, and it is unique in the architectural suite because it provided front-row, compartmentalized storage space. Ritual activities, including mortuary practices, apparently took place in Pit Structure 3, and in this sense, Pit Structure 3 is complementary to the other structures in the architectural suite. There is no wing wall in Pit Structure 3, and therefore there was no short-term storage space. The specialized storage space in Room 10 and the long-term storage in adjoining Room 8 may have compensated for the lack of short-term storage space in Pit Structure 3. The data from Architectural Suite 3 suggest that there were multiple infrahousehold groups that shared the domestic rooms, storage rooms, and pit structure.

### Pit Structure 4

The activities represented in Pit Structure 4 duplicate those represented in the other pit structures, but the relationship of this structure to rooms in the roomblock is unknown. Pit Structure 4 could have been affiliated with Architectural Suite 2. Alternatively, Pit Structure 4 could have been the residence of a separate household that used Rooms 8 and 10, in Architectural Suite 3, for storage. Pit Structure 4 has cooking, grinding, short-term storage, and active-storage areas, and mortuary activities were conducted in it at abandonment. Pit Structure 4 could have been a largely independent domestic unit, except that—unless its residents had access to Rooms 8 and 10—it would have lacked sufficient long-term storage space.

## Site-Wide Patterns

For the site as a whole, the repetition of entire architectural suites is the most obvious redundancy. A greater variety of tools was found in pit structures than in rooms, and many of these tools were used for manufacturing. The differences in the richness of the tool assemblages may be the result of storage patterns or abandonment and postabandonment processes. Alternatively, a wider variety of activities might have been performed in pit structures than in rooms. In particular, it appears that more manufacturing activities took place in pit structures than in rooms. For example, modified sherds, modified and edge-damaged flakes, bone awls, hammerstones, cores, and modified cobbles are all manufacturing tools, and they are much more abundant in pit structures than in rooms. This represents activity complementarity between pit structures in general and rooms in general. There is a notable lack of consistency between individual dwelling units. Dwelling units in Architectural Suites 1 and 3 are very similar to each other in their configurations, but they are very different from the arrangement of dwelling units in Architectural Suite 2, which has more domestic rooms but less storage space per square meter of domestic space than either of the other two architectural suites.

The only structures that might have contained suprahousehold activities or allowed suprahousehold access are Room 17 and the specialized storage rooms, Rooms 10 and 15. These three rooms are storage rooms that were accessible directly from the courtyard area, and therefore access might not have been controlled by a single household.

Cooking, food-processing (grinding), storage, and ritual activities are represented repeatedly in each architectural suite, but there are no activity areas or structures that are unique or that obviously were shared for suprahousehold activities. This probably does not mean that there were no integrated social gatherings or activities involving the entire roomblock group. Rather, it probably indicates that the group was small enough not to need any extra facilities to accommodate such gatherings. Specialized community facilities are more likely to be found in villages or communities of 200 people or more (Adler 1989; Wilshusen 1991). Rather than having specialized integrative structures, the inhabitants of the Duckfoot site probably used the pit structures for integrative social and ritual activities (Varien and Lightfoot 1989; Wilshusen 1989b).

## Relationship of Domestic Space to Long-Term and Specialized Storage Space

Patterns of structure use and the distribution of activity areas make it clear that there was great variability in access to long-term and specialized storage areas at Duckfoot. At least during the late period of occupation, the residents of Architectural Suites 1 and 3 had a higher proportion of long-term and specialized storage space relative to domestic space than did the residents of Architectural Suite 2. An explanation of where the residents of Pit Structure 4 stored their food has not been offered at all. In this section, I compare the relative amounts of long-term and specialized storage space in each architectural suite and address the following questions: Did the residents of each architectural suite have vastly different amounts of storage space, which a casual look suggests? How did the relative distribution of storage space change through time? Where did the residents of Pit Structure 4 store their food, and how did Pit Structure 4 fit into the preexisting architectural-suite configurations?

The changes in structure use during the occupation of Duckfoot produced changes in the amount of space devoted to long-term and specialized storage per household. Researchers with the Dolores Archaeological Program (Gross 1987; Kane 1986; Wilshusen 1988a) documented a substantial increase in the size of long-term storage rooms in sites in the Dolores River valley from A.D. 860 to 880. Gross (1987) attributed this increase to increases in the proportional contribution of agriculture to the diet, an increased need for long-term storage as a buffer against agricultural uncertainty, and an increase in the amount of ceremonial activity that involved feeding many outside individuals. At Duckfoot, the conversion of Rooms 10 and 15 from domestic to specialized storage rooms represents an increase in storage space at the expense of domestic space in Architectural Suites 1 and 3. The construction of Room 17 could have increased the long-term storage capacity of Architectural Suite 2. The addition of Pit Structure 4 increased domestic space, perhaps to compensate for the conversion of domestic rooms to specialized storage rooms.

Table 5.5 lists the floor areas of structures at Duckfoot. These data are used to evaluate the changes in floor space devoted to storage and domestic activities. In Table 5.6, I compare the amount of space devoted to long-term and specialized storage with the amount of space devoted to domestic activities for two general time periods, one early and one late. This requires making some assumptions about the use of structures in the early period. The area calculations for the early period assume that Room 17 and Pit Structure 4 had not yet been built, that Rooms 10 and 15 were domestic structures, and that Room 5 was used for long-term storage. During the late period, Rooms 10 and 15 were converted from domestic to specialized storage use in Architectural Suites 3 and 1, respectively; Room 17 was added as long-term storage space to Architectural Suite 2; and Room 5 was converted from long-term storage to domestic use. Pit Structure 4 was also a late addition, but it is kept separate in Table 5.6 to allow an evaluation of how its addition would have affected Architectural Suites 2 and 3.

There is only a 14.12-m$^2$ (6 percent) increase in total floor area between the early and late periods, but there is a 22.34-m$^2$ (30 percent) increase in long-term and specialized storage area, coupled with an 8.22-m$^2$ (5 percent) decrease in domestic space. This indicates a substantial change in priorities for the use of space across the entire site.

How were these changes expressed in individual architectural suites? During the early period, long-term storage space made up 34 percent, 39 percent, and 22 percent of the total space in Architectural Suites 1, 2, and 3, respectively. The residents of Architectural Suite 3 could have been at a disadvantage in that they might not have been able to store enough surplus food in productive years to sustain them through a period of bad years. By the late period, the proportion of storage space to total space had changed to 49 percent

Table 5.5. Floor Areas

| Structure | Area (m$^2$) |
| --- | --- |
| Architectural Suite 1 | |
| Room 1 | 11.46 |
| Room 2 | 7.25 |
| Room 3 | 7.00 |
| Room 15 | 11.30 |
| Room 16 | 22.95 |
| Pit Structure 1 | 14.92 |
| Architectural Suite 2 | |
| Room 4 | 8.93 |
| Room 5 | 6.16 |
| Room 6 | 7.53 |
| Room 7 | 8.92 |
| Room 14 | 3.85 |
| Room 17 | 5.22 |
| Room 11 | 9.99 |
| Room 12 | 11.75 |
| Room 13 | 13.67 |
| Pit Structure 2 | 20.60 |
| Architectural Suite 3 | |
| Room 8 | 5.71 |
| Room 9 | 4.06 |
| Room 18 | 3.69 |
| Room 10 | 11.98 |
| Room 19 | 12.61 |
| Pit Structure 3 | 23.95 |
| Architectural Suite Unknown | |
| Pit Structure 4 | 8.90 |

Table 5.6. Comparison of Domestic Space and Long-Term and Specialized Storage Space
During the Early and Late Periods

| | Early-Period Floor Areas (m$^2$) | | | | |
|---|---|---|---|---|---|
| | Architectural Suite 1 | Architectural Suite 2 | Architectural Suite 3 | Pit Structure 4 | Total |
| Storage | 25.71 | 35.39 | 13.46 | — | 74.56 |
| Domestic | 49.17 | 56.01 | 48.54 | — | 153.72 |
| TOTAL | 74.88 | 91.40 | 62.00 | — | 228.28 |
| | Late-Period Floor Areas (m$^2$) | | | | |
| | Architectural Suite 1 | Architectural Suite 2 | Architectural Suite 3 | Pit Structure 4 | Total |
| Storage | 37.01 | 34.45 | 25.44 | 0 | 96.90 |
| Domestic | 37.87 | 62.17 | 36.56 | 8.90 | 145.50 |
| TOTAL | 74.88 | 96.62 | 62.00 | 8.90 | 242.40 |

in Architectural Suite 1, 36 percent in Architectural Suite 2, and 41 percent in Architectural Suite 3. These percentages represent significant increases in storage space in Architectural Suites 1 and 3 and a slight decrease in Architectural Suite 2.

The question that remains is how the addition of Pit Structure 4 is related to changes in the use of rooms in the roomblock. Were the residents of Pit Structure 4 members of a separate household, or were they part of an existing household that occupied either Architectural Suite 2 or 3? The construction of Pit Structure 4 represents the addition of domestic space with no corresponding addition of long-term storage space. Even without considering Pit Structure 4, Architectural Suite 2 experienced a slight decline in its proportion of long-term and specialized storage space through time. If Pit Structure 4 was added to Architectural Suite 2 as domestic space, storage space would have decreased from 39 percent to 33 percent at a time when the percentage of storage space in the other architectural suites increased to over 40 percent.

If Pit Structure 4 was added to Architectural Suite 3, the proportion of long-term and specialized storage space to total space for the suite would have increased from its early level of 22 percent to 36 percent, making its proportion of storage space equal to that of Architectural Suite 2 during the late period. Furthermore, if the addition of Pit Structure 4 was concomitant with the conversion of Room 10 from domestic to specialized-storage space, the occupants of Pit Structure 4 would have had access to long-term storage by way of Room 10. This scenario suggests that Pit Structure 4 replaced Room 10 as a domestic structure in Architectural Suite 3.

# 6

# Network Analysis

One reason for studying architectural patterns and artifact distributions is that they are likely to reveal something about past human behavior. Archaeologists have come to recognize the difficulties in using the archaeological record to study problems of social organization. We wish to document patterns of behavior that can help us understand social interactions and the organization of social groups. Our clues are architecture, features, artifacts, and our records of their spatial distributions. We recognize that the physical remains in archaeological sites and the spatial relationships of those remains are influenced by numerous natural and cultural processes. Wilshusen concisely defined the problem:

> Archaeological data are primarily reflective of spatial relationships, and ethnological data are centered on social relationships. An archaeological taxonomy of social organization will have spatial and social aspects. An implicit assumption is that certain functional requirements of society will produce certain spatial patterns in architecture, features, and possibly artifacts [Wilshusen 1988b:636].

Social relationships and social organization influence the types and frequency of interactions that individuals and social groups have with each other. To the extent that social organization has an effect on the structure of activities and activity groups, it is possible that patterned social interactions may leave material traces that can be studied archaeologically.

In this chapter, I use network analysis (Leinhardt 1977; Plog 1977; Irwin-Williams 1977) in an attempt to bridge the inferential gap between a static material record in the present and a dynamic constellation of social interactions in the past. *Network analysis* refers to an approach used in the social sciences to analyze social interactions between nodes, with nodes being variously defined as individuals, groups, or locations. The focus in network studies is the interaction between individuals or the individuals who occupy a spatial node. For example, a network approach might be used to analyze the frequency of interaction between different departments in a corporation. To develop a more efficient management strategy, the corporation might combine or move closer together those departments that have the highest frequency of interaction. The interaction "density" in the corporate example might be measured by the number of trips or phone calls from one department to another or by the amount of time spent communicating between departments. Network analyses commonly use graphic displays (sociograms) in which nodes are represented by circles and interactions are depicted by lines between nodes. If the interactions have directionality (for example, from a supplier to a consumer), arrows may be used to indicate the direction of material or information flow. Alternatively, network data may be compiled into a matrix in which the cells contain binary or quantitative information about interactions between individuals. The matrix is amenable to quantitative analysis, but the graphic approach has a greater visual impact. To apply this approach archaeologically, we must make the assumption that certain social interactions can be measured by the effect that they have on the flow of materials.

## The Nested-Hierarchy Model

The nested-hierarchy model has both social and spatial aspects. The spatial aspects can be observed archaeologically, but the social aspects are of greater interest. Early Pueblo social organization may be understood best as a series of groups within larger groups, which were themselves contained within even larger groups, and so on. Individuals were grouped into households that were probably kin based and comparable to extended-family households. Within these households there were undoubtedly subgroups—such as nuclear families, married couples, unmarried adults, and groups of siblings—which are defined as dwelling groups. Households were also grouped into larger social groups, called roomblock groups, which we can define only on the basis of their residential clustering. These roomblock groups might have been organized on the basis of kinship or clan affiliation, and although we will never know what these affiliations were, we *can* address the behavioral relationships between households that shared a roomblock. Roomblock groups may have resided in relatively isolated hamlets, or they may have resided close to other roomblock groups to form a village group. A community was an even larger constellation, consisting of many roomblock groups residing in villages or hamlets or both. A community is loosely defined as a group of several hundred people, living in the same general area and having regular, face-to-face interaction. Although the nested-hierarchy model defines several social tiers, it does not imply a ranked or stratified society but, rather, an egalitarian society that is stratified horizontally. The implication is that decisions are made largely through a sequential consensus-building process, or sequential hierarchy (Johnson 1982, 1989). That is, in egalitarian societies, decisions are often made sequentially, beginning with nuclear families, then extended families, then courtyard groups, and so forth. Decision making and dispute resolution are handled from the bottom up rather than from the top down (Johnson 1982).

Spatially, each social tier in the nested-hierarchy model is associated with a particular set of architectural facilities or spatial configurations. The household is defined as the group that occupies an architectural suite, consisting of a pit structure and its associated rooms and courtyard area. A household may consist of several dwelling groups, which occupy separate dwelling units in the roomblock. A roomblock group is the group of households that occupies the same roomblock. The model presented here differs from previous models (e.g., Kane 1989) in the way that the household and its architectural facilities are defined. What I define here as the dwelling group, in previous versions was considered the household.

The nested-hierarchy model may be evaluated using network analysis because it ultimately is based on the activities and interactions of social groups within architecturally defined spaces. If we define individual rooms and pit structures as spatial nodes, then the social relationships of interest are those that involve the movement of individuals or the interactions of individuals between spatial nodes. The nested hierarchy of intracommunity organization could be illustrated as a series of nodes within nodes (Figure 6.1). Each household is represented by a spatial node (architectural suite) that has nested within it a cluster of smaller nodes (dwelling units) representing infrahousehold groups. The flow of information and materials, as well as interactions between people, should be greatest within the lower-order spatial nodes (for example, the dwelling group) and less frequent with each increase in the size of the node (that is, the household, the roomblock group, the hamlet group, the village group, and the community group).

As the structures in which social and ritual gatherings took place, pit structures probably played a role in socially integrating the different households in early Pueblo sites. Therefore, one would expect that physical traces of interaction between people in different households would appear in pit structures. For example, people from dif-

**Figure 6.1.** *Schematic illustration of the nested-hierarchy model of social organization.*

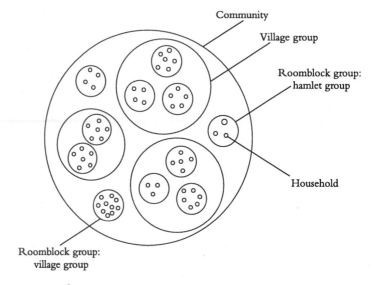

Community

Village group

Roomblock group: hamlet group

Household

Roomblock group: village group

ferent households might have come together for potluck dinners, to which guests would have brought a dish to share (Blinman 1989). Pottery vessels filled with food might then have been transported from one architectural suite to another or from a domestic room to a pit structure. One problem in applying the network concept archaeologically is finding materials whose movement can be tracked from one location to another; one possibility is pursued in this chapter.

The difficulty of using artifact relationships as indicators of social interaction is that other factors, such as discard, may have had a greater influence on the movement and deposition of artifacts than did the use-related activities that are of interest. At Duckfoot, most trash was disposed of in the midden area to the south of the pit structures, but as discussed in Chapter 3, some trash was also discarded onto structure floors. If we use the densities of orphan sherds on the floors of front rooms (excluding Rooms 14 and 17) and pit structures as a proxy for the abundance of trash on those floors (Table 6.1), it is clear that Rooms 15 and 19 and Pit Structure 2 are most likely to have had artifacts on their floors that were the result of discard rather than of use.

## Evaluating the Model

In the network analyses presented here, I use relational data from Duckfoot to evaluate the social aspects of the nested-hierarchy model. Relational data are those that consider the relationship be-

Table 6.1. Densities of Orphan Sherds from Floors of
Front Rooms and Pit Structures

| Structure | No. of Orphan Sherds | Area (m²) | Sherd Density |
|---|---|---|---|
| Room 10 | 154 | 11.98 | 12.9 |
| Room 11 | 158 | 9.99 | 15.8 |
| Room 12 | 72 | 11.75 | 6.1 |
| Room 13 | 469 | 13.67 | 34.3 |
| Room 15 | 1,057 | 11.30 | 93.5 |
| Room 16 | 267 | 22.95 | 11.6 |
| Room 19 | 684 | 12.61 | 54.2 |
| Pit Structure 1 | 330 | 14.92 | 22.1 |
| Pit Structure 2 | 1,146 | 20.60 | 55.6 |
| Pit Structure 3 | 247 | 23.95 | 10.3 |
| Pit Structure 4 | 379 | 8.90 | 42.6 |

NOTE: Rooms 14 and 17 are excluded. Counts include all orphan sherds from floors.

tween two or more items rather than consider simple attributes of
the items in isolation. In this chapter, I first examine accessibility
between rooms by inferring the locations of doorways. Doorways are
indicators of social interaction because they allow movement and
interaction between structures, and they allow the residents some
control over the interactions that take place. The doorway study
applies only to the roomblock and does not help us elucidate relationships between pit structures and room suites. Second, I present
the results of a pottery-refitting project in which pottery from the
floors of all front rooms and pit structures was analyzed to find
pieces of vessels that were broken and deposited in different structures. The importance of this study is that we can see the final
distribution of the parts of broken vessels, and we can make inferences about the parent vessels from which they came. The pottery-
refitting analysis focuses more on evaluating social interactions and
the movement of people between domestic rooms and pit structures.
Do the patterns of movement between domestic rooms and pit
structures conform to those predicted by the nested-hierarchy model?
Can we discern any patterned relationships between Pit Structure 4
and a particular room or room suite in the roomblock? These questions are addressed in this chapter.

## Architectural Data

What kinds of physical evidence would indicate social interaction or
human movement in prehistoric pueblos? One source of data used
by archaeologists in sites with preserved architecture is the interconnectivity of rooms by means of doorways or other passages (Dean

1969; Rohn 1965; Wilcox 1975). In addition to doorway access, architectural design may have enhanced or discouraged interactions. For example, two architectural suites may share a wall, but if the doorways open onto different courtyards that do not interconnect, then interaction would be restricted (e.g., Fewkes 1919; Rohn 1965, 1977). The nested-hierarchy model assumes that social interactions are more frequent and of longer duration among individuals who share cooking, storage, and sleeping facilities than among individuals who do not. A doorway that opens from a domestic room onto a courtyard gives the user of that domestic room the opportunity to interact frequently with others whose domestic-room doors open onto the same courtyard. In large cliff dwellings at Mesa Verde, the buildings in different courtyard groups are separated from one another in such a way that traffic from one courtyard to the next would have been restricted by walls or other physical features. Yet, compared with groups whose buildings were separated by great distances, the separate courtyard groups who shared a single rock shelter probably would have interacted relatively frequently.

The roomblock at Duckfoot is comparable to a courtyard unit in a cliff dwelling (Fewkes 1909:8; Rohn 1971:37–39) in that it consists of a cluster of rooms that open onto a common courtyard. I use architectural data at Duckfoot to infer the locations of doorways or openings in the interior walls of the roomblock. Interior doorways are one means of evaluating social interaction. The logic underlying the use of doorways to infer social interaction is fairly straightforward: Doorways allow physical access and movement of people and materials between rooms. Rooms connected by doorways are inferred to have been associated because doorways would have promoted physical movement and social interaction. Conversely, the absence of a doorway between rooms implies that human movement and interaction were restricted. On the basis of earlier versions of the nested-hierarchy model (e.g., Kane 1986), one would expect doorways to be in walls separating domestic rooms from their associated storage rooms but not in walls separating two domestic rooms. Alternatively, if an entire architectural suite is the domain of a single household, as I have argued in this volume, then one would expect interactions within architectural suites to have been facilitated, whereas those between architectural suites would have been restricted. In the following sections, I assess these two variations of the nested-hierarchy model to see if the data support one version over the other.

Models of social and spatial organization at Duckfoot would be different for the early and late periods of occupation, as discussed in Chapter 5. Early in the occupation, Rooms 10 and 15 were domestic structures in Architectural Suites 3 and 1, respectively. Room 17 and

Pit Structure 4 were not yet built. During the late period, Rooms 10 and 15 were converted to specialized storage rooms, Room 17 was added in Architectural Suite 2, and Pit Structure 4 was built. The relationship of Pit Structure 4 to social and architectural groups in the roomblock remains unclear.

### Doorway Slabs

The main problem with using doorway locations to interpret interior accessibility between rooms is that doorways are generally not preserved in mud-walled pueblos that are built in the open (that is, outside rock shelters). One way that doorway locations in collapsed wall rubble might be inferred is by the locations of the shaped sandstone slabs that were used as doors. Sites preserved in rock shelters throughout the region commonly have doorway cover slabs. The presence of a large, thin, rectangular, shaped sandstone slab on the floor or in the lower fill of a domestic room near a wall could be a clue to the location of a doorway. Well-shaped, rectangular sandstone slabs that clearly were not part of the collapsed wall but are the appropriate size to be doorway covers were found on the floor or in the fill near the floor in Rooms 13, 16, and 19. Furthermore, these slabs were found near the north walls of each room in places where they might have been used to cover doors leading to storage rooms. There is good reason to interpret these slabs as indicating the locations of doorways into storage rooms (Figure 6.2 and Table 6.2).

### Gaps in Interior Walls

At Duckfoot there are eight gaps 40 cm or wider in otherwise well-preserved interior walls of the roomblock (Figure 6.2), and I propose that these gaps may have been doorways. Our experience with known prehistoric doorways has been confined mostly to masonry structures and earth-walled structures built in protected rock shelters. In both cases, doorways typically have sills, or thresholds, that are raised approximately 20 to 90 cm above the floor. Because mud-walled structures built in open sites generally are not preserved well enough for the raised sills to have survived, such doorways may appear archaeologically as gaps in the walls. It is also possible that raised-sill passages were not the only types of doorways that existed during Pueblo I times—perhaps some were constructed as simple openings *without* sills. If the gaps in the walls at Duckfoot were the result of natural deterioration alone (that is, if they do *not* mark the locations of doorways), then one would expect them to occur more or less randomly. As Figure 6.2 and Table 6.2 illustrate, however, the gaps do not occur randomly but, rather, in walls between rooms in

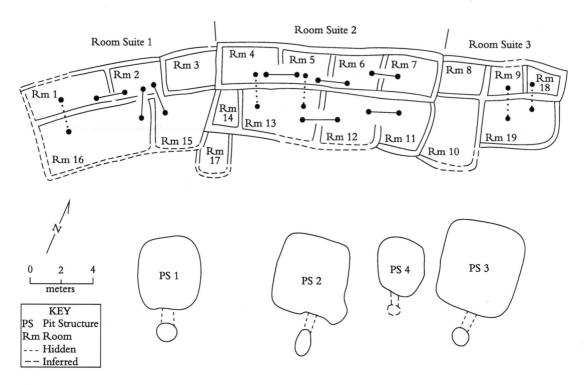

**Figure 6.2.** *Connections between rooms inferred on the basis of possible doorway locations. Dotted connections indicate doorways inferred on the basis of fallen door slabs; solid connections indicate doorways inferred on the basis of gaps in the walls.*

the same architectural suite. Three of the eight gaps are in Room Suite 1, connecting Room 2 with two adjacent front rooms (Rooms 15 and 16) and one back room (Room 1). The other five gaps are in Room Suite 2, connecting all four back rooms (Rooms 4–7) with each other and connecting the three domestic front rooms (Rooms 11–13) with each other. The question that remains is, How plausible is it that these gaps really were prehistoric doorways?

Some of the best examples of late Pueblo I doorways are in the masonry walls at McPhee Pueblo in the Dolores River valley (Brisbin et al. 1988). Seven doorways were recorded in interior walls, and these were probably in use during two sequential periods of occupation that involved the construction of several floors and significant remodeling. All of these doorways had raised sills that ranged in height from 17 to 92 cm above the floors, with an average height of 65 cm (Brisbin et al. 1988:Table 2.14). All seven interior doorways were in two adjoining dwelling units. Five of these doorways connected front (domestic) rooms with their adjoining back (storage) rooms. One doorway connected the front rooms of the two dwelling units with each other, and the seventh doorway connected the adjoining back rooms of the two dwelling units. The doorway that connected the two front rooms had a shaped sandstone (doorway

Table 6.2. Matrix of Accessibility Between Rooms

| Room ↓→ | Room Suite 1 | | | | | Room Suite 2 | | | | | | | | Room Suite 3 | | | | |
|---|---|---|---|---|---|---|---|---|---|---|---|---|---|---|---|---|---|---|
| | 1 | 2 | 3 | 15 | 16 | 4 | 5 | 6 | 7 | 11 | 12 | 13 | 14 | 8 | 9 | 18 | 19 | 10 |
| 1 | | | | | | | | | | | | | | | | | | |
| 2 | + | | | | | | | | | | | | | | | | | |
| 3 | − | − | | | | | | | | | | | | | | | | |
| 15 | + | + | − | | | | | | | | | | | | | | | |
| 16 | + | + | − | + | | | | | | | | | | | | | | |
| 4 | − | − | − | − | − | | | | | | | | | | | | | |
| 5 | − | − | − | − | − | + | | | | | | | | | | | | |
| 6 | − | − | − | − | − | + | + | | | | | | | | | | | |
| 7 | − | − | − | − | − | + | + | + | | | | | | | | | | |
| 11 | − | − | − | − | − | + | + | + | + | | | | | | | | | |
| 12 | − | − | − | − | − | + | + | + | + | + | | | | | | | | |
| 13 | − | − | − | − | − | + | + | + | + | + | + | | | | | | | |
| 14 | − | − | − | − | − | − | − | − | − | − | − | − | | | | | | |
| 8 | − | − | − | − | − | − | − | − | − | − | − | − | − | | | | | |
| 9 | − | − | − | − | − | − | − | − | − | − | − | − | − | − | | | | |
| 18 | − | − | − | − | − | − | − | − | − | − | − | − | − | − | + | | | |
| 19 | − | − | − | − | − | − | − | − | − | − | − | − | − | − | + | + | | |
| 10 | − | − | − | − | − | − | − | − | − | − | − | − | − | − | − | − | − | |

NOTE: Accessibility was determined on the basis of doorway locations. "+" denotes a doorway connection inferred on the basis of a wall gap or door-cover slab.

cover) slab next to it in the fill just above the final use surface of one of the rooms. The doorway connections within and between dwelling units at McPhee Pueblo were very similar to the type of interior connections that I infer from door slabs and gaps in the walls at Duckfoot.

The physical connections across dwelling-unit boundaries have important implications for our evaluation of the nested-hierarchy model. Researchers with the Dolores Archaeological Program (DAP) defined the dwelling unit as the architectural correlate of a household, whereas I have argued that an entire architectural suite is the architectural correlate of a household. According to the DAP version of the model, the main connection between the dwelling-unit-based households is their shared use of a pit structure. Consequently, pit structures were interpreted as having a predominant role in integrating separate households. On the contrary, I have argued that the pit structure is a predominantly domestic structure that serves as the focal point of a single household. Under this revised version of the nested-hierarchy model, the groups that occupy separate dwelling units are infrahousehold groups that are all part of the same household. Under the revised model, we would expect a greater degree of connection between dwelling groups within an architectural suite than we would expect under the original model.

I interpret the data from Duckfoot and McPhee Pueblo as supporting the revised model. The two doorways that connected rooms across dwelling-unit boundaries at McPhee are significant because their presence suggests that there was a significant social connection between the two dwelling groups. At Duckfoot, the connections within Room Suites 1 and 2 are much greater than would be expected if each dwelling unit represented a semiautonomous household. The connections between storage rooms in Room Suites 1 and 2 suggest that, although storage space within room suites was subdivided into smaller units, access between them was not obstructed. In Room Suite 2, both storage and domestic rooms are interconnected, which also supports the notion that the individuals using those domestic spaces were not members of separate households. If we add the doorways inferred on the basis of shaped door slabs, then the connections between structures would have provided very open access to rooms within Room Suites 1 and 2 but not between suites. In Room Suite 3, the doorway access is different. The presence of two door slabs supports the inference that domestic room 19 was connected to its adjoining storage rooms to the north, Rooms 9 and 18. However, there is no evidence of doorways between dwelling units in Room Suite 3.

The absence of a doorway between Room 10 and Room 19 in Room Suite 3 supports the interpretation that Pit Structure 4 was added by the residents of Architectural Suite 3 in conjunction with the conversion of Room 10 from domestic to specialized storage space. This could also mean that Room 8, as well as Room 10, was used for storage by the residents of Pit Structure 4. If this is true, then the use of Pit Structure 4 was equivalent to that of a domestic room and a pit structure combined.

## Pottery-Refitting Data

The reconstruction of pottery vessels allows us to study how sherds were dispersed after vessels were broken and provides a form of relational data that reveals something about the distribution of the parts of vessels that cannot be determined by looking at sherd attributes alone. The focus of this section is on parts of vessels recovered from the floors and roof fall strata of structures. Items found in these contexts are more likely to have been deposited by cultural processes than by natural, postabandonment processes.

The recycled pottery vessels called "sherd containers" were first recognized in the relatively uncluttered assemblage of de facto refuse from Pit Structure 1. Sherd containers are large sherds that were used as saucerlike containers, sometimes for cooking or heating food. The fact that these pieces of broken vessels had some recycling value meant that they were likely to stay in the systemic context after the parent vessels broke. In addition, the potential for reuse could have encouraged people to store (as provisional discard) larger pieces of broken vessels for future use. Such a practice could explain why so many partial vessels were found in structures, whereas smaller pieces were found in the midden area.

If individual households were manufacturing, using, and breaking their own pottery, then large sherds may have had recycling and curation value, but they would have had low trade value because neighboring households would have had large sherds from their own broken vessels. Consequently, the movement of such materials should have taken place within groups that shared material equipment or that exchanged materials primarily on the basis of generalized reciprocity, that is, within households or groups of economically linked households.

If partial vessels were stockpiled and eventually put back into use, then these sherds and their depositional contexts could provide the kind of relational tracer we need. The recycling value of large sherds could have provided a stimulus for people to move sherds around between structures within architectural suites or the roomblock cluster. If we found large sherds from the same vessel on the floors of different structures and if these sherds were not likely to have been dispersed naturally into these specific locations, they would provide a record of human activity that could be interpreted using network analysis. It is likely that some parts of vessels were discarded as secondary refuse in structures; these items should not be used as evidence of social interaction.

### Refitting Methods

Generally, archaeologists reconstruct vessels when clusters of similar sherds are found together. The reconstruction of vessels from Duckfoot involved a more comprehensive attempt to refit entire assemblages of sherds found within individual structures, followed by an attempt to match parts of vessels between structures. It was not possible to include every sherd from the site in this study, so the analysis was limited to seven front rooms (10–13, 15, 16, and 19) and all four pit structures. Sherds from all contexts in these structures were included in the analysis, but the emphasis was placed on sherds from floor and roof fall deposits.

The process resulted in a final total of 125 reconstructed vessels, including complete or nearly complete vessels, sherd containers, and partial vessels that were intact enough to get whole-vessel measurements such as volume. In addition, we documented over 500 "sherd refits" (SRs), which are sherds that fit together but do not form enough of the original vessel to be included in the "vessel-analysis" track. The lack of systematic treatment of all contexts has two interpretive implications: First, the absence of refits between back rooms and other structures cannot be regarded as significant. Second, sherds missing from partial vessels in structures may be accounted for in discard contexts that were not included in the analysis.

## Refitting Results

As a result of the refitting efforts, parts of nine pottery vessels were matched between the floors or features of front rooms and pit structures (Figure 6.3 and Table 6.3). Three sherd refits are made up of pieces found on the floors or in the roof fall deposits of multiple structures, and an additional 10 matches were made between parts of vessels in the postabandonment deposits of different structures (the latter are not included in Figure 6.3 or Table 6.3). The matches between floors and features of different structures are of interest in

**Figure 6.3.** *Connections between structures inferred on the basis of pottery-refitting results. Lines indicate sherd matches between structures (floor and roof fall contexts only).*

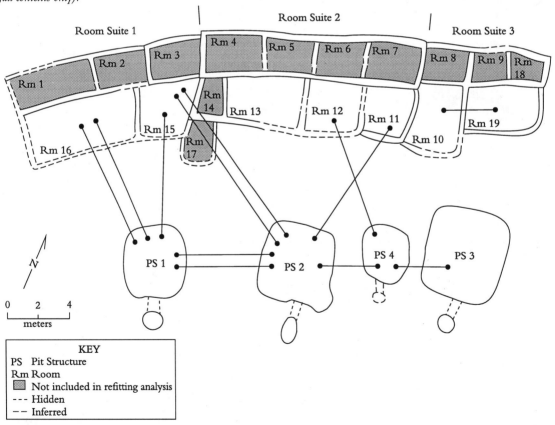

Table 6.3. Vessels and Sherd Refits from Floors and Roof Fall Deposits of Multiple Structures

| Item | Description | Context |
|------|-------------|---------|
| V 25 | Chapin Gray olla | Pit Structure 1, floor |
| | | Room 16, floor |
| V 32 | Bluff Black-on-red bowl | Pit Structure 1, floor |
| | | Pit Structure 2, floor |
| V 37 | Bluff Black-on-red bowl | Pit Structure 1, floor |
| | | Room 16, floor |
| V 81 | Moccasin Gray jar | Pit Structure 4, floor |
| | | Pit Structure 4, roof fall |
| | | Room 12, floor |
| | | Room 12, wall and roof fall |
| V 112 | Bluff Black-on-red bowl | Pit Structure 2, floor |
| | | Room 15, floor |
| V 127 | Moccasin Gray jar | Pit Structure 1, floor |
| | | Room 15, floor |
| V 128 | Chapin Gray jar | Pit Structure 3, floor |
| | | Pit Structure 3, roof fall |
| | | Pit Structure 4, floor |
| | | Pit Structure 4, roof fall |
| V 129 | Moccasin Gray jar | Pit Structure 2, floor |
| | | Pit Structure 1, floor |
| V 130 | Moccasin Gray olla | Pit Structure 2, floor |
| | | Pit Structure 2, Surface 2 |
| | | Pit Structure 2, wall and roof fall |
| | | Room 11, floor |
| | | Room 11, roof fall |
| SR 280 | Chapin Gray jar | Pit Structure 2, floor |
| | | Pit Structure 4, roof fall |
| SR 479 | red ware jar | Room 19, floor |
| | | Room 19, wall and roof fall |
| | | Room 10, roof fall |
| SR 543 | white ware bowl | Pit Structure 2, floor |
| | | Room 15, Feature 2 (floor) |

V = vessel; SR = sherd refit.

this study because the deposition of these items is best explained by acts of sharing or exchange rather than by discard behavior per se.

***Refits Within Architectural Suites.*** Architectural Suite 1 has the best intrasuite interconnectivity, with Pit Structure 1 having a total of three refit connections with front rooms 15 and 16. One of these, Vessel 127, includes a sherd container found on the floor of Pit Structure 1 and miscellaneous sherds discarded in Room 15. Architectural Suite 2 has only two intrasuite connections, if one includes

Pit Structure 4 in this suite. One vessel (Vessel 130) connected Pit Structure 2 with Room 11, and another (Vessel 81) connected Pit Structure 4 with Room 12. The latter connection is consistent with the interpretation that the occupants of Pit Structure 4 had their strongest affiliations with the residents of Architectural Suite 2. The only refit connection within Architectural Suite 3 is SR 479, which was reconstructed from sherds found in Rooms 10 and 19 (sherds from back rooms 9 and 18 also refit with SR 479, but because back rooms were not included systematically in the analysis, these connections are not indicated in Figure 6.3 or Table 6.3).

The rarity of refits between rooms in the same architectural suite is in part the result of the decision to not systematically examine sherds from front or back storage rooms. It also reflects the low sherd frequencies on the floors of many domestic rooms. There are no room connections that crossed the architecturally defined room-suite boundaries.

*Refits Involving Trash-Filled Structures.* More than half of the refitted items on floors and in roof fall deposits of multiple structures have some connection to Room 15 (three items) or Pit Structure 2 (six items). In fact, two refitted items, Vessel 112 and SR 543, were reconstructed from pieces found in both structures. Apparently, sherds and partial vessels from a variety of sources were discarded onto the floors of Room 15 and Pit Structure 2. Refits directly connect Pit Structure 2 with the two adjacent pit structures (Pit Structures 1 and 4) and two front rooms (Rooms 11 and 15). Although these connections are more likely the result of discard than of social interactions, they do provide valuable information about the abandonment of Pit Structure 2. Originally I hypothesized that Pit Structure 4 might have been built to replace Pit Structure 2, the roof of which would have been dismantled to provide salvageable timbers for the construction of Pit Structure 4. In this scenario, it was inferred that Pit Structure 2 was abandoned, trash was dumped on its floor, a partial human skeleton was placed in the northwest corner and surrounded with rocks, the roof was dismantled to salvage building timbers, and Pit Structure 4 was built to replace it while the village continued to be occupied. There are several indicators that suggest that this interpretation is incorrect. If Pit Structure 2 had been abandoned and dismantled while the rest of the hamlet continued to be occupied, one would expect trash to have been deposited on top of the collapsed roof because there would have been a large open pit in the middle of the site. However, the fill above roof fall in Pit Structure 2 does not contain trash deposits. Sherd refits that link items on the floor of Pit Structure 2 with items on the floors of Pit Structures 1 and 4 and Rooms 11 and 15 also contradict the hypothesis that Pit Structure 2 was dismantled before the destruction of the other structures at the site. The abandonment of Pit Structure 2 probably began slightly earlier than that of the other structures at the site, which would account for the accumulation of some trash on its floor. However, it probably was not dismantled until after Pit Structure 4 was built and until the rest of the structures at the site were being destroyed. The fact that pieces of the same broken vessels were present on the floor of Pit Structure 2 and on the floors of other structures that clearly were being used until the final abandonment of the site supports the revised abandonment sequence for Pit Structure 2. The abandonment of Pit Structure 2 was apparently more gradual than that of most other structures at the site. The trash on the floor consisted more of a scatter than an actual layer of accumulated debris, which suggests that the period in which Pit Structure 2 was used as a trash receptacle was probably fairly brief. In fact, the interpretation of many of the artifacts as trash is based on the presence of more-than-the-expected number of sherds that could not be refit into vessels. The cessation of domestic activities in Pit Structure 2 probably preceded the dismantling of its roof and the abandonment of the other structures by a matter of weeks or months rather than years.

*Refits Between Pit Structures.* One of the more interesting outcomes of the pottery-refitting project was the discovery of numerous refit connections between pit structures. Each pit structure has refit connections with its neighbors. The connections between Pit Structures 1 and 2 consist of sherds that form a partial vessel (Vessel 32) and a parent vessel (Vessel 129) whose two component parts are sherd containers. The connection between Pit Structures 3 and 4 is inferred on the basis of a parent vessel (Vessel 128) whose component parts are sherd containers: one on the floor of Pit Structure 3 and one on the floor of Pit Structure 4. The connection between Pit Structures 2 and 4 is made on the basis of a sherd refit, SR 280. If all the connections between pit structures involved Pit Structure 2, it would be easier to dismiss the relationship as related to discard rather than to social interactions. However, the relationship between Pit Structures 1 and 2, involving parent vessel 129, is very similar to the relationship between Pit Structures 3 and 4, involving parent vessel 128. These are the two cases in which a parent vessel is made up of sherd containers found on the floors of two different structures.

Refit relationships between pit structures consistently involve adjacent structures, and there are no connections across the site from one end to the other. The procedures used in the analysis gave refits between structures across the site a chance of discovery equal to that of refits between adjacent structures.

# Conclusions

Although the total number of sherd refits between structures is relatively small, the pattern of relationships as indicated by sherd refits and doorways is largely consistent with the expectations of the revised nested-hierarchy model. The revised model predicts that within a roomblock the most frequent interactions and movements of people and materials should be within architectural suites. This portion of the model is clearly supported by the inferred doorways within Architectural Suites 1 and 2. Probably the best-preserved doorways in any Pueblo I site are at McPhee Pueblo (Brisbin et al. 1988), where the interconnections between dwelling units are comparable to what I infer for Duckfoot. These doorway connections are significant because they strengthen my argument that the residents of the entire architectural suite were a single household. The doorways indicate that there was a more significant connection between the residents of different dwelling units in the same architectural suite than previous models of Pueblo I household organization would have suggested.

If an architectural suite is the space used by a single household, there should be relatively free movement of people between rooms and pit structures within an architectural suite. The best example of this pattern in the pottery-refit data is in Architectural Suite 1, where there are sherd-refit connections between Pit Structure 1 and Rooms 15 and 16. However, one cannot rule out the possibility that the connection between Pit Structure 1 and Room 15 is a result of the discard of sherds onto the floor of Room 15. There is a refit between Pit Structure 2 and Room 11, both of which are in Architectural Suite 2, and there are two connections between Pit Structure 2 and Room 15 (the latter in Architectural Suite 1), which may be the result of discard. Finally, there is a refit connection between Pit Structure 4 and Room 12, indicating movement of materials—and perhaps of people—between the two structures.

In presenting the nested-hierarchy model, I suggested that social interactions between households (across architectural-suite boundaries) were expected to be channeled through the pit structures because of the role that these structures played in integrating different households. This expectation is supported both by the inferred doorway data and the pottery-refit data. Interior doorways are found only within architectural suites, not between them. Also, pottery-refit connections between structures predominantly involve connections with pit structures. Some connections are between rooms and pit structures in the same architectural suite, some are between a room and a pit structure in different architectural suites, and others are between two pit structures.

The inference I draw from these relationships is that a domestic room is not a strong indicator of an economically independent household group. The basic minimum architectural suite consists of a pit structure and a combination of domestic and storage rooms. There is redundancy in certain activities such as food-preparation and cooking areas within the suite, but if domestic spaces and storage facilities were all interconnected through interior doorways, the groups occupying these spaces were not very strongly divided. The diversity of activities and artifact types in pit structures is greater than that in rooms, which suggests that the pit structure was a significant part of the basic economy of a household. Residential facilities generally include an entire suite of rooms and a pit structure. For a residential group to have had access to the basic set of domestic and economic activity areas, it would have needed access to this full architectural suite of facilities.

# 7

# Household Organization

*Most people in most societies at most times live in households, membership in which is usually based on kin relationships of marriage and descent, which are simultaneously a combination of dwelling unit, a unit of economic cooperation (at least in distribution and consumption), and the unit within which most reproduction and early childhood socialization takes place.*

—P. Kunstadter 1984:300

The concept of household is so familiar that we take it for granted, but one of the things that anthropology has taught us is the remarkable diversity in the way that households are organized in different cultures. In this chapter, I examine the organization of households at Duckfoot and consider the role of households in Pueblo I society. The Duckfoot site provides an opportunity to study in detail some aspects of household organization in a late Pueblo I hamlet. This chapter addresses basic questions of household archaeology: How large were Pueblo I households? How were households organized, and what role did they play in the community? What is the relationship, or fit, between architectural units and the household groups they contained? Anthropologists since the 1950s have made a distinction between the *family*, as a kinship group, and the *household*, as a coresident group that shares in domestic and economic activities (Bender 1967). In archaeology, the household is the preferred unit of analysis because it is defined behaviorally rather than structurally. That is, the household is a social group defined on the basis of the activities it performs rather than on the basis of the kin relations of its members. Ashmore and Wilk (1988:6) defined a household as "the group of people that shares in a maximum definable number of activities, including one or more of the following: production, consumption, pooling of resources, reproduction, coresidence, and shared ownership." This definition of household emphasizes the activities and patterned associations between activity groups. In this volume, I have attempted to identify both the dominant activity systems that leave a material signature and the patterned associations between them.

Some patterned variation in household size and composition may be explained by natural developmental cycles that most households experience through time. Fortes (1958) introduced the concept of a developmental cycle in domestic groups and argued that what might be considered different types of families (for example, nuclear vs. extended) may be nothing more than different phases of development of a single household. Fortes (1958) defined three distinct phases in the developmental cycle: (1) the *expansion* phase, lasting from the marriage of two people to the end of their family procreation (that is, the period during which offspring are economically, affectively, and jurally dependent on their parents); (2) the *dispersion,* or *fission,* phase, which begins with the marriage of the oldest child and continues until the marriage of the youngest; and (3) the *replacement* phase, which starts with one or more of the children beginning to take over the family estate and ends with the death of the parents and their full replacement in the social structure of the family. Although the members of a household in Pueblo I times may not have been a single family, similar cycles of change probably played a role in determining the size and composition of the household.

## Household Size

The size and configuration of early Pueblo households are significant because the way we define households and their architectural correlates influences our estimates of population size and our perceptions of how the prehistoric organizations compare with other tribal societies cross-culturally. Attempts to determine prehistoric population size always rely on some type of quantitative transformation from a physical parameter that can be measured at sites to a population derived from some equivalent units in the ethnographic record. The exact transformation depends on the scale of the study and the resolution of the archaeological attribute being measured. Archaeological parameters that have been used to estimate population include roofed area (Naroll 1962; LeBlanc 1971), area of roomblock rubble on the modern ground surface (Schlanger 1985, 1987; Wilshusen 1991), vessel volume (Turner and Lofgren 1966; Blinman 1986), and hearth size (Ciolek-Torrello and Reid 1974). The remaining part of the equation requires a knowledge of average cross-cultural household size. How consistent are household sizes cross-culturally? The following section addresses that question.

## Variation in Household Size

In societies in which residence is not based on nuclear-family households, the rules of residence often imply that large and complex households should be the norm. For example, a matrilocal family (Eggan 1950:29) consisting of a woman, her husband, her unmarried sons, and her married daughters and their husbands and children, might number 10 or more. In preindustrial Europe, extended or multiple-family households may have consisted of 15 or more persons (Laslett [1972:18], summarizing the work of French social reformer Frédéric Le Play, 1806–1882). Burch (1972) noted, however, that such large households are rarely average or modal. Laslett (1972) also noted that, despite differences in household structure and rules of residence and inheritance, mean household size has been relatively constant over time and space. In England, average household size has ranged between 4.0 and 5.5 from the seventeenth to the twentieth centuries, with an overall mean of approximately of 4.75. The historical data from England compare favorably with those from other regions of the world, including western Europe, eastern Europe, colonial America, and Japan. Average household size for this worldwide historical sample ranged from 4.2 to 7.0, and the percentage of multiple- or extended-family households ranged from 3 to 56 percent (Laslett 1972).

Other researchers have pondered the discrepancies between the ideal and real sizes of households and have offered a variety of explanations. Some argue that economic factors limit the size and composition of households, whereas others stress the social and psychological difficulties of maintaining large, complex household groups (Burch 1972). Other researchers have focused on the role that demographic factors play in limiting household size. Levy (1965) argued that actual family structures have been similar in societies of all times and places, regardless of the structural ideals. Laslett's (1972:Table 1.15) worldwide sample showed that households of more than two generations are rare except in Nishinomiya, Japan, where three-generation households consistently make up 30 percent of all households.

## Household Size in Historic Pueblos

One might ask if household size in historic pueblos conforms to the worldwide averages discussed above. Throughout the twentieth century, Western Pueblo households have been composed of compound or extended families organized by principles of matrilineal descent and matrilocal residence; each household typically has occupied a suite of contiguous rooms (Eggan 1950). Data from the *Eleventh*

*Census of the United States: 1890* (Census Office 1894:183) indicate that the average household size at Zuni in the late nineteenth century was 5.7 persons and that the average Hopi household consisted of 5.5 persons. Kroeber's (1917:124) 1915–1916 census of Zuni families showed a mean household size of 7.56, and Li (1937:75) confirmed that this estimate was still accurate in the 1930s. On the basis of the 1941 census data, Eggan (1950) estimated average household size at Acoma to be approximately 6. In 1960, the average Hopi household was 5.8 persons, and at Zuni the average was 7.3 (Hillery and Essene 1963:305). These numbers are of particular interest because they support Laslett's (1972) contention that average household size is relatively constant, regardless of family structure and rules of residence and inheritance.

Although the average size of a historic Pueblo household is consistent with cross-cultural averages, the variation in size is apparently quite large. In 1934, Beaglehole (1935:42) conducted a census of two Hopi villages, Shipaulovi and Mishongnovi, and calculated the average household sizes to be 6.25 and 6.83 persons, respectively. She noted that these averages were larger than estimates of 4.8 and 5.4 that had been recorded in 1900. Beaglehole, following Kroeber (1917), defined *household* as "the house unit in which a number of people live around a single hearth" (Beaglehole 1935:42). She noted that households ranged from two to 10 persons at Shipaulovi and from two to 11 persons at Mishongnovi. Beaglehole also noted that among the 51 households there were 12 with two to four persons each and 23 households with eight to 11 persons each.

The above summary suggests that it is reasonable to infer that Pueblo I households, on average, consisted of five to eight individuals. It also suggests that if there were extended-family-type households during the Pueblo I period, some households would have been large, but the sizes of these households would have been offset by the existence of smaller households to bring the average back to within the cross-cultural average.

## Household Size at Duckfoot

On the basis of cross-cultural studies, one might expect household size in prehistoric pueblos to have ranged from two to 12 and to have averaged between five and eight persons. The average values are quite consistent with those used by previous researchers to estimate local and regional populations (Schlanger 1988; Wilshusen 1991). The problem arises not in deciding the correct size of an average household but in recognizing the architectural correlate of an early Pueblo household. Previous versions of the nested-hierarchy model (e.g., Kane 1986) assumed that each household in late Pueblo I times was represented by a domestic front room. Therefore, each pit structure was interpreted as serving the needs of roughly 10 to 20 persons, and a small hamlet like Duckfoot would have had an estimated population of 40 to 80 persons.

I propose that the estimated population of 40 to 80 persons at Duckfoot is too large. The data presented in this volume support the interpretation that each household is represented by an architectural suite rather than by a dwelling unit. If each architectural suite had been occupied by a household averaging five to eight persons, then the population of Duckfoot would have been more on the order of 15 to 24 persons. Brown (1987), in a worldwide study, documented a cross-cultural average of 6.2 m$^2$ of roofed area per person. Dividing the total roofed area of 242.4 m$^2$ at Duckfoot (late in the occupation) by this average produces an estimated population of 39 persons. Dohm (1990) conducted a study of roofed space per person in modern Southwestern cultures and proposed that roofed space per person increases with sedentism and increased settlement aggregation. Data assembled by Dohm (1990:Table 3) indicate an average of 17.7 m$^2$ of roofed space per person in 22 modern Pueblo villages in New Mexico and Arizona. Applying this factor to Duckfoot, with a total roofed space of 242.4 m$^2$, yields an estimate of 13.7 persons at the site. Nineteenth- and twentieth-century Navajo settlements (Dohm 1990:Table 1) that were occupied year round had an average of 9.7 m$^2$ of roofed space per person. Applying this factor yields an estimated population of 25.0 at Duckfoot. If roofed space per person increases with sedentism and degree of settlement aggregation, then one might expect that the amount of roofed space per person at Duckfoot would fall somewhere between the modern Pueblo and Navajo estimates. If so, these estimates could be used as boundaries for an estimated total population of between 14 and 25 persons and household populations of between five and eight persons. These estimates are substantially lower than those listed above, which were derived from a previous version of the nested-hierarchy model. I believe that the lower population estimates are more likely to be correct.

# Household Activities

Wilk and Netting (1984) recommended abandoning classifications of households that are based on morphology and structure. Instead, they advocated identifying classes of household activities, including coresidence, production, distribution, genetic and social reproduction, and generational transmission of wealth, property, and rights. The groups that perform these activities may overlap to varying degrees, or they may overlap entirely and be one and the same. Defining households in a particular social setting does not require that each set of overlapping activities be the same. The household is the smallest group whose members have the maximum amount of economic, social, and behavioral interdependence. In the following sections, I define various activities and discuss the groups that might have performed them. Different kinds of activities may be organized at different social scales or at different levels in the social organization.

## Coresidence

Household membership is often synonymous with coresidence, so much so that considerable attention has been devoted to cases in which the two are not perfectly congruent. Buildings to some extent condition the size and composition of household groups. David (1971) noted in his study of the Fulani that the lower the capital outlay or labor required to construct a building or complex of buildings, the greater the fit between it and its personnel throughout the use life of the structure. Conversely, the more permanent a building and the greater its cost, the less perfect the fit (Kidder 1958). Rapoport (1990:11) addresses the fit between architectural spaces and the activities they enclose, which is also relevant to this discussion: "If architecture encloses behavior tightly, then activities will tend to shape architecture. . . . If, on the other hand, activities are contained only loosely, then their impact on form will be greatly reduced."

The attempt in Chapter 5 to separate early and late patterns of structure use and interaction at Duckfoot were aimed at sharpening our understanding of the fit between architecture and activities. Group size and composition and anticipated use of structures might have had a strong influence on the initial design of the architectural facilities at Duckfoot. Through time, the walls stayed the same, but the use of architectural spaces changed in response to the composition of the groups and the organization of activities. Consequently, the fit between the original design and the eventual use of structures became looser through time. Only by looking at internal features can we infer the changes in structure use.

Identifying coresident groups in Pueblo I settlements is difficult because it is not always clear which activities define coresidence. In addition, some activities that may be important in defining coresidence, such as sleeping, may not leave archaeological traces. Coresidence can be difficult to define ethnographically, so we should not be surprised that it is difficult to infer from archaeological data. Identifying the coresident group would not be an issue if the living room, the kitchen, and the bedrooms were all under one roof. The problem arises when there are multiple roofs and, in some cases, multiple kitchens and living rooms. Identifying coresident groups is also difficult in situations in which the groups that use these different areas consist of different, but overlapping, membership.

At Duckfoot, the redundancy of domestic activities in domestic rooms implies that for at least part of the year the coresident group was the dwelling group. Redundancy of domestic activities between domestic rooms and pit structures could be explained either by seasonal differences in the use of front rooms and pit structures or by the pit structure being occupied by a separate dwelling group. The principal arguments against the interpretation that pit structures and domestic rooms were occupied by different individuals are that the residents of the pit structures would have lacked direct access to long-term storage rooms, and the residents of domestic rooms would have lacked direct access to manufacturing and ritual facilities. Alternatively, the redundancy of domestic activities between domestic rooms and pit structures might have been the result of seasonal differences in the intensity of use of the two types of structures and not a result of differences in the individuals who used them. If domestic rooms and pit structures were used on a seasonal basis, then the coresident group could have changed its size and membership on a seasonal basis. That is, each domestic room might have housed a small coresident dwelling group during the warm months, whereas each pit structure might have housed a larger coresident household group and more diverse activities during the winter. It could well be that more manufacturing and ceremonial activities took place in the pit structures in the winter, when mobility was restricted by short days and cold temperatures, as well as by mud and snow.

Schlanger (1987) considered the implications of shared use of pit structures by multiple nuclear-family households, each of whom had their own domestic surface rooms at Dolores. She proposed that if multiple households based in domestic rooms moved into a single pit structure during the winter, the open floor area of the pit structure would had to have been large enough to accommodate the appropriate number of people. Estimating that a person would need at least 1.5 m² of open floor for sleeping, she concluded that, before A.D. 800, pit structures could have accommodated households consisting of two or three dwelling groups, but all available floor space would have been occupied. After A.D. 800, there is less pit structure space than domestic-room space, and Schlanger (1987:577) concluded that the pit structures could not have accommodated entire households. Schlanger's conclusions are based on an assumption that each dwelling unit was the residence of a (nuclear-family) group with an average population of five individuals.

The amount of sleeping space available in structures is less than the total area of the structures, because a certain portion of the floor space of pit structures and domestic rooms is taken up by hearths, fire pits, short-term storage features, and grinding areas. To compare available sleeping space between structures at Duckfoot, I subtracted the amount of space consumed by such features and activity areas from the total floor space of individual structures. The available floor areas of domestic rooms and pit structures during the late period of occupation at Duckfoot are listed in Table 7.1 by architectural suite, with Pit Structure 4 kept separate. For the site as a whole, open space in pit structures is less than that in domestic rooms. There is only about 75 percent as much space available in pit structures as there is in domestic rooms. In Architectural Suites 1 and 2, available sleeping space in the pit structures is less than half (approximately 45 percent) of that available in domestic rooms, whereas in Architectural Suite 3, sleeping space in Pit Structure 3 is about 75 percent greater than that in domestic room 19. If we translate floor area into people space, as Schlanger did, then in Architectural Suite 1 there was sleeping space for 14 persons in Room 16, but only six persons could have slept in Pit Structure 1. In Architectural Suite 2, there would have been room for 22 sleepers in the domestic rooms, whereas Pit Structure 2 would have accommodated only 10. In Architectural Suite 3, the domestic room would have slept seven, the pit structure, 12. Pit Structure 4 had sleeping space for only four persons.

If the domestic rooms in Architectural Suites 1 and 2 were filled to capacity during the warm months, Pit Structures 1 and 2 could not have accommodated the total group in the winter. In Architectural Suite 3, the pit structure would have had ample space to accommodate a full house from Room 19. If the rooms were used predominantly during the warm months, there might have been greater flexibility in where people slept, because there probably would have been no need for them to sleep in rooms with hearths.

Table 7.1. Available Floor Areas During the Late Period

|  | Floor Area ($m^2$) | | |
|  | Pit Structures | Domestic Rooms | Total |
| --- | --- | --- | --- |
| Architectural Suite 1 | 14.9–5.0 =  9.9 | 23.0–1.0 = 22.0 | 31.9 |
| Architectural Suite 2 | 20.6–5.5 = 15.1 | 41.6–7.5 = 34.1 | 49.2 |
| Architectural Suite 3 | 24.0–5.0 = 19.0 | 12.6–1.5 = 11.1 | 30.1 |
| Pit Structure 4 | 8.9–2.5 =  6.4 | — | 6.4 |
| TOTAL | 50.4 | 67.2 | 117.6 |

NOTE: Available floor area is the total floor area minus the approximate area occupied by storage features, hearths, fire pits, and grinding areas.

In the winter months, however, the nights are cold enough that the warmth of the pithouse and the fire in its hearth might have been essential. The available space in the pit structures might be a good indicator of population potential. The estimated numbers of individuals that could have slept in Pit Structures 1, 2, 3, and 4 are six, 10, 12, and four, respectively. Combined, these numbers suggest a maximum winter population of 32 individuals. Taken as an upper limit, this number agrees relatively well with the population estimate presented above that was calculated assuming an average of five to eight persons per architectural suite.

## Production

*Production* refers to human activities, including housekeeping and domestic labor, that result in the procurement of resources or an increase in their value (Wilk and Netting 1984). Production and distribution form the economic base of a household, and several studies suggest that household size and structure change in response to changing economic strategies. Scheduling, which includes both the timing and sequencing of tasks, is perhaps the most important factor affecting production. Wilk and Netting (1984) hypothesized that the more simultaneous the labor requirements of major productive tasks and the more diverse the productive tasks within the yearly cycle, the larger the size of the minimal group involved in production. In the absence of some other need for larger groups, linear tasks arranged in a simple yearly cycle favor the small household as the minimal production group. Hegmon (1991), in a simulation of food-sharing strategies modeled on Hopi subsistence practices, found that groups of small, autonomous households who share only their food surplus are more successful than either small households that do not share or larger groups that share completely. Sahlins (1957) found that, on Fiji, widely dispersed resources were exploited most efficiently by large, extended-family households. Netting (1986) documented that Kofyar household size increased when families moved to an area where larger, cooperative agricultural labor forces could produce greater marginal returns than could small, independent groups. During Pueblo I times, the technology of agricultural production was simple, with no elaborate methods of farming, food collecting, or water control that required large groups or labor pools. If Wilk and Netting's hypothesis is correct, one would expect relatively small, independent households during the Pueblo I period.

Production includes subsistence activities, such as farming, hunting, and gathering of food and other resources, but it also includes the construction of buildings and other facilities. Construction can be construed as an aspect of production in terms of the labor and materials invested by a group in order to meet their needs for domestic activities and storage. I argued in Chapter 2 that the early phases of construction at Duckfoot involved the construction of three suites, each consisting of a distinct set of structures, including one pit structure, two to three domestic rooms, and three to five storage rooms. At Duckfoot, the production group for basic housing facilities would have been the group that built and occupied an architectural suite. Smaller groups might have been responsible for food production, but the evidence of how architectural suites were built suggests that the group that built the entire architectural suite was a cooperative work group.

Further support for this interpretation comes from the distribution of the tools of production. Tool classes other than those used for food preparation and consumption were categorically more abundant and more ubiquitous in pit structures than in above-ground rooms at Duckfoot. These artifacts include a variety of manufacturing tools and materials for making pottery, which suggests that tool and pottery manufacture were organized at the level of the household. Regardless of whether the tools were used or merely stored in the pit structures, they were found in locations where the entire group occupying the architectural suite would have had access to them. It is also clear that certain ritual activities took place predominantly in pit structures and were organized at the level of the household (Varien and Lightfoot 1989). It is possible that some aspects of production were organized at the level of the dwelling group, but it is likely that income and labor were pooled across the entire household on the basis of generalized reciprocity.

During Pueblo I times, household architectural facilities were aggregated into roomblocks, hamlets, villages, and communities, and it is likely that the suprahousehold organizations represented by these architectural clusters played a role in decision making, defense, and controlling access to land and other resources. The construction and use of large, integrative facilities such as great kivas (Lightfoot 1988; Lightfoot et al. 1988) probably would have involved cooperation across the entire community. The presence of community-wide structures suggests that there may have been community-wide leadership, although there is little indication that the leaders attained much wealth, status, or ruling power (Kane 1989). Even at large Pueblo I sites, there are no indications of elite residences, suprahousehold storage facilities, or high-status goods. The absence of community storage facilities where surpluses could have been stored for redistribution suggests that production was not organized at the level of the roomblock or community. At least agricultural production and residential building construction appear to have been organized at the level of the household. Some of the larger settlements, especially the more formalized villages such as McPhee Village (Brisbin et al. 1988), had oversize integrative pit structures, the construction of which probably involved cooperation at the level of the roomblock group or village. Wilshusen (1988d) argued that people during the Pueblo I period did not have powerful elite leaders but, rather, were self-regulated through religious ritual.

## Distribution

*Distribution,* which includes food storage, preparation, and consumption, refers to the movement of material from producers to consumers. Households typically are characterized by the pooling of economic resources and generalized reciprocity, in which there is no strict accounting of repayment for goods or services. Patterns of distribution provide a basis for determining household boundaries because the rules for exchange within households are often different from those that govern exchange between households.

The distribution group is not necessarily perfectly congruent with the production group as defined above. At Duckfoot, the arrangement of storage facilities and domestic activity areas is perhaps the best indicator of patterns of distribution and, hence, the size of the group involved in sharing food and other goods. In Chapter 6, I described doorway access between domestic rooms and storage rooms in different dwelling units at McPhee Pueblo in the Dolores River valley. At Duckfoot, Architectural Suite 1 has two front rooms and three back rooms, with one back room (Room 2) potentially being accessible from both front rooms (Rooms 15 and 16). The results of the doorway study also suggest that storage rooms within the same architectural suite may have been interconnected. If storage rooms were interconnected and largely accessible from the front rooms in an architectural suite, then the argument that each front room represents a separate unit of storage and distribution is weakened. In Room Suite 2, all the storage and living rooms (except perhaps Rooms 14 and 17) are potentially interconnected, which again suggests that the group that occupied a single domestic room had little autonomy with respect to distribution. The presence of separate hearths and grinding areas in each domestic room, however, supports the argument that cooking, food preparation, and eating were conducted separately by the groups that used these rooms. On the other hand, the hearth and food-preparation facilities in pit structures apparently were accessible to everyone in the architectural suite.

As was discussed in the section on production, the absence of roomblock, village, or community storage facilities suggests that distribution was not managed at a suprahousehold level. If there had been some managerial elite or some other type of centralized authority, one would expect to find centralized storage and redistribution facilities. The absence of storage facilities beyond those controlled by the dwelling group and the household suggests that distribution was handled entirely by the dwelling group and the household. Although food was consistently stored at the dwelling-group and household levels, the success of roomblock and village groups could have been based on agreements to assist in productive tasks and to share food or at least food surpluses.

## Reproduction

*Reproduction* refers both to biological replacement of individuals and to the care and socialization of children, which in effect validates and reproduces the social groups and the organization of those groups. Providing child care requires a constant labor investment, and that labor can be organized in a variety of ways. Pooling labor for child care could have been an advantage that came along with aggregation into roomblocks and villages. Large households and roomblock groups would have had an advantage over small, isolated households because a smaller proportion of the labor force would have been committed to child care. Pooling labor for child care allows more of the population to be involved in farming, collecting, or other aspects of production.

## Transmission

*Transmission* refers to the transfer of land, property, roles, and rights from one generation to the next. When land is plentiful, its transmission is generally based on group affiliation, such as lineage or village; as land becomes scarce and difficult to obtain, rights to its access are increasingly restricted and eventually controlled by households or individuals (Wilk and Rathje 1982). As Pueblo I population density increased in the northern Southwest, access to, and transmission of, land (the means of production) would have become increasingly important and increasingly vested in households. This could have stimulated an increase in average household size because household members would have been less likely to separate and lose access to suitable farmland. Adler (1992) looked at a worldwide, cross-cultural sample of small-scale agricultural groups to determine why communal access to land is associated with some agricultural strategies but not with others. He showed that communal (multiple-household) access to land is associated with groups that have an intermediate intensity of agricultural labor investment, whereas household or individual access to land is associated with both very low and very high agricultural labor investment. All indications are that the agricultural strategy during Pueblo I times involved relatively low labor investments—there was no irrigation, elaborate ground preparation, or field-enclosure system. Both the relative scarcity of land and the low-intensity agricultural strategy suggest that access to land and transmission of land and other property were probably controlled at the household level. Although the rights to have access to land were probably vested in individual households, protection of those rights, or claims, may have been taken up by suprahousehold groups at the level of the roomblock, village, or community group. The larger group could have maintained the authority to ensure the land-transmission rights of its constituent households.

## The Household and the Dwelling Group

I have departed from previous studies of Pueblo I household organization in identifying the household as the group that occupied an architectural suite rather than the group that occupied a dwelling unit. Recent studies of household organization in Latin America and the Caribbean indicate that there is not a perfect correspondence between coresidence and the other spheres of household activity:

> It is common to find groups that eat together, work together, share child rearing and other obviously domestic activities but live in separate houses. Anthropologists should not be forced to abandon the term *household* for describing or discussing these units or to resort to tortuous terms like *nonresidential extended family* [Wilk 1984:223; italics in original].

In his study of households of the Kekchi Maya of Belize, Wilk (1984) defined several types of household organization on the basis of production and distribution rather than coresidence. Wilk's typology reflects the inherent variability of households within a single culture or a single settlement. A household consisting of one dwelling unit is called an *independent household*. Households composed of multiple dwelling units are called *household clusters*, some of which Wilk defined as *tight household clusters*. A tight household cluster in a Kekchi Mayan settlement is essentially a single household in terms of production and distribution, but its members occupy several buildings located close together. Tight household clusters share all food and income, and they exchange labor according to an explicit rule of generalized reciprocity rather than the rule of balanced reciprocity that is normal between households. "Each dwelling unit within the household cluster has its own hearth and kitchen area, but in a tight cluster more than half of the meals each week are eaten by all the cluster members together in one kitchen" (Wilk 1984:225).

During the late period at Duckfoot, there was only one domestic room apiece in Room Suites 1 and 3, each representing a household composed of a single dwelling group. The household organization in Architectural Suites 1 and 3 may have been comparable to Wilk's independent household. Room Suite 2, on the other hand, had three front domestic rooms and one back domestic room, representing three, or possibly four, dwelling groups that together formed a single household. The household that occupied Architectural Suite 2 may have been similar to what Wilk defined as a tight household cluster. It is likely that household size was variable in the Pueblo I period in the northern Southwest, just as it is in all cultures today.

Households at Duckfoot may have been extended-family-type households that incorporated a number of nuclear-family groups or dyads (Adams 1960). Residential dyads might have existed in a variety of forms, including a maternal dyad, which is composed of a mother and one or more children, or a conjugal adult dyad, which is composed of a man and a woman (Adams 1960). These smaller infrahousehold groups may have been the dwelling groups that occupied separate living rooms in each architectural suite. Through time, the size and composition of households could have changed because of the developmental cycle of domestic groups, which includes such events as marriage, birth, death, group fission, and the like. As the size and composition of the social groups changed, the architectural configurations and the use of structures would have changed as well. Thus, one would expect variations in the architectural configurations of the household facilities because of differences in household size and composition, as well as in the number of infrahousehold groups requiring separate living rooms.

## The Household, the Roomblock Group, and the Community

In historic and modern Pueblo societies, extended-family households are the most common form in both the Eastern and Western Pueblos (Dozier 1965; Eggan 1950). Although this recent pattern cannot necessarily be assumed to have held for prehistoric Pueblo households, it is possible that the household form is deeply rooted in Pueblo prehistory. In most modern Pueblo societies, there are nonlocalized lineage and clan groups above the level of the household, and some scholars believe that these suprahousehold groups may have been localized some time in the past (Dozier 1965:40; Eggan 1950:299–300). Most modern Pueblo societies have village or multiple-village communities. According to Dozier (1965:41), "While some of these structures [village or multiple-village communities] may have a bias or inclination toward unilineality and its members may be relatives, there are no specific conditions of kinship for membership."

During the Pueblo I period, several levels of social organization above the level of the household were represented architecturally by roomblock clusters, hamlets, villages, and community clusters, each of which had a social correlate. The roomblock group consisted of a number of households who lived in adjoining residences. In many instances, the roomblocks were much larger than the one at Duck-foot, and often several roomblocks were clustered together to form villages. Although much of the population during the A.D. 850–880 period was living in villages, small, single-household residential sites did not disappear entirely (Schlanger 1987; Orcutt 1987). The small sites that were contemporaneous with villages probably had social, political, or religious affiliations with other hamlets and villages to form communities.

On the basis of population aggregation and spacing in the Dolo-res River valley, Kane (1989:318) inferred a three-tier hierarchical settlement system from A.D. 840 to 920. The third, or highest, tier was represented by the seven largest villages, each of which contained five or more roomblocks. Settlements in the second, or middle, tier consisted of one to three roomblocks, whereas the third, or lowest, tier consisted of settlements with fewer than six rooms and some-times lacking a pit structure. Within this hierarchical scheme, Duck-foot would be considered a second-tier settlement. Kane concluded that the settlement data at Dolores offered some support for his hypothesis that there were emerging political elites (following Light-foot 1984) associated with population aggregation and village for-mation in the mid–A.D. 800s. The data supporting the political-elite model included the three-tier hierarchy of settlements and the fact that villages were not strongly associated with the best agricultural locations. However, architectural and mortuary data did not support the political-elite model (Kane 1989).

Wilshusen (1991) looked at Pueblo I villages in the larger region of southwestern Colorado and showed that the pattern of a village and its surrounding community of smaller sites was not limited to the Dolores River valley. He recorded 30 Pueblo I villages including one, the Cirque site, that is 3 km east of Duckfoot. The Cirque site is the closest contemporaneous village to Duckfoot, and the two may have been part of a single Pueblo I community, which suggests that residents of the two sites probably had regular face-to-face contact, as well as strong social and political ties. Warm, dry climatic condi-tions during the mid– to late A.D. 800s apparently caused many people to favor settlements at higher elevations, and most of the population in the northern Southwest moved to elevations above 2010 m (Petersen 1989). The congregating of population in the more restricted high-elevation areas of the Southwest led to an increase in population density, which in turn probably increased the competition for arable land and other limited resources in the higher-elevation areas that were suitable for farming. At an elevation of approximately 1900 m, the Cirque community, including Duck-foot, was the only community recorded by Wilshusen (1991) that was below the 2010-m threshold. The population density of the Cirque community was lower than that of contemporaneous com-munities in the Dolores area; it is possible that this community developed as a result of the fissioning of households from Dolores. Even though the low-elevation areas were probably more susceptible to crop failure caused by drought, the fields in the Cirque commu-nity would have been less susceptible to crop failure caused by frost. Thus, the Cirque community might have provided a buffer against food shortages that resulted from short growing seasons at Dolores. Similarly, the Pueblo I communities at Dolores could have provided a buffer against food shortages in the Cirque community resulting from drought.

Increases in population density in the upland areas of the north-ern Southwest could have affected how group decisions were made. Problems might have stemmed from attempts to reach a consensus among too many individuals or independent households. It is well known that large groups tend to be more complex than small groups, and Johnson (1982) argued that these increases in social complexity may be the result of societies developing mechanisms for decision making and problem resolution. Johnson argued that there are biological constraints on human information-processing capabili-ties that limit the size of consensual, "task-oriented" organizations. As the number of decision-making units (for example, individuals or households) increases to a number greater than six, the group tends to undergo stress, evidenced by decreasing consensus and decreasing member satisfaction with group decisions. This stress can be reduced by one of three means: (1) development of a nonconsensual political (vertical) hierarchy, (2) group fission, or (3) institution of a consen-sual sequential (horizontal) hierarchy. The sequential solution in-volves the aggregation of smaller social units into larger, and thus fewer, entities that may attain a consensus more easily. For example, households aggregate into roomblock groups, which may then reach a consensus more easily than they could have among several hundred independent households. A decision between roomblock groups may then be achieved more easily than among their more numerous constituent households simply because there are fewer decision-making entities involved. Lower-order groups (in this case, households) are subject to minimum coercion from higher-order groups, and satisfaction remains high because the lower-order groups maintain their fission option (Johnson 1989). The coalescence of population into higher-elevation farmlands during the Pueblo I period resulted in higher population densities that would have created stress in decision making and conflict resolution. Roomblock groups and villages might have evolved as a means of reducing stress (Johnson 1982, 1989) as an alternative to fission or the creation of vertical (simultaneous) hierarchies. In fact, the Cirque community could have been composed of household and roomblock groups who had exercised their fission option and moved out of the higher-elevation areas, into the hotter, drier, lower-elevation area.

## Household Organization Through Time

I have considered the size of households, the types of activities that households perform, the distribution of those activities at Duckfoot, and the role of households within the hamlet and the larger community. It is also important to consider household organization through time. In the northern Southwest, there are dramatic variations in the degree of aggregation and in settlement density through time. There are also dramatic changes in architectural patterns. Despite these changes, the architectural suite consisting of a pit structure and a cluster of rooms is the basic structural component for hundreds of years.

During the Basketmaker III period (A.D. 500–750), a typical residential suite consisted of a shallow pit structure and several shallow, isolated storage structures. Each pit structure is thought to have represented a single household. The beginnings of the Pueblo I period were marked in part by a change in architecture: Pit structures became deeper, and they were associated with suites of contiguous, above-ground rooms that included multiple domestic rooms and storage rooms. This change is often referred to as the pithouse-to-pueblo transition, and in the earlier model of social organization, it was interpreted as signaling a change in household organization (Kane 1986). Each dwelling unit was believed to represent a household, and pit structures were interpreted as multiple-household structures representing two to three households. At the same time that the pithouse-to-pueblo transition was taking place, the population was aggregating into villages. A dramatic increase in the estimated population of the Dolores River valley in the mid– to late A.D. 800s was inferred to be at least partly a result of this change in household organization. The alternative that I have presented in this volume is that, during the Pueblo I period, the household remained centered around a pit structure, as it had in Basketmaker III times. The above-ground facilities became more specialized, storage technology improved, and ample room for storing food surpluses was made a regular part of every pueblo. The addition of multiple domestic structures in each architectural suite allowed individuals and infrahousehold groups more privacy, which was demanded by the increased population density and the aggregation of households into hamlets and villages.

I believe that individual architectural suites, such as those at Duckfoot, were the facilities of a household and that this architectural pattern, once established during the Pueblo I period, persisted until the end of the thirteenth century. Prudden (1903) identified "unit-type" house mounds, consisting of single kivas and their associated room suites, at Pueblo II sites. These small, unit-type pueblos were built throughout the Pueblo II and Pueblo III periods. When population aggregated into villages during the Pueblo II and III periods, the villages were made up of clusters of "kiva suites" (Bradley 1992), with each kiva suite consisting of a kiva and its associated suite of rooms. Even though masonry styles, settlement patterns, and architectural patterns changed through time, the basic elements of the architectural suite endured. It seems quite possible that the basic elements of the architectural suite persisted through time because the architectural suite was the basic facility of a household. The facility was functionally adequate to meet the domestic, storage, and ritual needs of an ancestral Pueblo household, and it had its roots in the earliest Pueblo period.

# References

Adams, E. C.
1983 The Architectural Analogue to Hopi Social Organization and Room Use, and Implications for Prehistoric Northern Southwestern Culture. *American Antiquity* 48:44–61.

Adams, K. R.
1993 Carbonized Plant Remains. In *The Duckfoot Site, Volume 1: Descriptive Archaeology,* edited by R. R. Lightfoot and M. C. Etzkorn, pp. 195–220. Occasional Papers, no. 3. Crow Canyon Archaeological Center, Cortez, Colorado.

Adams, R. N.
1960 An Inquiry Into the Nature of the Family. In *Essays in the Science of Culture in Honor of Leslie A. White,* edited by G. E. Dole and R. L. Carneiro, pp. 30–49. Thomas Y. Crowell, New York.

Adler, M. A.
1989 Ritual Facilities and Social Integration in Nonranked Societies. In *The Architecture of Social Integration in Prehistoric Pueblos,* edited by W. D. Lipe and M. Hegmon, pp. 35–52. Occasional Papers, no. 1. Crow Canyon Archaeological Center, Cortez, Colorado.
1992 Land Tenure Systems and Prehistoric Land Use: Perspectives from the American Southwest. Paper presented at the 57th Annual Meeting of the Society for American Archaeology, Pittsburgh.

Adler, M. A., and M. D. Varien
1991 The Changing Face of the Community in the Mesa Verde Region, A.D. 1000–1300. Paper presented at the Anasazi Symposium, Mesa Verde National Park, Colorado.

Adler, M. A., and R. H. Wilshusen
1990 Large-Scale Integrative Facilities in Tribal Societies: Cross-Cultural and Southwestern US Examples. *World Archaeology* 22:133–145.

Ahlstrom, R. V. N.
1985 *The Interpretation of Archaeological Tree-Ring Dates.* Ph.D. dissertation, University of Arizona. University Microfilms, Ann Arbor.
1989 Tree-Ring Dating of Pindi Pueblo, New Mexico. *Kiva* 54:361–384.

Ascher, R.
1961 Analogy in Archaeological Interpretation. *Southwestern Journal of Anthropology* 17:317–325.
1968 Time's Arrow and the Archaeology of a Contemporary Community. In *Settlement Archaeology,* edited by K. C. Chang, pp. 43–52. National Press Books, Palo Alto.

Ashmore, W., and R. R. Wilk
1988 Household and Community in the Mesoamerican Past. In *Household and Community in the Mesoamerican Past,* edited by R. R. Wilk and W. Ashmore, pp. 1–27. University of New Mexico Press, Albuquerque.

Beaglehole, P.
1935 Census Data from Two Hopi Villages. *American Anthropologist* 37:41–54.

Bender, D. R.
1967 A Refinement of the Concept of Household: Families, Co-Residence, and Domestic Functions. *American Anthropologist* 69:493–504.

Berger, Edward F.
1993 *Crow Canyon.* Southwest Research and Educational Services, Sedona, Arizona.

Binford, L. R.
1962 Archaeology as Anthropology. *American Antiquity* 28:217–225.
1964 A Consideration of Archaeological Research Design. *American Antiquity* 29:425–441.
1981 Behavioral Archaeology and the "Pompeii Premise." *Journal of Anthropological Research* 37:195–208.

Binford, L. R., and S. R. Binford
1966 A Preliminary Analysis of Functional Variability in the Mousterian of Levallois Facies. In *Recent Studies in Paleoanthropology,* edited by J. D. Clarke and F. C. Howell, pp. 238–295. *American Anthropologist* 68(2), part 2.

Blalock, H. M.
1979 *Social Statistics.* 2nd. ed. Rev. McGraw-Hill, New York.

Blinman, E.
1986 Technology: Ceramic Containers. In *Dolores Archaeological Program: Final Synthetic Report,* compiled by D. A. Breternitz, C. K. Robinson, and G. T. Gross, pp. 595–609. Bureau of Reclamation, Engineering and Research Center, Denver.
1988a *The Interpretation of Ceramic Variability: A Case Study from the Dolores Anasazi.* Unpublished Ph.D. dissertation, Department of Anthropology, Washington State University, Pullman.
1988b Justification and Procedures for Ceramic Dating. In *Dolores Archaeological Program: Supporting Studies: Additive and Reductive Technologies,* compiled by E. Blinman, C. J. Phagan, and R. H. Wilshusen, pp. 501–544. Bureau of Reclamation, Engineering and Research Center, Denver.

1989   Potluck in the Protokiva: Ceramics and Ceremonialism in Pueblo I Villages. In *The Architecture of Social Integration in Prehistoric Pueblos,* edited by W. D. Lipe and M. Hegmon, pp. 113–124. Occasional Papers, no. 1. Crow Canyon Archaeological Center, Cortez, Colorado.

1991   Adjusting the Pueblo I Chronology: Implications for Culture Change at Dolores and in the Mesa Verde Region at Large. Paper presented at the Anasazi Symposium, Mesa Verde National Park, Colorado.

Bohannon, P.
1963   *Social Anthropology.* Holt, Rinehart, and Winston, New York.

Bradley, B. A.
1992   Excavations at Sand Canyon Pueblo. In *The Sand Canyon Archaeological Project: A Progress Report,* edited by W. D. Lipe, pp. 79–97. Occasional Papers, no. 2. Crow Canyon Archaeological Center, Cortez, Colorado.

Breternitz, D. A., C. K. Robinson, and G. T. Gross (compilers)
1986   *Dolores Archaeological Program: Final Synthetic Report.* Bureau of Reclamation, Engineering and Research Center, Denver.

Breternitz, D. A., A. H. Rohn, Jr., and E. A. Morris (compilers)
1974   *Prehistoric Ceramics of the Mesa Verde Region.* Ceramic Series, no. 5. Museum of Northern Arizona, Flagstaff.

Brew, J. O.
1946   *Archaeology of Alkali Ridge, Southeastern Utah.* Papers of the Peabody Museum of American Archaeology and Ethnology, vol. 21. Harvard University, Cambridge.

Brisbin, J. M., A. E. Kane, and J. N. Morris
1988   Excavations at McPhee Pueblo (Site 5MT4475), a Pueblo I and Early Pueblo II Multicomponent Village. In *Dolores Archaeological Program: Anasazi Communities at Dolores: McPhee Village,* compiled by A. E. Kane and C. K. Robinson, pp. 62–403. Bureau of Reclamation, Engineering and Research Center, Denver.

Bronitsky, G., and R. Hamer
1986   Experiments in Ceramic Technology: The Effects of Various Tempering Materials on Impact and Thermal Shock Resistance. *American Antiquity* 51:89–101.

Brooks, R. L.
1993   Household Abandonment Among Sedentary Plains Societies: Behavioral Sequences and Consequences in the Interpretation of the Archaeological Record. In *Abandonment of Settlements and Regions: Ethnoarchaeological and Archaeological Approaches,* edited by C. M. Cameron and S. A. Tomka, pp. 178–187. Cambridge University Press, Cambridge.

Brown, B. M.
1987   Population Estimation from Floor Area: A Restudy of "Naroll's Constant." *Behavior Science Research* 22(1–4):1–49.

Brown, D. E.
1982   Great Basin Conifer Woodland. In Biotic Communities of the American Southwest—United States and Mexico, edited by D. E. Brown, pp. 52–57. *Desert Plants* 4(1–4).

Burch, T. K.
1972   Some Demographic Determinants of Average Household Size: An Analytic Approach. In *Household and Family in Past Time,* edited by P. Laslett and R. Wall, pp. 91–102. Cambridge University Press, Cambridge.

Cameron, C. M.
1991   Structure Abandonment in Villages. In *Archaeological Method and Theory,* vol. 3, edited by M. B. Schiffer, pp. 155–194. University of Arizona Press, Tucson.

Cassells, E. S.
1983   *The Archaeology of Colorado.* Johnson Books, Boulder, Colorado.

Census Office
1894   *Eleventh Census of the United States: 1890.* Report on Indians Taxed and Indians Not Taxed in the United States (Except Alaska). House of Representatives Miscellaneous Document, 340(15). Department of the Interior, Washington, D.C.

Ciolek-Torrello, R. S.
1978   *A Statistical Analysis of Activity Organization: Grasshopper Pueblo, Arizona.* Ph.D. dissertation, University of Arizona. University Microfilms, Ann Arbor.

1985   A Typology of Room Function at Grasshopper Pueblo, Arizona. *Journal of Field Archaeology* 12:41–63.

Ciolek-Torrello, R., and J. J. Reid
1974   Change in Household Size at Grasshopper. *The Kiva* 40:39–47.

Clarke, D. L.
1968   *Analytical Archaeology.* Methuen, London.

Cordell, L. S., S. Upham, and S. L. Brock
1987   Obscuring Cultural Patterns in the Archaeological Record: A Discussion from Southwestern Archaeology. *American Antiquity* 52:565–577.

David, N.
  1971 The Fulani Compound and the Archaeologist. *World Archaeology* 3:111–131.

Deal, M.
  1985 Household Pottery Disposal in the Maya Highlands: An Ethnoarchaeological Interpretation. *Journal of Anthropological Archaeology* 4:243–291.

Dean, J. S.
  1969 *Chronological Analysis of Tsegi Phase Sites in Northeastern Arizona*. Papers, no. 3. Laboratory of Tree-Ring Research, Tucson.
  1978a Independent Dating in Archaeological Analysis. In *Advances in Archaeological Method and Theory*, vol. 1, edited by M. B. Schiffer, pp. 223–255. Academic Press, New York.
  1978b Tree-Ring Dating in Archeology. In *Anthropological Papers*, no. 99, pp. 129–163. University of Utah, Salt Lake City.

DeBoer, W. R.
  1985 Pots and Pans Do Not Speak, Nor Do They Lie: The Case for Occasional Reductionism. In *Decoding Prehistoric Ceramics*, edited by B. A. Nelson, pp. 347–357. Southern Illinois University Press, Carbondale.

Decker, K. W., and L. L. Tieszen
  1989 Isotopic Reconstruction of Mesa Verde Diet from Basketmaker III to Pueblo III. *Kiva* 55:33–47.

Dohm, K.
  1990 Effect of Population Nucleation on House Size for Pueblos in the American Southwest. *Journal of Anthropological Archaeology* 9:201–239.

Dozier, E. P.
  1965 Southwestern Social Units and Archaeology. *American Antiquity* 31:38–47.

Eddy, F. W., A. E. Kane, and P. R. Nickens
  1984 *Southwest Colorado Prehistoric Context: Archaeological Background and Research Directions*. Office of Archaeology and Historic Preservation, Colorado Historical Society, Denver.

Eggan, F.
  1950 *Social Organization of the Western Pueblos*. University of Chicago Press, Chicago.

Egloff, B. J.
  1973 A Method for Counting Ceramic Rim Sherds. *American Antiquity* 38:351–353.

Ericson, J. E., D. W. Read, and C. Burke
  1972 Research Design: The Relationships Between the Primary Functions and the Physical Properties of Ceramic Vessels and Their Implications for Ceramic Distributions on an Archaeological Site. *Anthropology UCLA* 3(2):84–95.

Etzkorn, M. C.
  1993a Other Pottery Tools. In *The Duckfoot Site, Volume 1: Descriptive Archaeology*, edited by R. R. Lightfoot and M. C. Etzkorn, pp. 147–152. Occasional Papers, no. 3. Crow Canyon Archaeological Center, Cortez, Colorado.
  1993b Sherds. In *The Duckfoot Site, Volume 1: Descriptive Archaeology*, edited by R. R. Lightfoot and M. C. Etzkorn, pp. 131–135. Occasional Papers, no. 3. Crow Canyon Archaeological Center, Cortez, Colorado.

Fewkes, J. W.
  1909 *Antiquities of the Mesa Verde National Park: Spruce-Tree House*. Bureau of American Ethnology Bulletin, no. 41. Smithsonian Institution, Washington, D.C.
  1919 *Prehistoric Villages, Castles, and Towers of Southwestern Colorado*. Bureau of American Ethnology Bulletin, no. 70. Smithsonian Institution, Washington, D.C.

Fitting, J. E., and J. R. Halsey
  1966 Rim Diameter and Vessel Size in Wayne Ware Vessels. *Wisconsin Archaeologist* 47:208–211.

Fortes, M.
  1958 Introduction. In *The Developmental Cycle in Domestic Groups*, edited by J. Goody, pp. 1–15. Papers in Social Anthropology, no. 1. Cambridge University, Cambridge.

Gilman, P. A.
  1987 Architecture as Artifact: Pit Structures and Pueblos in the American Southwest. *American Antiquity* 52:538–564.

Glennie, G. D.
  1983 *Replication of an* A.D. *800 Anasazi Pithouse in Southwestern Colorado*. Unpublished Master's thesis, Department of Anthropology, Washington State University, Pullman.

Glennie, G. D., and W. D. Lipe
  1984 Replication of an Early Anasazi Pithouse. Paper presented at the 49th Annual Meeting of the Society for American Archaeology, Portland, Oregon.

Griffitts, E. A.
  1987 Analysis of the *Phaseolus* Remains from the Dolores Project Area. In *Dolores Archaeological Program: Supporting Studies: Settlement and Environment*, compiled by K. L. Petersen and J. D. Orcutt, pp. 248–253. Bureau of Reclamation, Engineering and Research Center, Denver.

Gross, G. T.
  1987 *Anasazi Storage Facilities in the Dolores Region:* A.D. *600–920*. Ph.D. dissertation, Washington State University. University Microfilms, Ann Arbor.

Hally, D. J.
1986 The Identification of Vessel Function: A Case Study from Northwest Georgia. *American Antiquity* 51:267–295.

Hantman, J. L.
1983 *Social Networks and Stylistic Distributions in the Prehistoric Plateau Southwest.* Ph.D. dissertation, Arizona State University. University Microfilms, Ann Arbor.

Hartwig, F., and B. E. Dearing
1979 *Exploratory Data Analysis.* Quantitative Applications in the Social Sciences, Sage University Paper, no. 7-16. Sage Publications, Beverly Hills.

Hayden, B., and A. Cannon
1983 Where the Garbage Goes: Refuse Disposal in the Maya Highlands. *Journal of Anthropological Archaeology* 2:117–163.

Hayes, A. C.
1964 *The Archeological Survey of Wetherill Mesa, Mesa Verde National Park, Colorado.* Archeological Research Series, no. 7-A. National Park Service, Washington, D.C.

Hayes, A. C., and J. A. Lancaster
1975 *Badger House Community, Mesa Verde National Park.* Publications in Archeology, no. 7E. National Park Service, Washington, D.C.

Hegmon, M.
1989 Social Integration and Architecture. In *The Architecture of Social Integration in Prehistoric Pueblos,* edited by W. D. Lipe and M. Hegmon, pp. 5–14. Occasional Papers, no. 1. Crow Canyon Archaeological Center, Cortez, Colorado.
1991 The Risks of Sharing and Sharing as Risk Reduction: Interhousehold Food Sharing in Egalitarian Societies. In *Between Bands and States,* edited by S. Gregg, pp. 309–329. Southern Illinois University Press, Carbondale.

Hegmon, M., W. Hurst, and J. R. Allison
1991 Production for Local Consumption and Exchange: Comparisons of Early Red and White Ware Ceramics in the San Juan Region. Paper presented at the 56th Annual Meeting of the Society for American Archaeology, New Orleans.

Henrickson, E. F., and M. M. A. McDonald
1983 Ceramic Form and Function: An Ethnographic Search and an Archeological Application. *American Anthropologist* 85:630–643.

Hill, J. N.
1966 A Prehistoric Community in Eastern Arizona. *Southwestern Journal of Anthropology* 22:9–30.
1970a *Broken K Pueblo: Prehistoric Social Organization in the American Southwest.* Anthropological Papers, no. 18. University of Arizona, Tucson.
1970b Prehistoric Social Organization in the American Southwest: Theory and Method. In *Reconstructing Prehistoric Pueblo Societies,* edited by W. A. Longacre, pp. 11–58. University of New Mexico Press, Albuquerque.

Hillery, G. A., Jr., and F. J. Essene
1963 Navajo Population: An Analysis of the 1960 Census. *Southwestern Journal of Anthropology* 19:297–313.

Hoffman, J. M.
1993 Human Skeletal Remains. In *The Duckfoot Site, Volume 1: Descriptive Archaeology,* edited by R. R. Lightfoot and M. C. Etzkorn, pp. 253–296. Occasional Papers, no. 3. Crow Canyon Archaeological Center, Cortez, Colorado.

[Honeycutt, L., and J. Fetterman]
1991 *Indian Camp Ranch at Cortez: Archaeology at Work, Preserving the Anasazi Legacy for the Future.* Indian Camp Ranch Report, no. 1. Archie and Mary Hanson, Templeton, California.

Irwin-Williams, C.
1977 A Network Model for the Analysis of Prehistoric Trade. In *Exchange Systems in Prehistory,* edited by T. K. Earle and J. E. Ericson, pp. 141–151. Academic Press, New York.

Johnson, G. A.
1982 Organizational Structure and Scalar Stress. In *Theory and Explanation in Archaeology: The Southampton Conference,* edited by C. Renfrew, M. J. Rowlands, and B. A. Segraves, pp. 389–421. Academic Press, New York.
1989 Dynamics of Southwestern Prehistory: Far Outside—Looking In. In *Dynamics of Southwest Prehistory,* edited by L. S. Cordell and G. J. Gumerman, pp. 371–389. Smithsonian Institution Press, Washington, D.C.

Jorgensen, J.
1975 A Room Use Analysis of Table Rock Pueblo, Arizona. *Journal of Anthropological Research* 31:149–161.

Kane, A. E.
1986 Prehistory of the Dolores River Valley. In *Dolores Archaeological Program: Final Synthetic Report,* compiled by D. A. Breternitz, C. K. Robinson, and G. T. Gross, pp. 353–435. Bureau of Reclamation, Engineering and Research Center, Denver.
1989 Did the Sheep Look Up? Sociopolitical Complexity in Ninth Century Dolores Society. In *The Sociopolitical Structure of Prehistoric Southwestern Societies,* edited by S. Upham, K. G. Lightfoot, and

R. A. Jewett, pp. 307–361. Westview Press, Boulder, Colorado.

Kane, A. E., and C. K. Robinson (compilers)
1988 *Dolores Archaeological Program: Anasazi Communities at Dolores: McPhee Village.* Bureau of Reclamation, Engineering and Research Center, Denver.

Keesing, F. M.
1958 *Cultural Anthropology.* Rinehart, New York.

Kent, S.
1984 *Analyzing Activity Areas.* University of New Mexico Press, Albuquerque.

Kidder, A. V.
1958 *Pecos, New Mexico: Archaeological Notes.* Papers, vol. 5. Robert S. Peabody Foundation for Archaeology, Andover, Massachussetts.

Kroeber, A. L.
1917 *Zuni Kin and Clan.* Anthropological Papers, vol. 18, part 2. American Museum of Natural History, New York.

Kunstadter, P.
1984 Cultural Ideas, Socioeconomic Change, and Household Composition: Karen, Lua, Hmong, and Thai in Northwestern Thailand. In *Households: Comparative and Historical Studies of the Domestic Group,* edited by R. M. Netting, R. R. Wilk, and E. J. Arnould, pp. 299–329. University of California Press, Berkeley.

Laslett, P.
1972 Introduction: History of the Family. In *Household and Family in Past Time,* edited by P. Laslett and R. Wall, pp. 1–89. Cambridge University Press, Cambridge.

LeBlanc, S.
1971 An Addition to Naroll's Suggested Floor Area and Settlement Population Relationship. *American Antiquity* 36:210–211.

Leinhardt, S.
1977 *Social Networks: A Developing Paradigm.* Academic Press, New York.

Levy, M. J., Jr.
1965 Aspects of the Analysis of the Family. In *Aspects of the Analysis of Family Structure,* edited by A. J. Coale, L. A. Fallers, M. J. Levy, Jr., D. M. Schneider, and S. S. Tomkins, pp. 1–63. Princeton University Press, Princeton.

Li, A.
1937 Zuni: Some Observations and Queries. *American Anthropologist* 39:62–76.

Lightfoot, K. G.
1984 *Prehistoric Political Dynamics: A Case Study from*

*the American Southwest.* Northern Illinois University Press, DeKalb.

Lightfoot, R. R.
1988 Roofing an Early Anasazi Great Kiva: Analysis of an Architectural Model. *The Kiva* 53:253–272.

Lightfoot, R. R., A. M. Emerson, and E. Blinman
1988 Excavations in Area 5, Grass Mesa Village (Site 5MT23). In *Dolores Archaeological Program: Anasazi Communities at Dolores: Grass Mesa Village,* compiled by W. D. Lipe, J. N. Morris, and T. A. Kohler, pp. 561–766. Bureau of Reclamation, Engineering and Research Center, Denver.

Lightfoot, R. R., and M. C. Etzkorn (editors)
1993 *The Duckfoot Site, Volume 1: Descriptive Archaeology.* Occasional Papers, no. 3. Crow Canyon Archaeological Center, Cortez, Colorado.

Lightfoot, R. R., M. C. Etzkorn, K. R. Adams, and D. N. Walker
1993 Introduction. In *The Duckfoot Site, Volume 1: Descriptive Archaeology,* edited by R. R. Lightfoot and M. C. Etzkorn, pp. 1–13. Occasional Papers, no. 3. Crow Canyon Archaeological Center, Cortez, Colorado.

Lightfoot, R. R., M. C. Etzkorn, and M. D. Varien
1993 Excavations. In *The Duckfoot Site, Volume 1: Descriptive Archaeology,* edited by R. R. Lightfoot and M. C. Etzkorn, pp. 15–129. Occasional Papers, no. 3. Crow Canyon Archaeological Center, Cortez, Colorado.

Lipe, W. D., and M. Hegmon
1989 Historical and Analytical Perspectives on Architecture and Social Integration in the Prehistoric Pueblos. In *The Architecture of Social Integration in Prehistoric Pueblos,* edited by W. D. Lipe and M. Hegmon, pp. 15–34. Occasional Papers, no. 1. Crow Canyon Archaeological Center, Cortez, Colorado.

Lipe, W. D., T. A. Kohler, M. D. Varien, J. N. Morris, and R. R. Lightfoot
1988 Synthesis. In *Dolores Archaeological Program: Anasazi Communities at Dolores: Grass Mesa Village,* compiled by W. D. Lipe, J. N. Morris, and T. A. Kohler, pp. 1213–1276. Bureau of Reclamation, Engineering and Research Center, Denver.

Lipe, W. D., J. N. Morris, and T. A. Kohler (compilers)
1988 *Dolores Archaeological Program: Anasazi Communities at Dolores: Grass Mesa Village.* Bureau of Reclamation, Engineering and Research Center, Denver.

Martin, P. S.
1938 *Archaeological Work in the Ackmen-Lowry Area, Southwestern Colorado, 1937.* Anthropological Series,

vol. 23, no. 2. Field Museum of Natural History, Chicago.

1939   *Modified Basket Maker Sites: Ackmen-Lowry Area, Southwestern Colorado, 1938.* Anthropological Series, vol. 23, no. 3. Field Museum of Natural History, Chicago.

Merbs, C. F.
1989   Patterns of Health and Sickness in the Precontact Southwest. In *Columbian Consequences, Volume 1: Archaeological and Historical Perspectives on the Spanish Borderlands West,* edited by D. H. Thomas, pp. 41–55. Smithsonian Institution Press, Washington, D.C.

Mills, B. J.
1989   Integrating Functional Analysis of Vessels and Sherds Through Models of Ceramic Assemblage Formation. *World Archaeology* 21:133–147.

Mindeleff, V.
1891   A Study of Pueblo Architecture: Tusayan and Cibola. In *Eighth Annual Report of the Bureau of Ethnology, 1886–1887,* pp. 3–228. Smithsonian Institution, Washington, D.C.

Montgomery, B. K., and J. J. Reid
1990   An Instance of Rapid Ceramic Change in the American Southwest. *American Antiquity* 55:88–97.

Morgan, L. H.
1965   *Houses and Houselife of the American Aborigines.* Reprinted. University of Chicago Press, Chicago. Originally published 1881, Contributions to North American Ethnology, vol. 12, U.S. Government Printing Office, Washington, D.C.

Morris, E. H.
1919   Preliminary Account of the Antiquities of the Region Between the Mancos and La Plata Rivers in Southwestern Colorado. In *Thirty-Third Annual Report of the Bureau of American Ethnology, 1911–1912,* pp. 155–205. Smithsonian Institution, Washington, D.C.

1939   *Archaeological Studies in the La Plata District, Southwestern Colorado and Northwestern New Mexico.* Publication, no. 519. Carnegie Institution of Washington, Washington, D.C.

Morris, J. N.
1988   Excavations in Area 8. In *Dolores Archaeological Program: Anasazi Communities at Dolores: Grass Mesa Village,* compiled by W. D. Lipe, J. N. Morris, and T. A. Kohler, pp. 873–932. Bureau of Reclamation, Engineering and Research Center, Denver.

Naroll, R.
1962   Floor Area and Settlement Population. *American Antiquity* 27:587–589.

National Climate Center, Environmental Data and In-

formation Service, National Oceanic and Atmospheric Administration
1983   *Climate Normals for the U.S. (Base: 1951–1980).* Gale Research, Detroit.

Netting, R. M.
1986   *Cultural Ecology.* Waveland Press, Prospect Heights, Illinois.

Netting, R. M., R. R. Wilk, and E. J. Arnould
1984   Introduction. In *Households: Comparative and Historical Studies of the Domestic Group,* edited by R. M. Netting, R. R. Wilk, and E. J. Arnould, pp. xiii–xxxviii. University of California Press, Berkeley.

Orcutt, J. D.
1987   Changes in Aggregation and Spacing, A.D. 600–1175. In *Dolores Archaeological Program: Supporting Studies: Settlement and Environment,* compiled by K. L. Petersen and J. D. Orcutt, pp. 617–648. Bureau of Reclamation, Engineering and Research Center, Denver.

Pauketat, T. R.
1989   Monitoring Mississippian Homestead Occupation Span and Economy Using Ceramic Refuse. *American Antiquity* 54:288–310.

Petersen, K. L.
1988   *Climate and the Dolores River Anasazi: A Paleoenvironmental Reconstruction from a 10,000-Year Pollen Record, La Plata Mountains, Southwestern Colorado.* Anthropological Papers, no. 113. University of Utah, Salt Lake City.

1989   AT LAST! Why the Anasazi Left the Four Corners Region. *Canyon Legacy* 1:19–24.

Petersen, K. L., V. L. Clay, M. H. Matthews, and S. W. Neusius
1987   Implications of Anasazi Impact on the Landscape. In *Dolores Archaeological Program: Supporting Studies: Settlement and Environment,* compiled by K. L. Petersen and J. D. Orcutt, pp. 146–184. Bureau of Reclamation, Engineering and Research Center, Denver.

Petersen, K. L., and J. D. Orcutt (compilers)
1987   *Dolores Archaeological Program: Supporting Studies: Settlement and Environment.* Bureau of Reclamation, Engineering and Research Center, Denver.

Plog, F.
1974   *The Study of Prehistoric Change.* Academic Press, New York.

1977   Modeling Economic Exchange. In *Exchange Systems in Prehistory,* edited by T. K. Earle and J. E. Ericson, pp. 126–140. Academic Press, New York.

Prudden, T. M.
1903   The Prehistoric Ruins of the San Juan Water-

shed in Utah, Arizona, Colorado, and New Mexico. *American Anthropologist* 5:224–288.

Rapoport, A.
1990 Systems of Activities and Systems of Settings. In *Domestic Architecture and the Use of Space,* edited by S. Kent, pp. 9–20. Cambridge University Press, Cambridge.

Roberts, F. H. H., Jr.
1925 Report on Archaeological Reconnaissance in Southwestern Colorado in Summer of 1923. *Colorado Magazine* 2:1–80.
1930 *Early Pueblo Ruins in the Piedra District, Southwestern Colorado.* Bureau of American Ethnology Bulletin, no. 96. Smithsonian Institution, Washington, D.C.

Robinson, C. K., G. T. Gross, and D. A. Breternitz
1986 Overview of the Dolores Archaeological Program. In *Dolores Archaeological Program: Final Synthetic Report,* compiled by D. A. Breternitz, C. K. Robinson, and G. T. Gross, pp. 3–50. Bureau of Reclamation, Engineering and Research Center, Denver.

Rohn, A. H.
1965 Postulation of Socio-Economic Groups from Archaeological Evidence. In *Contributions of the Wetherill Mesa Archaeological Project,* assembled by D. Osborne, pp. 65–69. Memoir, no. 19. Society for American Archaeology, Washington, D.C.
1971 *Mug House, Mesa Verde National Park, Colorado.* Archeological Research Series, no. 7-D. National Park Service, Washington, D.C.
1977 *Cultural Change and Continuity on Chapin Mesa.* Regents Press of Kansas, Lawrence.

Sahlins, M. D.
1957 Land Use and the Extended Family in Moala, Fiji. *American Anthropologist* 59:449–462.

Schiffer, M. B.
1972 Archaeological Context and Systemic Context. *American Antiquity* 37:156–165.
1976 *Behavioral Archaeology.* Academic Press, New York.
1985 Is There a "Pompeii Premise" in Archaeology? *Journal of Anthropological Research* 41:18–41.
1987 *Formation Processes of the Archaeological Record.* University of New Mexico Press, Albuquerque.

Schlanger, S. H.
1985 *Prehistoric Population Dynamics in the Dolores Area, Southwestern Colorado.* Ph.D. dissertation, Washington State University. University Microfilms, Ann Arbor.
1987 Population Measurement, Size, and Change, A.D. 600–1175. In *Dolores Archaeological Program:*

*Supporting Studies: Settlement and Environment,* compiled by K. L. Petersen and J. D. Orcutt, pp. 568–613. Bureau of Reclamation, Engineering and Research Center, Denver.
1988 Patterns of Population Movement and Long-Term Population Growth in Southwestern Colorado. *American Antiquity* 53:773–793.

Schlanger, S. H., and R. H. Wilshusen
1993 Local Abandonments and Regional Conditions in the North American Southwest. In *Abandonment of Settlements and Regions: Ethnoarchaeological and Archaeological Approaches,* edited by C. M. Cameron and S. A. Tomka, pp. 85–98. Cambridge University Press, Cambridge.

Seymour, D. J., and M. B. Schiffer
1987 A Preliminary Analysis of Pithouse Assemblages from Snaketown, Arizona. In *Method and Theory for Activity Area Research: An Ethnoarchaeological Approach,* edited by S. Kent, pp. 549–603. Columbia University Press, New York.

Smith, M. F. J.
1985 Toward an Economic Interpretation of Ceramics: Relating Vessel Size and Shape to Use. In *Decoding Prehistoric Ceramics,* edited by B. A. Nelson, pp. 254–309. Southern Illinois University Press, Carbondale.

Steponaitis, V. P.
1983 *Ceramics, Chronology, and Community Patterns: An Archaeological Study at Moundville.* Academic Press, New York.

Stevenson, M. G.
1982 Toward an Understanding of Site Abandonment Behavior: Evidence from Historic Mining Camps in the Southwest Yukon. *Journal of Anthropological Archaeology* 1:237–265.

Stodder, A. W.
1987 The Physical Anthropology and Mortuary Practice of the Dolores Anasazi: An Early Pueblo Population in Local and Regional Context. In *Dolores Archaeological Program: Supporting Studies: Settlement and Environment,* compiled by K. L. Petersen and J. D. Orcutt, pp. 336–504. Bureau of Reclamation, Engineering and Research Center, Denver.

Sullivan, A. P., III
1974 Problems in the Estimation of Original Room Function: A Tentative Solution from the Grasshopper Ruin. *The Kiva* 40:93–100.

Thompson, R. H., and W. A. Longacre
1966 The University of Arizona Archaeological Field School at Grasshopper, East Central Arizona. *The Kiva* 31:255–275.

Turner, C. G., II, and L. Lofgren
    1966   Household Size of Prehistoric Western Pueblo
    Indians. *Southwestern Journal of Anthropology* 22:117–
    132.

Turner, R. M.
    1982   Great Basin Desertscrub. In Biotic Communi-
    ties of the American Southwest—United States and
    Mexico, edited by D. E. Brown, pp. 145–155. *Desert
    Plants* 4(1–4).

Varien, M. D.
    1984   *Honky House: Replication of Three Anasazi Sur-
    face Structures.* Unpublished Master's report, Depart-
    ment of Anthropology, University of Texas, Austin.

Varien, M. D., and R. R. Lightfoot
    1989   Ritual and Nonritual Activities in Mesa Verde
    Region Pit Structures. In *The Architecture of Social
    Integration in Prehistoric Pueblos,* edited by W. D. Lipe
    and M. Hegmon, pp. 73–87. Occasional Papers, no.
    1. Crow Canyon Archaeological Center, Cortez,
    Colorado.

Vivian, R. G., and P. Reiter
    1965   *The Great Kivas of Chaco Canyon and Their Re-
    lationships.* Monograph, no. 22. School of American
    Research, Santa Fe.

Waterworth, R. M. R., and E. Blinman
    1986   Modified Sherds, Unidirectional Abrasion, and
    Pottery Scrapers. *Pottery Southwest* 13(2):4–7.

Whallon, R., Jr.
    1969   Rim Diameter, Vessel Volume, and Economic
    Prehistory. *Michigan Academician* 2(2):89–98.

Wilcox, D. R.
    1975   A Strategy for Perceiving Social Groups in
    Puebloan Sites. In *Chapters in the Prehistory of East-
    ern Arizona, IV,* authored by P. S. Martin, E. B. W.
    Zubrow, D. C. Bowman, D. A. Gregory, J. A. Hanson,
    M. B. Schiffer, and D. R. Wilcox, pp. 120–174.
    Fieldiana: Anthropology, no. 65. Field Museum of
    Natural History, Chicago.

Wilk, R. R.
    1984   Households in Process: Agricultural Change
    and Domestic Transformation Among the Kekchi
    Maya of Belize. In *Households: Comparative and His-
    torical Studies of the Domestic Group,* edited by R. M.
    Netting, R. R. Wilk, and E. J. Arnould, pp. 217–244.
    University of California Press, Berkeley.

Wilk, R. R., and R. M. Netting
    1984   Households: Changing Forms and Functions.
    In *Households: Comparative and Historical Studies of
    the Domestic Group,* edited by R. M. Netting, R. R.
    Wilk, and E. J. Arnould, pp. 1–28. University of
    California Press, Berkeley.

Wilk, R. R., and W. L. Rathje (editors)
    1982   Archaeology of the Household: Building a
    Prehistory of Domestic Life. *American Behavioral
    Scientist* 25(6).

Wilshusen, R. H.
    1984   Engineering the Pithouse to Pueblo Transi-
    tion. Paper presented at the 49th Annual Meeting
    of the Society for American Archaeology, Portland.
    1986   The Relationship Between Abandonment
    Mode and Ritual Use in Pueblo I Anasazi Proto-
    kivas. *Journal of Field Archaeology* 13:245–254.
    1988a   Architectural Trends in Prehistoric Anasazi
    Sites During A.D. 600 to 1200. In *Dolores Archaeo-
    logical Program: Supporting Studies: Additive and Re-
    ductive Technologies,* compiled by E. Blinman, C. J.
    Phagan, and R. H. Wilshusen, pp. 599–633. Bureau
    of Reclamation, Engineering and Research Center,
    Denver.
    1988b   Household Archaeology and Social Sys-
    tematics. In *Dolores Archaeological Program: Supporting
    Studies: Additive and Reductive Technologies,* compiled
    by E. Blinman, C. J. Phagan, and R. H. Wilshusen,
    pp. 635–647. Bureau of Reclamation, Engineering
    and Research Center, Denver.
    1988c   The Pitstructure to Pueblo Transition: An Al-
    ternative to McGuire and Schiffer's Explanation. In
    *Dolores Archaeological Program: Supporting Studies: Ad-
    ditive and Reductive Technologies,* compiled by E.
    Blinman, C. J. Phagan, and R. H. Wilshusen, pp.
    703–708. Bureau of Reclamation, Engineering and
    Research Center, Denver.
    1988d   Sipapus, Ceremonial Vaults, and Foot Drums
    (Or, a Resounding Argument for Protokivas). In
    *Dolores Archaeological Program: Supporting Studies: Ad-
    ditive and Reductive Technologies,* compiled by E.
    Blinman, C. J. Phagan, and R. H. Wilshusen, pp.
    649–671. Bureau of Reclamation, Engineering and
    Research Center, Denver.
    1989a   Architecture as Artifact—Part II: A Com-
    ment on Gilman's "Architecture as Artifact: Pit
    Structures and Pueblos in the American South-
    west." *American Antiquity* 54:826–833.
    1989b   Unstuffing the Estufa: Ritual Floor Features
    in Anasazi Pit Structures and Pueblo Kivas. In *The
    Architecture of Social Integration in Prehistoric Pueblos,*
    edited by W. D. Lipe and M. Hegmon, pp. 89–111.
    Occasional Papers, no. 1. Crow Canyon Archaeo-
    logical Center, Cortez, Colorado.
    1991   *Early Villages in the American Southwest: Cross-
    Cultural and Archaeological Perspectives.* Ph.D. disserta-
    tion, University of Colorado. University Microfilms,
    Ann Arbor.

Wood, W. R., and D. L. Johnson
1978  A Survey of Disturbance Processes in Archae-ological Site Formation. In *Advances in Archae-ological Method and Theory,* vol. 1, edited by M. B. Schiffer, pp. 315–381. Academic Press, New York.

Wright, M. K.
1990  *Sandstone and Cornmeal: Experimental Use of Early Pueblo Maize Grinding Tools from Southwestern Colo-rado.* Unpublished Master's thesis, Department of Anthropology, Washington State University, Pullman.